台灣影像歷史系列

開台尋跡

A Collection of the Visual History of Taiwan

Strolling the Old Trails

台灣傳承文化
T.H.L
Taiwan Heritage Co., Ltd.

為台灣歷史留下見證

台灣島國四面環海，斯土斯民千百年來匯萃淤連，歷史長河沖積成獨特的時空流域，曾昔以降鋪陳出獨特的歷史、人文、風土、政治、社群、乃至外環國際諸端勢力的對應互動，遂成像疊影成福爾摩莎美麗島國豐富多元的強韌屬性…有緬舊懷古的敦厚，既往錮結的悲情，亦有展望未來的願憬與無限可能。

數百年來，島境台灣的住民新陳交迭，各方外來勢力與本土文化凝聚交融，諸端因緣造就族群共同記憶，在歷史時空的方方面面廓構版圖，世代交替傳承迄今…斯土斯民秉承母親血理的先天本能，發揚島國住民山海包容的豪情；是以我們誠實返照歷史，摯誠面對族群與族群之間的深層命題；《台灣影像歷史系列》的出版，有幸能蒐羅、典藏先民祖輩的跫跡步履，以專業的觀點編造輯成，串連海內外所有台灣人社群的原鄉夢憬。

歷史乃文化紮根、淤葉連枝，史料文物之陳敘重組，是過去先民汗血滴凝的忠實見證。遠自荷蘭時代到日治的殖民統治世代，「台灣傳承文化」將數千件蒐藏史料文物，分類造冊為《見證台灣總督府》、《台灣總督府官葉》、《典藏手繪封》、《斯土繪影》、《高砂春秋》、《蓬萊舊庄》、《海國圖索》、《開台尋跡》、《台灣古書契》、《殖產方略》十部影像目錄。《台灣影像歷史系列》匯集海內外台灣學術界與民間耆宿之智慧精華，歷時多年重新修訂結輯出版；內造力求超然詳實，外緣得幸與讀者諸君共體台灣承傳文化的內蘊真諳。

《台灣影像歷史系列》與實證文物的延展，需要您的熱誠參與，透過城市聚落的巡迴展覽與精美複製文物的普羅推廣，冀望古早台灣的人文地物，能以最真摯的容顏展現於本土地域乃至國際舞台，讓海內外台灣子民無論身處故鄉或異鄉，皆能傳續歷史的傳承與使命，永續福爾摩沙美麗島的壯闊襟懷。

台灣傳承文化事業 謹誌

FROM THE PUBLISHER

Attesting to Taiwan's History

On Taiwan, this island surrounded on all sides by the high seas, a unique people has coalesced and spread forth over thousands of years. The long river of history has formed a distinct catchment area of time and space. Here, an assortment of historical events, cultures, folk customs, politics, ethnic groups and even external influences has interacted reciprocally, creating a diverse tapestry of overlapping images, and carving out the rich and tenacious character of Formosa. This beautiful island nation harbors a sincere fondness for its past, along with a tragic sense of its history of aspirations confined, yet it gazes at the future with a spirit of hope and unbounded possibility.

For several centuries, new waves of immigrants have settled alongside communities of earlier residents. An array of outside forces has merged with local cultures, and this chain of cause and effect has forged a collective ethnic memory, a broad and complex legacy passed from generation to generation to the present day... The blood of this people carries the instincts of its forebears, and this land has nurtured a lofty spirit of tolerance as broad as the mountains and the seas. So it is that we honestly reflect upon our history, and sincerely address the issues that exist at a deep level among our society's various communities. It is our good fortune, through the publication of A Collection of the Visual History of Taiwan, *to retrace the footprints of our ancestors. Thoughtfully collected and professionally edited, this series of visual records sincerely conveys the aspirations which the Taiwanese people, at home and abroad, hold toward their homeland.*

History is the process through which culture sets down roots, and grows verdant, interweaving branches. The presentation and reorganization of historical materials is a testimony to the blood, sweat and tears of the island's original settlers. Taiwan's cultural legacy, from as far back as the period of Dutch colonization through the era of Japanese rule, has been collected in thousands of historical documents, separated into different categories and presented in ten separate volumes: Witness - The Colonial Taiwan; Postcards Issued By Taiwan Governor's Office; Postcard Drawings - The Rare Collection; The Drawings of That Land - The Interpretation of Taiwan; The Exquisite Heritage - The Culture and Arts of Taiwan Aborigines; The Abodes in the Bygone Era - Taiwan's Town and Country Settlements; The Landscape of the Island Country - The Development of the Natural Geography of Taiwan; Strolling the Old Trails; Archaic Land Documents of Taiwan; and The Schemes of Production - Taiwan's Industrial Development. A Collection of the Visual History of Taiwan *brings together the essence of the insights of Taiwan's scholarly community, both at home and abroad, and the wisdom of the older generation throughout society - revised, edited and published as a fresh perspective on the island's long history. We have striven to be unbiased, detailed and thorough, and are fortunate to share with each of you the true inside story of Taiwan's cultural inheritance.*

A Collection of the Visual History of Taiwan, *and the authentic witness which these documents bear, requires your heartfelt participation. Through a series of exhibitions in major cities and the public dissemination of these exquisitely reproduced pictorial records and documents, it is our desire to present, in the local arena and on the international stage, the most genuine representation of the people, culture and geography of early Taiwan. Ultimately, we hope to bestow the children of Taiwan, living on both native and foreign soil, with the heritage and mission of our collective history, so that the expansive heart of this beautiful island of Formosa will beat in perpetuity.*

Respectfully,
"Taiwan Heritage"

編　序

空間的歷史長河

本書是針對台灣早期開發的幾個城鎮聚點，作定點式的巡遊及介紹，讓昔日的地景風貌躍然紙上，從古城堡、老街、到古建築的歷史空間向度和深度上，可以恰如其份的拿捏。其中對於歷史陳述所擷取的重點不免失衡，然而就一本針對社會大衆而定位的歷史書籍，本書所作的旨在概念性的強化歷史空間印象，至於相關的歷史命題，只是基於一個歷史邏輯的追索、聯想與初探，而得以有請專家爲文釐清的機會，本書的任務，也就在於對某些歷史命題作某種程度的衍生與整合，重現衆人眼前。基於篇幅所限，並遷就於現有的影像資料，呈現了跳躍式的影像組合，尤以〈土地開發〉一章爲甚。

〈老街紀行〉把歷史線索追溯至50年、100年，甚至於更早的清領時期的台灣。屋舍與街道之變，由今昔圖片的對照下，緬懷之外，竟有一份唏噓之歎，今日台灣地景的混亂，直指空間美感的淪喪與文化修持的薄弱，甚至是權力的更張重塑。

日治期間基於殖民政策，依據先天條件和後天環境評估的三大港市，以及殖台期間從事現代化都市計劃的藍圖，不管是具有誇耀的企圖，抑或在執行計劃過程中所展現的對台灣人民及歷史文化的意義，或以都市計劃的專業眼光去評價，皆非本書所關照的，僅針對客觀事實的政策措施作描述。

有關〈古築物語〉，主要撰文者王志鴻先生，以其建築的專業背景，及長期對台灣史蹟的鑽研，對古建築物的建築特色多所著墨，俾以一窺台灣曾經擁有的閩、日、西等豐富的建築風貌，並旁述每棟建築因改朝換代、制度更替所牽動的面貌演化，更加耐人尋味。前古風史蹟研究會會長姚其中先生，則以史蹟解說的方式及角度，帶領讀者作紙上導覽。

在台灣現存的都市公園的空間裡，我們隱然感受到日治時期的地域氣氛和結構。本書〈現代都市的表徵——公園〉中所述及的，幾乎都留存至今，這不由得讓我們想追溯至日治期間，日本人在台灣所規劃的公園，其終極考量和特色，也想探究當時都市公園的定位與整體都市規劃的關係究竟爲何？

其次關於日本時代的驛站原貌，至今也都已逐漸消失，在〈驛站巡禮〉一章裡，我們網羅各地的驛站風情，並著眼於建築特色的介紹，更將難得一見，由總督府交通局所發行的各地驛站戳，以原戳本羅列，在印刷上儘量要求忠於原戳顏色，一方面又可當成版畫藝術欣賞。當然其他饒具地方風土趣味的風景戳及地方鳥瞰圖，也在本書陸續刊出。

台灣傳承文化　總編輯

FROM THE EDITOR

An Historical Spatial Continuum

This book contains a place-by-place overview and introduction of several cities and townships developed in the early history of Taiwan. This approach allows us in this book to present in a very lively manner the old-time appearances of places and scenery in Taiwan. The historic dimension and depth of old fortresses, streets and buildings are adequately portrayed. Although the historical landmarks featured herein are not exhaustive or balanced in representation, as a historical publication targeted at the mass readership, this book strives to strengthen people's conception of historical space. Relevant historical themes are highlighted in an attempt to pursue, relate and explore historical logic by retaining experts to prepare essays for clarification of historical issues. The underlying principle of this book is to present to the readers a certain degree of derivation and integration with respect to specific historical themes. However, images in the book, especially those in "Strolling on Old Streets," are arranged in a somewhat discontinuous fashion, due to the constraint of length.

The historical threads in "Strolling on Old Streets" date back to 50 or 100 years ago, or even an earlier period of time when Taiwan was under the reign of China's Ching Dynasty. The buildings and streets went through considerable transformation, as a comparison of pictures taken in different time periods reveals. This evolution inspires a strong sense of nostalgia. The chaotic countenance of Taiwan's land and scenery today indicates the deterioration of spatial aesthetics, inadequate preservation of culture and even reshuffling of power.

This book does not concern itself with the ostentatious intentions revealed by the development projects for the three harbor cities during Japan's colonial rule of Taiwan, or by modern urban plans undertaken during the same period. Nor does the book intend to explore the historical or cultural implications for Taiwan and the Taiwanese people as demonstrated in the implementation process of the projects or plans. Neither is it the intention of this book to evaluate the urban plans of that time period from a professional perspective. The focus of the book is actually to describe the facts associated with the policies of that era.

The main contributor to "Antique Buildings" is Mr. Wang Chih- hung, who has devoted considerable efforts to describing the architectural characteristics of antique buildings, thanks to his professional background and long-term studies of Taiwan's history. His essays have brought to light the rich Fukienese, Japanese or Western features of different buildings that were once prevalent across the landscape of Taiwan. His succinct accounts of the transformation of the appearance of the buildings due to changes of governments or political systems are particularly interesting. Mr. Yiao Chih-chung, the former chairman of the Kufen Association of Historic Sites Studies, takes the readers on a guided tour through the book by providing an overview of historic sites.

Existing parks in Taiwan's cities reveal the atmosphere, structure and administration of the previous regime in Taiwan. Most of the parks described in "Parks- - Symbols of Urban Development" exist today, reminding us of the ultimate considerations behind these parks developed by Japan during its colonial rule of Taiwan, as well as their characteristics. The parks have also brought to the fore the question of how the definition and orientation of the parks during that time were related to the overall urban plans.

Today, the original outlook of railway stations during the Japanese era is nowhere to be found. In "History of railway Stations," we have pooled together tidbits of Railway stations in different places, focusing on the introduction of architectural characteristics. A precious feature of the book is that the stamps issued for the railway stations by the Transportation Bureau under the Taiwan Governor's Office are displayed as they originally appeared. Special attention was devoted to preserving the original coloring of the stamps during the printing process, so that the stamps can also be appreciated as block prints. The book also includes other stamps of indigenous scenery, as well as bird's-eye-view pictures of various places.

Editor-in-Chief
Taiwan Heritage Co., Ltd.

目　錄 Contents

土地開發
Land Deveopment

城堡舊事
Fortress Stories

老街紀行
Strolling on Old Streets

目　錄 Contents

古築物語
Antique Buildings

目 錄 Contents

目　錄 Contents

設施 Construction

19世紀由紐約Ackerman出版公司石版印刷的台灣地圖

Nineteenth Century map of Taiwan, which was printed in monochrome lithography by Ackerman Publishing Company in New York.

RH-001

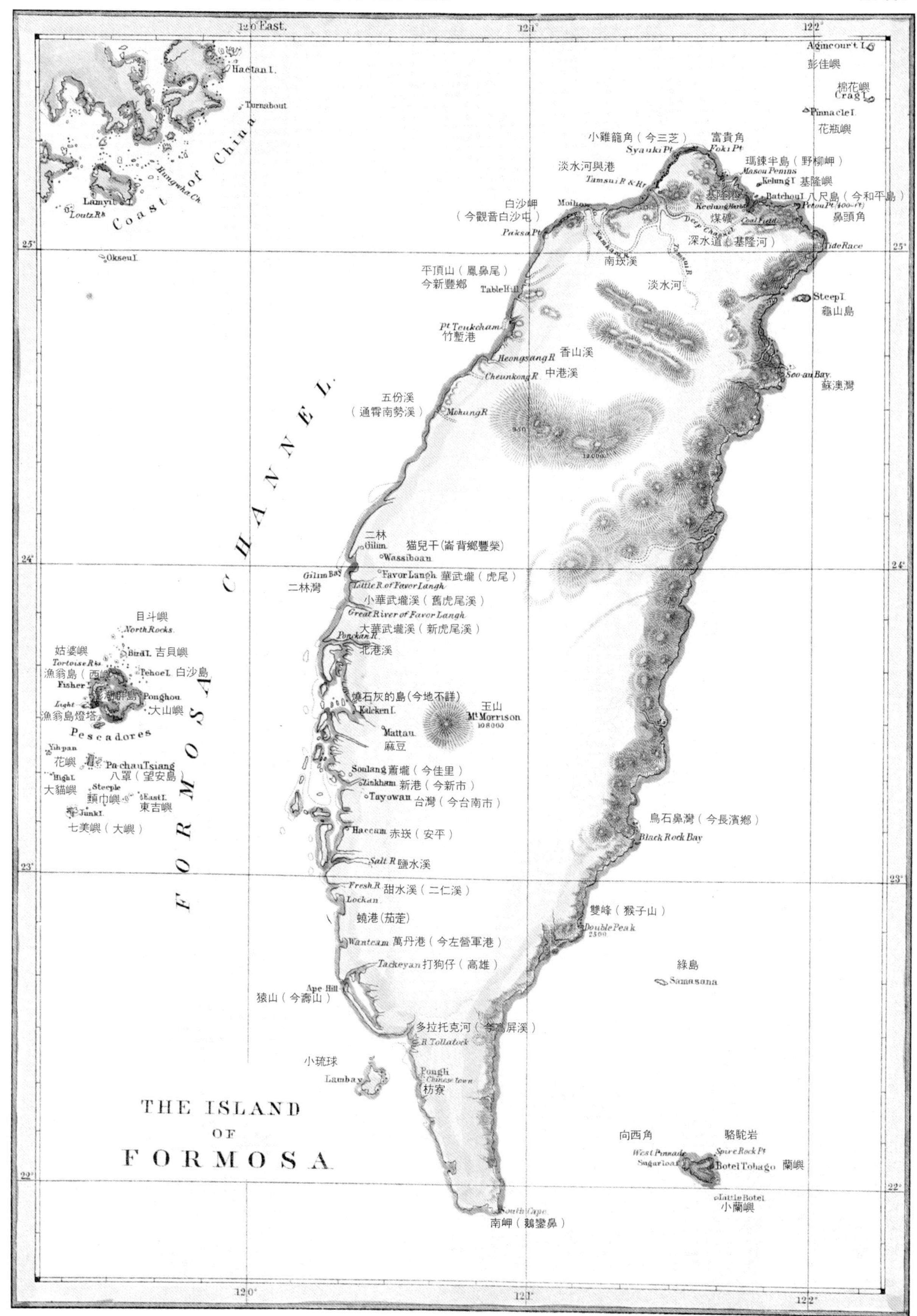

中文地名翻譯：師大地理系　吳進喜老師

Mandarin Translator：Mr. Wu, Jin-hsi

土地開發
Land Development

台灣土地的拓墾自南宋時漢人已移入澎湖；荷據時期已進入雲林、嘉義、台南、高雄若干據點；清季以降，拓墾遍及全島；日治之後，台灣東部及山地陸續開發，日人都市計劃的著力，同時也爲城市定位和空間結構奠下基礎。

The land development of the Taiwan area began with the immigration of Han Chinese to the Penghu island group during the Southern Sung dynasty (around the 13th century AD). During the rule of the Dutch, settlements of the Han people began to appear on Taiwan island proper, in Yulin, Chiayi, Tainan and Kaohsiung. In the Ching dynasty, settlements of Han Chinese spread throughout the island. During the Japanese era, eastern Taiwan and mountainous areas were gradually developed. The dedication of the Japanese to urban planning laid the foundation and the spatial frameworks for the cities of Taiwan.

日人對
台灣土地開發的主力
—城市開發
及其序位

台灣土地在清領時期多已開發，日人治台後新拓之地，多爲山地及東部地區。然而日人對台灣土地開發主要的貢獻在於都市計畫，爲台灣今日城鎮的形成奠下基礎。由於台北爲日人治台之政治、經濟的中心，故最早實行市區改正工事。東部的花蓮、台東則因交通的開發而興。高雄則因高雄港及左營海軍基地而取代台南成爲南部最大城。台中的建設主要是爲了避免人口過度集中於北、高兩地，再加上新高港市的計畫而進行。日治時期的城市開發序位、依次爲；

一、台北市：台北市的市區改正工事起於明治28年(1895)，隨著都市人口的擴張及建築物的增加，而進行了幾次都市更新及區域擴大。

二、澎湖馬公：澎湖馬公街由於是澎湖廳治所在地，又是陸軍要塞及海軍要港，在明治39年(1906)進行都市計畫。

三、台東市街：明治41年(1908)，台東街開始了市區改正的工事。大正15年(1926)和花蓮間有了鐵路相連，但是仍然不及西部大城的發展。

四、花蓮港市計劃：明治42年(1909)，花蓮由於花蓮港市計畫而興起，但是眞正發展則要等到昭和6年(1931)，蘇花臨海道路完成後，才和台東正式成爲新興市鎮。

五、基隆港市：因爲地近台北，基隆港又爲北部最主要的國際港，所以在明治42年(1909)，開始了市區改正的工事，再加上設有要塞司令部及對日貿易的關係，而成爲台灣兩大港市之一。

六、高雄港市計劃：高雄市因爲高雄港的擴建而成爲新興都市，並且取代台南成爲南部第一大港市。高雄市的市區改正工事於大正6年(1917)動工。

七、新竹市都市計劃：新竹市在改隸以前，街道及市街規劃甚爲零亂，乃於大正9年(1920)進行市區改正工事，開始發展工商業。

八、台中港市發展：台中市爲台灣中部大城，是中部米、果菜及砂糖的集散地，在大正10年(1921)進行市區改正，在新高港都市計畫案中，則計畫以此兩市（台中市、新高市）作爲台灣的第三都市。

九、彰化市：彰化市伴隨著交通、商業的發展，而於大正10年(1921)開始市區改正，市勢的進展及規模隨工事的發展而擴張。

十、台南市：台南市原爲南部大城，但市區街道極不規則，而於大正10年(1921)進行市區改正，並擴大範圍。但是爲了保存古蹟及重要建築物而未完全改正。

十一、嘉義市：嘉義市在大地震後，原有屋舍大多損毀，加以阿里山開墾伐木的推行，需要一個基地，而在大正10年(1921)進行市區改正。

十二、屏東市：屏東市是屬於熱帶農業都市，在大正10年(1921)，因人口膨脹而開始市區改正的工事。

十三、宜蘭市：宜蘭市原爲東海岸的最大都市，又爲官廳、公司、銀行的集中地，在昭和6年(1931)進行市區改正工事。

註83、91、129、150

Urban Development

The Focus of Japanese Developmental Efforts in Taiwan

Much of Taiwan's land area had been developed during the Ching Dynasty. During the Japanese era, developmental efforts were focused on the mountain areas and eastern Taiwan. However, the greatest contribution of the Japanese remained in the field of urban planning and reconstruction, which paved the way for the formation of present-day city layouts. Taipei, which was the hub of political and financial activities during the period, was the first city to undergo reconstruction. In eastern Taiwan, the construction of railroads and highways brought prosperity to the cities of Hualien and Taitung. Kaohsiung replaced Tainan as the largest city in southern Taiwan, following the development of Kaohsiung Harbor and the Tzouying Naval Base. In central Taiwan, development in Taichung City was meant to help ease population congestion in Taipei and Kaohsiung, and at the same time, supplement the development and construction of Taichung Harbor. Arranged in chronological order, city reconstruction and development projects during the Japanese era were as follows:

1 Taipei: The re-planning of Taipei City started in 1895 during the 28th year of the Meiji era. The city underwent several phases of reconstruction and expansion to accommodate the increase in population and building construction.

2 Makung in Penghu: Makung was the site of the Penghu prefecture hall and a major army base and naval port. Urban planning started in 1906.

3 Taitung: Urban planning in Taitung City started in 1908, and railroad tracks connecting the city to Hualien were completed in 1926 during the 15th year of the Taisho era. Despite this, however, city development still lagged behind that in the cities of western Taiwan.

4 Hualien : Hualien prospered due to the construction and development of Hualien Harbor in 1909. But it was not until 1931, with the completion of the coastal highway connecting Hualien and Su'ao, that the city, together with Taitung, became the two newly developed cities on the island.

5 Keelung: Due to its proximity to Taipei, Keelung

became the major international port in northern Taiwan. Urban reconstruction started in 1909, which, together with trade with Japan, made Keelung one of the two major trading ports in Taiwan.

6 Kaohsiung: The expansion of the Kaohsiung Port helped in the development of Kaohsiung City, which took over Tainan as the largest port in southern Taiwan. Urban reconstruction started in 1917.

7 Hsinchu: Hsinchu City, whose streets were formerly not properly laid out and were hard to locate, started urban reconstruction in 1920 in order to develop into a commercial and industrial area.

8 Taichung: Taichung City, one of the major cities in central Taiwan, was also the trading hub for rice, vegetables, and refined sugar. Urban reconstruction started in 1921. Under the plan, Taichung City, together with Kaohsin City, were jointly to become the third most important municipal area on the island.

9 Changhua: Urban reconstruction in Changhua stated in 1921. As traffic and commercial activities grew, the city also grew and expanded accordingly.

10 Tainan: Tainan City was one of the major cities in southern Taiwan. Reconstruction started in 1921 to correct the poorly-planned city streets and to expand the city's borders. The reconstruction, however, was restricted in scope, due to the need to preserve part of the city's historical relics.

11 Chiayi: Most of the buildings in Chiayi City were destroyed after a big earthquake. Reconstruction started in 1921 to rebuild the city and help facilitate the emerging logging activities in the Ali mountain area.

12 Pingtung: A tropical agricultural city, Pingtung City underwent reconstruction in 1921 due to increased population.

13 Ilan: The largest city in the coastal region of eastern Taiwan, Ilan City was also the site of government offices, business establishments, and banks. Urban reconstruction started in 1931.

台灣土地拓墾歷程（荷據時期至清領時期）

	時間	拓墾區域	拓墾概況
澎	南宋		漢人移入
湖	明萬曆		漢人移民定居
北	明鄭時期	台北一庄	實行屯田
		北路27堡計有：麻豆堡、鐵線橋堡、哆囉嘓東堡、果毅後堡、太子宮堡、鹽水港堡、下茄苳堡、龍蛟潭堡、鹿仔草堡、大坵田西堡、打貓南堡、嘉義西堡、大槺榔西堡、大槺榔東堡、打貓東堡、他里霧堡、斗六堡、沙連堡、北港西堡、馬芝堡、線東堡（彰化）、大肚堡、苗栗三堡、桃澗堡、芝蘭堡、基隆堡、金包里堡	鄭氏屯墾或招佃開墾並自南崁溪登陸
		唭里岸至關渡之道路	
		八里坌——蘆洲——海山口	漢人入墾
		營盤（新莊街）	屯兵——將撤守的兵營改爲田園租予農民
		南崁、北投	永曆25年(1671)鄭經時代漢人集團入墾
		溪水、基隆、金包里（今金山）	明永曆29年(1675)
	清康熙20年(1681)	復修荷人舊城址	
	清康熙末年	竹塹、南勢、西勢、北勢	王世傑由竹塹登陸拓及南、西、北勢
	清康熙48年	大加蚋堡	福建人陳建年開墾
	清雍正、乾隆年間	北部平原	
部	清嘉慶年間	三貂嶺——噶瑪蘭	
中	明鄭時期	南投、雲林各一庄	實行屯田
	清康熙36年	半線（今彰化）、牛罵（今清水）	半線一帶由施氏與其子施長齡、楊志甲、吳溶、張萬振等人由鹿港登陸，或由台南、諸羅北上
	清康熙49年	大肚溪以北、日南、後壠	
部	清嘉慶年間	埔里盆地	
南	荷據時期	雲林、嘉義、台南、高雄等若干據點	仍以台南市爲中心，北自北港、蕭壠、麻豆、灣裡（今台南縣安定鄉）、茄投（今台南縣善花鎮）、新港、大目降，南至阿公店（今高雄岡山）
	明鄭時期	台南縣16庄、高雄縣市共16庄、屏東一庄	實行屯田
		東門外	墾闢菜園
	清康熙末	諸羅、斗六門、恆春枋山、楓港、羅漢門——林邊下淡水溪和東港溪流域	
部	清乾隆、嘉慶年間	南部平原	
東	清道光	越中央山脈移墾後山卑南覓	
部	清同治末年	寶桑、奇萊	

註109、110、111

Different Stages of Taiwan Settlement (From the Dutch Era to the Ching Dynasty)

	Period	Area of Settlement	Settlement Status
Penghu	Sung Dynasty, 1127-1279		Han Chinese moved in
	Ming Dynasty		Han Chinese settled
Northern Taiwan	Ming Dynasty	Taipei	Stationed armies in the countryside to engage in farming
		The 27 Divisions (*Pao*) of the North	Stationed armies in the countryside to engage in farming; hired local peasants
		Road from Chilian to Kuantu	
		Palipen, Luchou, Haishankou	Han Chinese settled
		Yingpan (Hsinchuang)	Stationed armies in the countryside to engage in farming; military base stations converted into farm lands
		Nankan, Peitou	Mass settlement by Han Chinese (1671)
		Hsishui, Keelung, Chinpaoli (present-day Chinshan)	1675
	Kanghsi Reign during the Ching Dynasty (1681)	Restoration of the former Dutch fortress	
	Last years of the Kanghsi Reign	Chuchien, Nanshih, Hsishih, Peishih	Wang Shih—chieh landed in Chuchien, development expanded to Nanshih, Hsishih, and Peishih
	Kanghsi Reign (1709)	Tachi—ena	Chen Chian-nian, a native of Fujian province, settled in the area
	Yungcheng and Chienlung Reigns, Ching Dynasty	Northern plains	
	Chiaching Reign, Ching Dynasty	Santiao Cape, Kemalan	
Central Taiwan	Ming Dynasty	Nantou, Yunlin	Stationed armies to engage in farming
	Kanghsi Reign, Ching Dynasty (1697)	Panhsien (present-day Changhua), Niuma (present-day Chingshui)	In the Panhsien area, Shih Chang ling and others landed in Lukang; others moved north via Tainan and Chulo
	Kanghsi Reign, Ching Dynasty (1710)	North of Tatu River, Chihnan, Houlung	
	Chiaching Reign, Ching Dynasty	Puli basin	
Southern Taiwan	Dutch era	Yunlin, Chiayi, Tainan, Kaohsiung	Tainan was the hub, extending north to Peikang, Hsialung, Natou, Wanli (present-day Anting village in Tainan), Chiehtou (present-day Shanhua village in Tainan), Hsinkang, Tamuchiang; extending south to Ahkungtien (present-day Kangshan in Kaohsiung County)
	Ming Dynasty	16 villages each in Tainan and Kaohsiung, one in Pingtung	Stationed armies to engage in farming
		Area outside of Tungmen	Cultivated vegetable farms
	Last years of the Kanghsi Reign, Ching Dynasty	Chulo, Touliumen, Fangshan in Hengshun, Feng-kang, Lohanmen	
	Chienlung and Chiaching Reign, Ching Dynasty	Southern plains	
Eastern	Taokuang Reign, Ching Dynasty	Across the Central Mountain Range	
Taiwan	Last years of the Tungchi Reign, Ching Dynasty	Saishang, Chilai	

北台灣的臍帶——淡水河

《明史》〈外國傳〉中，有段關於淡水河的描述：「淡水河中多大溪，流入海，水澹，故曰淡水洋。」

淡水河發源於大霸尖山，其上游之新店溪、大料崁溪在台北縣江子翠匯合成爲淡水河，迂迴於台北盆地之間，爾後在關渡附近又匯流基隆河向北流至淡水港注入台灣海峽。全長159公里，流域面積廣達2726平方公里。淡水河流域左岸包括鶯歌、山子脚、樹林、新莊；右岸則是三峽、土城、板橋；進入台北市後更流經萬華、大稻埕等早期台灣繁極一時的地區，可說是台灣北部最重要的河川，尤其和早期北台灣的發展息息相關，彷彿是台北盆地的一條臍帶。

從極盛到落寞

淡水地區早在明萬曆年間即與大陸通商，至西荷殖民時期、明鄭時期仍屬要地。到了清代，淡水便成爲北台灣主要的出入港口。咸豐10年（西元1860年）中英法北京條約正式開淡水爲通商港口後，更趨繁華，道路、碼頭、堤防等設施日益完整。後來因爲泥沙淤積，港面日益縮小；再加上基隆港的興建及淡水線鐵路的修築，使得淡水港經濟、交通樞紐之地位逐一被取代而漸趨沒落，如今僅具漁港之性質。

根據昭和17年（西元1942年）的統計，當時淡水港每年漁產量約爲300萬公斤，之後便逐年遞減。光復後，省政府研擬了修復漁港的計畫，以挽救淡水港的沒落。

航運聯絡重站

淡水河早期擔負了十分重要的航運連絡工作，《台灣府志》中記載：「淡水港在八里坌，海口水程十里至關渡門，内有大港分爲二港，西南至擺接社止，東北至峰仔峙止，番民往來俱用蟒甲者，刳獨木以爲舟也，澳内可艙數百……内地商船，間亦到此。」由此可見清代早期淡水河流域舟船往來的大致情形。乾隆57年（西元1792年）八里坌開港，與福州五虎門及蚶江通商後，淡水河艋舺——八里坌間之船舶航行更盛；咸豐10年後，淡水——大稻埕間機動船隻來往頻繁；而新店、大料崁、基隆河一帶因爲生產茶葉的關係，水運也很興盛。

日治時期貨物集散地

日治時期，大稻埕成爲全省貨物的集散地，連帶提升了淡水河的重要性。當時，中部之木材、樟腦、日用品，在大稻埕集中經河運輸出；而由中國大陸或日本輸入的貨物則由淡水港進入經河運至大稻埕；由基隆進口者亦多利用小型輪船運送至淡水，再經河運至大稻埕。

明治 33 年（西元 1900 年）爲極盛時期，每日均有日商機動船 9 艘，往返於淡水——大稻埕間；帆船之往來更是頻仍。之後因河底積沙，機動船每日僅可於午前後往復一次，到了淡水線鐵路通車後便廢航，近年，便無水運可言。

註 16、17、19、21、123

日治時代的淡水河口港內景觀

A scene of the harbor on the estuary of Tanshui River during the Japanese era.

RH-002

Tanshui River Umbilical Cord of Northern Taiwan

In the *Overseas Stories*, the *Ming History*, there is a description about Tanshui River: "Containing a large number of tributaries and flowing into the sea, the river, with its fresh water, is called Tanshui [denoting *Fresh Water* in Mandarin]."

With a length of 159 km and a catchment area of 2726 square kilometers, Tanshui River originates on Mt. Tapa-chien. Its upstream system is formed along with Hsintien Creek and Takokan Creek, which join the Tanshui at Chiang-tzutsui, Taipei County. With the confluence of these rivers, Tanshui River then meanders within the Taipei Basin and connects with Keelung River in the vicinity of Kuantu before moving all the way north to Tanshui Harbor and emptying into the Taiwan Strait. The catchment area of Tanshui River includes Yingke, Shantzuchiao, Shulin, and Hsinchuang to its left, and Sanhsia, Tucheng and Panchiao to its right. Upon entering Taipei City, the river travels through places like Wanhua and Tataocheng, prosperous places in the early days of Taiwan. Tanshui River is indeed one of the most important rivers in Northern Taiwan. With its close connection with the development of Northern Taiwan in its early days, the river may be described as the umbilical cord of Taipei Basin.

From Prosperity to Downfall

The Tanshui area traded with the Chinese mainland as early as the Wanli reign of the Ming dynasty and was able to maintain its key trading position while being dominated by first the Spaniards, then the Dutch and Cheng Cheng-kung (a general from the Ming dynasty who came to Taiwan to establish resistance against the government of the newly established Ching dynasty). Before the establishment of the Ching dynasty, Tanshui had become the main harbor for the exit and entrance of Northern Taiwan. Under the Peking Treaty of 1860, signed jointly by the Chinese, British and French, Tanshui was officially declared a trading port, and this declaration contributed to more prosperity, as well as better roads, piers and embankments in Tanshui. However, Tanshui s status as an economic and transportation hub was gradually replaced due to the siltation and shrinkage of Tanshui Harbor, as well as to the establishment of Keelung Harbor and Taipei s railway link with Tanshui. Today, Tanshui is merely a fishing port.

According to the statistics released in 1942, Tanshui Harbor enjoyed an annual fishing turnover of 3 million kg, a volume subsequently on the decline each year. Following the retrocession of Taiwan, the Provincial Government of Taiwan crafted plans to renovate the fishing port to save Tanshui from further decline.

Major Post for Navigational Communication

Tanshui River played a vital role of navigational communication in its early days. The Taiwan Province Annals have this to say: Palifen, in the northern part of Tanshui Harbor, is 10 "*li*" (about one third of a mile) away from the Kuantu gate, dividing the harbor into two ports, ranging from Paichiehshih in the southwest to Fengtzuchih in the northeast. The aborigines, who relied exclusively on boat transportation, created canoes for that purpose. The harbor can accommodate hundreds of vessels. Business from the hinterland has extended to this harbor. This account provides a general overview of the shipping and navigation of the Tanshui river basin in the early Ching dynasty. In 1792, Palifen was established as a port. Following the initiation of its trade with Wuhumen and Hanchiang of Fuchou, navigation exchanges between Mengka and Palifen were getting busier and busier. Since the 10th year of the Hsienfeng reign of the Ching dynasty (1860), there was an increasing exchange of motor vessels between Tanshui and Tataocheng. In the meantime, shipping among Hsintien, Takokan and Keelung River was also in full swing due to the production of tea in these areas.

Cargo Center during Japanese Era

During Japanese Occupation, Tataocheng became the most important cargo center of Taiwan, raising the importance of Tanshui River. In these days, wood, camphor and daily supplies from Central Taiwan converged in Tataocheng before their outward shipment via Tanshui River. Cargo imported from the Chinese mainland or Japan was shipped to Tataocheng from Tanshui Harbor via Tanshui River. For cargo entering Keelung Harbor, small boats were used for shipping to Tataocheng via Tanshui.

The year 1900 saw the heyday of this shipping route. There were nine motor vessels owned by Japanese companies traveling between Tanshui and Tataocheng on a daily basis; exchange of sailboats between the two places was even more frequent.

Later on, motor vessels could travel to and from the two places only once in the morning or in the afternoon, due to the siltation of the river. The route was abandoned following the operation of the Tanshui railway line. Today, there is virtually no shipping on the river.

滬尾、商港、紅毛城

淡水古名滬尾，爲土著語 Hoba 轉音而來，爲河口之意。漢人譯爲滬尾，以指海濱捕魚處之末端（「滬」字原意爲在潮間帶所築以攔魚之竹柵）。

明崇禎元年（西元 1628 年），西班牙人佔滬尾，命名爲「卡西多爾」（Casidor），淡水河則名爲「契馬諾」（Kimalon）。翌年建聖多明峨城（San Domingo，民間稱紅毛城）。崇禎 15 年，荷蘭人奪佔滬尾。日後明鄭及清廷均將紅毛城作爲駐軍之要塞。

咸豐 8 年（西元 1858 年），中英、中法天津條約明定安平、淡水爲通商口岸。次年，因清軍於大沽口炮擊英國換約艦隊，引發第二次英法聯軍東來，與清廷簽訂北京條約（咸豐 10 年），淡水始正式開港。在同治、光緒年間，淡水成爲北台灣第一大港，洋樓林立，其中茶葉爲輸出物之大宗。商務最盛時可停泊兩千噸級之輪船。

但由於淡水爲一河口港，因此受淡水河沖積而漸趨淤淺。而基隆之港口形勢優越，光緒 17 年（西元 1891 年）後基隆與臺北間鐵路通車，商務更盛。日本殖民台灣之後，淡水與基隆的地位相互消長，明治 37 年（光緒 30 年，西元 1904 年），基隆商務超越淡水，日後遂完全取代之。

註 84、95、151

RH-003

1860年代的淡水爲商務繁華的黃金時代，1904年時，其地位已被基隆所取代

The 1860s saw Tanshui's glory of commercial prosperity. By 1904, Tanshuei's status was replaced by Keelung.

Fuwei, Commercial Harbor, San Domingo

Fuwei, the old name of Tanshui, was derived from Hoba, an aboriginal name, denoting the river mouth. The aboriginal name was translated by the Han people into Fuwei (the prefix *"fu"* originally refers to the bamboo gate for the interception of fish in the intertidal area, and the suffix *wei* means tail orend), meaning the end of the sea-shore fishery.

In 1628 (the first year of the Chungchen reign of the Ming dynasty), the Spaniards occupied Fuwei and renamed it Casidor. In the meantime, the Tanshui River was renamed Kimalon. The Spaniards established San Domingo (known as the *Red Hair's Citadel* to the Taiwanese). In 1642, the Dutch seized Fuwei. Later on at the beginning of the Ching dynasty, Cheng Cheng-kung used San Domingo as a fortress guarded by military forces.

In 1858, Anping and Tanshui were opened as trading ports under the Sino-British and Sino-French agreements entered into at Tienchin. The next year, the Ching dynasty entered into the Treaty of Peking with the second coalition forces of Britain and France, which had attacked China because the troops of the Ching dynasty had shelled the British fleet passing through Taku on their way to exchanging ratified agreements with the Chinese government. Under the Treaty of Peking, Tanshui officially became a trading port. During the Tungchih and Kuanghsu reigns, Tanshui became the largest harbor in Northern Taiwan, with myriads of modern buildings and tea as the mainstay of its export. Tanshui could accommodate 2000-ton class steamboats in the heyday of its commercial operation.

Because Tanshui was located at the mouth of Tanshui River, it was gradually subject to siltation as a result of the alluvial effect of Tanshui River. In contrast, Keelung Harbor burgeoned with commercial activities, thanks to its geographical advantages and the launch of the railway link between Taipei and Keelung in 1891. During Japanese Occupation, Tanshui was losing ground in its tug- of-war with Keelung and was surpassed by Keelung in 1904, which subsequently took the place of Tanshui completely.

走過三世紀——八里遺勝

淡水隔河相望之八里，舊名八里坌，爲原住民語譯音。西班牙人稱爲 Parian，荷蘭人則稱 Parrigon。明鄭時以此地爲往來大陸與台灣船隻之補給港。清領台之後，厲行海禁，康熙 50 年（西元 1711 年）於八里坌設淡水營守備。雍正 10 年（西元 1732 年）設八里坌巡檢，並升淡水營守備爲淡水都司。翌年海禁解除，八里坌與鹿仔港（鹿港）、鹿耳門（台南安平）同列爲官方許可之移民口岸，八里之商業爲之大盛，遠在對岸滬尾之上；但因淤積及漢人向內陸開發之故，使八里坌之發展受影響。乾隆 24 及 32 年，都司營與巡檢先後改駐艋舺、新莊。嘉慶元年（西元 1796 年），淡水河氾濫，沖毀八里坌城牆、街道，居民大舉移往滬尾後，就此没落。民國 80 年，內政部決議，定八里之大坌坑遺址爲一級古蹟。

註 84、95、151

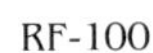

日治時代的淡水港

Tanshui Harbor during the Japanese era.

The Pali Relics — A History of Three Centuries

Originally called Palifen, Pali, whose designation was a translation of the aboriginal language, is located on the side of Tanshui River opposite Tanshui. Pali was called Parian by the Spaniards and Parrigon by the Dutch. During the rule of Cheng Cheng-kung, Pali functioned as a supply port for vessels traveling between the Chinese mainland and Taiwan. When the Ching dynasty conquered Taiwan, a ban on maritime transportation was imposed and the Tanshui Battalion was established in Palifen in 1711. In 1732, the Palifen Patrol was established, and the Tanshui Battalion was promoted and became the Tanshui Garrison. The maritime ban was lifted the next year, and Palifen, Lutzaikang (Lukang) and Luerhmen (Anping, Tainan) were officially open as ports of immigration, contributing to Pali's prosperous commercial activities, which far exceeded those of Fuwei at the other side of Tanshui River.

However, the siltation of Palifen and the inland migration of Han Chinese hampered the development of Palifen. In 1760 and 1767 (the 24th and 32nd years of the Chienlung Reign), the Garrison and Patrol moved to Mengka and Hsinchuang, respectively. The glory of Pali was ended in 1796 when the flooding of Tanshui River destroyed the ramparts and streets of Palifen, causing the residents to migrate to Fuwei on a massive scale. In 1991, the Ministry of Interior declared the Tafenkung relics of Pali a grade-one historical monument.

基隆地名探源與沿革

Evolution of the Name "Keelung" (chicken coop)

基隆舊稱雞籠，原是平埔族 Kétagalan （凱達格蘭）人的居住地，雞籠二字更是省去 taga 之後所成 kelan 的譯音。大雞社、雞籠社、大雞籠社均指此地。西元 1875 年清朝在此設立台北分防通判時，改地名爲「基隆」，取其「基地昌隆」之意，一直沿用至今。光緒 13 年 （1887 年） 台灣建省，設基隆廳隸屬台北府；日治時期設有基隆支廳；1920 年後改爲基隆郡，屬台北州；1924 年稱基隆市；光復後基隆列爲省轄市之一。

註 94

Plains aborigines of the Ketagalan tribe once lived in Keelung. The name was derived from the homophone "kelan," which was Ketagalan without the syllables "taga." The Chinese word "Keelung," literally means "chicken coop," and sounds very similar to "kelan" when prounced in the Taiwanese dialect. The region was renamed Keelung in 1875 during the Ching Dynasty. The name (pronounced *chilung* in Mandarin) was derived from the first and last words of the phrase *chi ti chang lung*, which meant "a prosperous base station." In 1887, the province of Taiwan was created and a Keelung prefecture hall was established under the supervision of the Taipei government. In 1920, the Keelung area was changed to Keelung County, which was under the supervision of Taipei prefecture. The region was further renamed to Keelung City in 1924, and came under the direct supervision of the Taiwan provincial government.

RH-004

新興都市海山口——新莊

新莊一帶原爲原住民「武勝灣社」的所在地。因地處淡水河沿岸，土地肥沃，且有商船往來，形成台北地區最早的商業都市，新莊原名「新庄」，即爲新興聚落。

新莊又因位於海山（鶯歌、三峽一帶）之出入要地，及舊時淡水河帆船航線中段，故有人稱其爲「海山口」或「中港街」。

註 16、123、154、161

RH-005

日治時代的新莊市街

A street scene of Hsinchuang during the Japanese era.

Hsinchuang Emerging City

Hsinchuang is the former site of Wulaowan Shih, an aboriginal settlement. Located along Tanshui River, Hsinchuang was blessed with rich soil and the traffic of commercial vessels, thus becoming the first commercial city in the Taipei area. The name Hsinchuang denotes a new settlement.

In addition, Hsinchuang was once called Haishankou or Chungkangchieh, because of its strategic location, controlling the exit and entrance of Haishan (Yingke and Shanhsia) and also situated along the midsection of the Tanshui River where busy traffic of sailboats used to take place.

泰山鄉原名山脚

山脚位於泰山鄉東北隅，在新莊的西北方。泰山鄉原隸屬台北州新莊郡新莊街，民國 39 年 3 月 1 日自新莊獨立出來成爲泰山鄉。 註 16、20

日治時代的山腳信用合作社 RH-006

Hsintien Cooperative of Shanchiao during the Japanese era.

Shanchiao- Previous Name of Taishan

Shanchiao was situated in the northeast of Taishan and in the northwest of Hsinchuang. In the past, Taishan was under the administration of Hsinchuang City, Hsinchuang County, Taipei Prefecture. On March 1, 1950, Taishan became a township independent of Hsinchuang.

新店 因碧潭而發跡

Green Lake — The Rise of Hsintien

碧潭地屬台北縣新店，位於新店溪西岸，水深而碧。相傳在清道光年間，泉州安溪人林章呑等在河寬水碧，積深潴潭的岸邊設店；而詩人遊客時常會集此地，日久成街，故名爲新店。碧潭自古又名石壁潭。日治時期碧潭名列台灣十二勝之一，當時鐵、公路交通都很方便，碧潭是鐵路新店線的終點。

註 92、95、154、158、160

With deep and green water, Green Lake (Pitan) is located on the west bank of Hsintien Creek in Hsintien, Taipei County. Legend has it that during the Taokuang Reign of the Ching dynasty, Li Chang- tuan and others established stores along the riverbank where water was green and deep; the place was called Green Lake. It was frequented by poets and tourists and naturally became a city called Hsintien (meaning *new store*). Called Stone Wall Lake in ancient times, Green Lake was listed as one of the 12 wonders of Taiwan during Japanese Occupation, with convenient railway and highway transportation. It was the last stop of the Hsintien railway.

新店之名因商集群聚碧潭而來，圖為日治時代的碧潭

The name" Hsintien" was derived from the convergence of businesses in Greek Lake. This picture depicts Greek Lake during the Japanese era.

RH-007

回首幾多淘金夢

日治時期東部礦業探勘

一談到早期花蓮的開發，便不能不談到砂金。當東來的葡萄牙人驚歎台灣爲「福爾摩沙」時，就稱今天的花蓮港附近爲「金河」。再加上荷蘭人、中國人、日本人先後在花蓮的採金活動的黃金傳說，爲早期東台灣的開發史，編織了許多慾望與浪漫的冒險故事。

最早有計劃探採金鑛的是曾經據有台灣北部的西班牙人，待荷蘭人驅逐西班牙人後，曾於1645年底組成一支爲數三百多人的遠征隊到花蓮採金。其後鄭克塽也曾派人至此，但皆所獲無多。此後砂金傳説雖時有所聞，但卻不再有大規模的採金行動。

及至日治時期，總督府及日本企業才又開始探鑛行動。在尋金的過程中，銅、鎳、石綿等鑛藏也逐漸被發現，但最引人注目的還是金鑛。1925年總督府派遣技師在立霧溪河口及加禮宛原野探勘砂金，歷經三年而無所獲。翌年，卻有來自日本内地的鑛山專家橫堀治三郎，在日本國内大肆宣傳，稱東台灣砂金蘊藏量至少有40億圓。40億圓究竟值多少？若以當時五口之家每月所需之柴米油鹽等費用爲60圓計，40億圓可謂天文數字。

一時間，不知有多少人因橫堀的宣傳而平添夢想，但多次探勘的總督府，卻未因世間的鼓噪而有所動。直至1934年，立霧溪中游又傳發現金鑛，淘金風潮更難抑止，總督府於是公告准許淘採砂金規定。兩年後，總督府組織了「東部台灣開發調查委員會」，派遣「東台灣資源調查團」入山調查。另繼1939年於立霧溪中游發現蘊藏量豐富的含金高位段丘後，又在和平南溪、木瓜溪、壽豐溪、萬里橋溪、馬太鞍溪、清水溪等處也有類似的發現。其後，總督府除宣佈保留東部砂金鑛區權外，也開始建設自太魯閣峽口至仙寰橋的「產金道路」。似乎有意進行大規模的採金行動，但最後仍無大展獲。

正當淘金熱潮的1936年，在立霧溪河口左岸一日人的鑛區内，挖掘出大量的金棒、金簪、加工用具、陶器壺等，並有二百多具人骨出土。關於此些遺跡的來源，衆説紛紜。其中甚至有17世紀初前來採金而遭原住民殺害之西班牙人遺骨的説法。然而如此大規模的發現，卻在淘金聲浪中遭淹没，並没有引發特別注目，只成爲淘金進行曲中一小段不和諧的揷曲罷了！

三百多年的淘金夢，得圓夢者幾希？如荷蘭東印度公司與台灣總督府，雖投下莫大的資金及人力，但終皆以不符合經濟效益而作罷。究其原因，乃在於立霧溪的砂金是段丘砂金，有時雖集中在砂礫層下部，而使得下游出現大量砂金。但除非眞正著手開發溪流砂金，否則難有大斬獲。然而，爲了一圓淘金夢而進行的各種調査，卻無意中爲原住民、地質探勘等研究留下許多珍貴的資料，則是作古的拜金先人所始料所未及的吧！

Gold Rush—

Mining Exploration of Eastern Taiwan during the Japanese Era

Placer gold played a particularly important role in the early development of Hualien. The area around Hualien Harbor was called Golden River by the Dutch who were dazzled by the beauty of Taiwan, which they referred to as Formosa, during their exploration of the Orient. Stories about the gold-digging activities of the Dutch, Chinese and Japanese were also prevalent, contributing to a wealth of adventures--adventures of desire and romance--in the early history of Taiwan's development.

The first organized effort to exploit gold was made by the Spaniards who occupied northern Taiwan. In 1645 after dislodging the Spaniards, the Dutch sent a gold-digging team of 300 explorers on an exploration tour to Hualien. Later in history, Cheng Ko-shuang also sent people to Hualien, again to no avail. From then on, large-scale exploitation of gold was no longer attempted, in spite of sporadic accounts of placer gold being discovered in this area.

Gold mining in Hualien had not been attempted until the colonial rule of Japanese when the Taiwan Governor's Office and Japanese companies resumed gold exploration. In the process, deposits of copper, nickel and asbestos were gradually discovered, even though gold mines still commanded the most attention. In 1925, the Governor's Office sent technicians on an exploration tour to the estuary of Liwu Creek and the field of Chialiwan, and three years later they returned empty-handed. The following year, a mining expert by the name of Yokobori Jizaburo put forward a hypothesis that there was about 4 billion yen worth of gold deposits in eastern Taiwan. The figure of 4 billion yen was at that time astronomical, judging from the fact that the monthly cost of living for a family of five was 60 yen.

The conjecture of Yokobori inspired fantasies of gold-digging, but the Governor's Office, which had made several futile attempts, was hardly moved. It was not until 1934 when discovery of gold deposits in midstream Liwu Creek was reported again, making it difficult for the Japanese rulers to stem the tide of the gold rush, that the Governor's Office finally issued a decree, authorizing gold-digging activities. Two years later, the Governor's office organized the Research Committee for Exploration of Eastern Taiwan and sent a research group on a field trip to study the resources in eastern Taiwan. In 1939, gold-rich hills in the midstream of Liwu Creek were discovered, followed by similar discoveries in Hopingnan Creek, Papaya Creek, Fengshou Creek, Wanli Bridge Creek, Mataian Creek and Chingshui Creek. Later, the Governor's Office claimed mining rights in eastern Taiwan and began to develop the Golden Path between Taroko Gorge and Hsienhuan Bridge. The seeming attempt of the Governor's Office to embark upon large-scale exploitation of gold ended up with few results.

In 1936 when the gold rush was in full swing, a large quantity of gold bars, gold hairpins, processing tools and ceramic kettles, along with over 200 skeletons, were unearthed in a Japanese-operated mine on the west bank along the estuary of Liwu Creek. Accounts differed with respect to the origin of the relics. Some even believed that the remains belonged to the Spaniards killed by the indigenous people in the 17th century during their gold exploration in Taiwan. However, such a spectacular discovery did not receive due attention during the gold rush and was in the end reduced to a mere episode of discord.

The gold rush for nearly three centuries produced few success stories. The East Indian Company of Holland, as well as the Governor's Office in Taiwan, devoted considerable amount of resources and man power to exploration for gold, only to abort their attempts for lack of economy of scale. The reason behind such failure is that the placer gold in Liwu Creek was underneath a bench. Although large quantities of gold sometimes emerged in downstream areas as a result of gold concentration in the bottom layers of gravel, no real progress could be made without full- scale exploitation of the placer gold in the catchment area. Nevertheless, the investigation and research conducted for the exploration of gold left behind invaluable information for the study of the indigenous people and geology--a result never intended by the gold diggers.

原鄉的再殖——日治時代官營移民村

1910年2月，來自日本四國德島縣的九户移民，抵達花蓮的吉安，揭開了日治時代「官營移民」的序幕。這種以建設純日本式農村爲目的的移民村，始於今吉安之「吉野村」，至1917年止，陸續建立了「豐田」、「林田」二村，成了著名的「三移民村」。

鉅資移民爲哪端？

在日本統治之下，日台兩地人員流動頻繁，自1909至1917年間，總督府年年投下鉅資，在花蓮從事農業移民，可稱得上是日治台灣史上的一項創舉。官營移民的目的何在？據《官營移民事業報告書》中，可明顯看出是基於台灣統治之需；一方面以作爲大和民族向熱帶地區發展的實驗；並可調節日本農村之過剩人口；另在國防及同化上也可發揮作用。

原住民被迫流放

增加日人移民以厚植日本在台之勢力雖是日本治台的既定政策，但三移民村的建立卻是一波三折。日本據台之初，即調查全台適宜大規模移民之地，吉野村一帶原即是移民預定地之一。然而此地恰爲南勢阿美族人「七脚川」社之地，如何將此地闢爲移民村實爲一棘手問題。因此，當1908年七脚川社阿美族人反抗時，不啻是爲移民村的建設提供了絶佳機會。總督府隨即對該族人進行大規模的軍事征討，並將殘存族人集體移往他處，其故地則被重劃爲移民村用地。因此，如果説吉野村之成立史即是七脚川社阿美族人之流放史也不爲過。至於豐田與林田二村，則原是製糖公司爲確保甘蔗源，招攬契約農民所闢成的。其後因經營不善，改由總督府接手，並轉爲後來的移民村。

優勢族群——花蓮的日本人

移民之初，總督府授予每户三甲地以供開墾之用，並約定闢成後承認其業主權。各村的主要收入源都是甘蔗、煙草等經濟作物。吉野村因地近花蓮市區，得以販賣蔬果、香蕉乾等而有較豐富的副業收入，是三村中最富裕的，而有模範農村之譽。而戴著白頭巾，牽著滿載蔬果的牛車沿街叫賣的日本女人，也成了花蓮的「名物」(名產)。

在社區結構方面，各村都有聯外道路，並有輕便鐵路供運送甘蔗之用。水利方面則是灌溉渠道，排水道、飲用水道一應俱全。村外圍設有防禦野獸侵襲的木柵，内部則有移民指導所(廳辦事處)、醫療所(公醫)、郵局、小學、警察派出所、青年會集會所等公共設施，並有神社、傳教所、火葬場、墓地等，舉凡照顧村人生老病死的相關設施皆配備齊全。由於村内不允許漢人及原住民移住，且刻意使村内外保持隔離狀態，結果三移民村都得以維持日本農村的風貌。

「清晨，在沁涼清新的空氣中醒來，眼前一片濃蔭中，點在著有廣闊庭園的內地式房舍。耳邊時聞穿著和式服飾的兒童嬉笑聲，彷佛置身內地般，實爲到東部來最愉快的一刻」。像這樣遊客筆下的移民村，不知讓多少客居台灣的日人抒解其思鄉情懷！

赤貧的優勢族群

然而，儘管總督府對移民村的建設投下大筆資金，但移民卻普遍稱窮。很多人在未獲得業主權時便已將所耕地抵押殆盡。甚至有日人向鄰近開雜貨店的漢人借貸時，所能抵押的卻只是移民間互相借貸的借據。而移民村之所以赤貧的原因，一般皆歸咎於其對風土之不適；也有人指稱其在台灣耕作所需付出的勞力，遠大於其於日本之所需，因此，即使辛勤耕作，也很難求其能與漢人有相同的收穫。更何況其中有些原是遊手好閒之輩，缺乏刻苦之開墾意志，更難期待能有所成了。

結果，投下鉅資建設的移民村，卻根本未能達到總督府早先預定的目標。特別是想以官營移民村救濟日本農村經濟的凋弊，及同化台灣人等目標上，與早先所預期的相去更遠。移民村最後的作用，恐怕只是提供一個純日本人的模範農村，作爲部份在台日本人緬懷原鄉、抒解鄉愁的寄情對象罷了！

Official Immigrant Villages during Japanese Rule

In February, 1910, nine Japanese families arrived at Chian, Hualien from Tokushima Prefecture, Shikoku, Japan, as a prelude to government-encouraged immigration during the Japanese era. This type of immigrant village established for developing pure Japanese agricultural communities began with Yoshino Village, which is Chian today, followed by Toyota and Hayashida villages. Together, these villages were generally known as the Three Immigrant Villages during the era of Japanese rule.

Purposes of Immigration

Japan's rule over Taiwan was characterized by frequent exchanges of people between Taiwan and Japan. Between 1909 and 1917, the Taiwan Governor's Office committed huge funds annually to agricultural immigration to Hualien. This was an unprecedented policy throughout Japan's rule of Taiwan, which is open to one question: What was the purpose of officially sponsored immigration? According to the Report on Official Immigration, it is apparent that this policy was required for Japan's rule of Taiwan. On the one hand, Japan intended to conduct an experiment in which the Japanese were relocated to develop tropical areas. On the other hand, the surplus population of farming folk in Japan could be adjusted. In addition, immigration of this nature could also facilitate Japan's national security, as well as the assimilation of the Taiwanese into Japanese society.

Indigenous People Forced into Exile

Although it was a set policy of Japan to rule Taiwan by increasing the population of Japanese immigrants to strengthen Japan's influence in Taiwan, the establishment of the three immigrant villages went through considerable hardships. In the early days of Japanese rule, Japan conducted surveys to identify places in Taiwan appropriate for mass immigration. The vicinity of Yoshino Village was one of the places designated for immigration. However, this area was already occupied by the Chichiao Village of the Ami tribe, and how to clear this land for immigration was a difficult question for the Japanese rulers. The uprising by the Ami tribe of Chichiao Village in 1908 provided a great opportunity for the development of immigrant villages. The Taiwan Governor's Office launched a large-scale military offensive against the indigenous rebels and subsequently relocated the remaining tribespeople elsewhere. Their land was then repartitioned for the development of immigrant villages. Therefore, it is not an exaggeration to equate the establishment of Yoshino Village with the exile of the Ami tribe of Chichiao Village. As for Toyota and Hayashida, they were originally established by farmers contracted by a sugar company to secure the supply of sugarcane. Poorly managed, the villages were taken over by the Governor's Office and later became immigrant villages.

Privileged Population--The Japanese in Hualien

During the initial phase of immigration, the Governor's Office granted each family three hectares of land for development purposes and agreed to their ownership of the land upon completion of land development. The villages depended for their income on cash crops, such as sugarcane and tobacco. Yoshino Village was nicknamed the model village, for its ability to generate more income, as compared with the other two villages, by the additional sale of vegetables and dried bananas, thanks to their geographical proximity to Hualien City. Sitting on an ox cart loaded with vegetables, the Japanese women in a kerchief selling vegetables door-to-door became a specialty of Hualien.

In terms of village infrastructure, they were connected with other places by a number of roads, with ready access to railways for the transportation of sugarcane. There were also small canals for irrigation purposes, as well as sluiceways and waterways for drinking water. In addition, the villages were encircled by picket fences erected to ward off the intrusion of wild animals. Internally, there were immigration offices, hospices, post offices, elementary schools, police stations, and meeting halls for youth clubs, along with Shinto shrines, churches, crematoriums, and cemeteries. In other words, these villages featured a complete array of facilities to accommodate the life, death and illness of the villagers. Because neither Han Chinese people nor indigenous people were allowed to move in, the three villages were able to maintain the appearances of typical Japanese villages.

"In the morning, I woke up in a farm house with a spacious yard, just like back home (Japan). Basking in the fresh air of the village, I was greeted by the lovely greenness of the trees, along with the laughter of the children in kimono. This was the happiest moment of my stay in eastern Taiwan, because I felt very much at home." Such was a typical expression in the diaries of Japanese visitors in Taiwan. In fact, the villages helped alleviate the nostalgia of the Japanese visiting Taiwan during that time.

Privileged Population in Poverty

Despite huge funding committed by the Governor's Office to the development of the immigrant villages, poverty among the immigrants was a common phenomenon. Some Japanese even took loans from the Han Chinese running grocery stores in the neighborhood by mortgaging IOUs issued among the villagers borrowing from each other. The poverty of the villages can probably be explained by the inability of the villagers to adjust to the new environment. Some said that they had to commit more labor to the tillage of the farmland in comparison with farming in Japan, and that even if they worked very hard, it was very difficult to reap harvests comparable to those of the Chinese. In addition, some of the immigrants had been loiterers back in Japan, and they lacked the diligence and willingness to cultivate the farmland; therefore, a desirable outcome from the development project could hardly be expected.

In the end, the immigrant villages which had cost the Taiwan Governor's Office a fortune failed to meet the objectives of the Governor's Office. Even worse, the villages turned out to be detrimental to the realization of the previous objective of the Japanese rulers: to salvage the withering agricultural industry in Japan and to assimilate the Taiwanese subjects by means of the official immigrant villages. In the final analysis, the immigrant villages only served as model villages for the Japanese and places for alleviating the homesickness of the Japanese in Taiwan.

RH-008

吉野村是日治時代東部官營移民村之一

Yoshino Village is one of the official immigration villages in eastern Taiwan during the Japanese era.

薪材之鄉吉野村

吉野村，即今之花蓮縣吉安鄉治所在，原名七脚川，爲阿美族語之音譯。其義爲薪柴甚多之地。日治後漸有日人移墾於此，西元 1910 年起，實行官營移民，日移民達 2 百 40 餘戶。光復後，日移民除部份日籍技術人員外，共遣回一萬 7 千餘人，並改稱吉安。

圖中屋舍爲傳統日人農村屋舍。

Chi Yeh Village--Country of Firewood

Originally named Chichiaochuan, a translation from the language of the Ami tribe meaning a place rich with firewood, Chi Yeh village has become Chi-an of Hualien County today. Japanese settlements emerged during Japanese era, and migration to this village was encouraged by the government, contributing to over 240 Japanese families in the village. After the retrocession of Taiwan, a total of 17,000 Japanese were sent back to Japan, with the exception of certain Japanese technicians, and the village was renamed as Chi-an.

This picture depicts a traditional Japanese farmhouse.

從番社、牧場到飛機場——加禮宛曠野

加禮宛曠野位在花蓮支廳平野區美崙山北面（今花蓮市郊、新城鄉境內），即今日之嘉里村、美崙溪以北之地統名加禮宛。加禮宛源自部落名，清咸豐3年，原居宜蘭之平埔族移居此地，以加禮宛爲中心建竹林、七結、武暖、談秉、瑤歌、加禮宛六社，統稱加禮宛社，是奇萊平埔族加禮宛五社所在地。加禮宛爲東部多山環境中少有的小平原，史載：「此地土地平廣膏腴甲於後山」。日治以後放牧草原，是爲加禮宛牧場，占地70922甲，畜養黃牛、水牛等。圖即放牧情景。日後在此設陸軍飛行場，爲平野天然機場，大正4年(西元1915年)曾舉行飛航大會，昭和11年(西元1936年)8月，日本航空株式會社闢臺北花蓮港航線時始設航空站，五年後以缺油停航。光復後民國50年（西元1961年）7月機場混凝土瀝青路面跑道動工，接著設置民航局花蓮航空站，設備也屢經擴充而更加完善，目前爲一具有夜航設備之軍民合用機場。此外，機場以東有民國65年開發完成的美崙工業區。

Chialiwan Field--From Aboriginal and Village prairie to Airfield

Chialiwan Field is located in the north of Mt. Meilun, Ping Yeh District, Hualien (or Hsincheng today, the suburbs of Hualien City). The present-day Chiali village is formerly known as Chiali Yuan. Places north of Meilun Creek are collectively called Chialiwan, a tribe name, and are where Chialiwan Wu Village of the Chilai tribe used to be. In 1853, plains aborigines from Ila, moved into the region, and built six villages, collectively know as the Chiali Yuan communities. Chialiwan is one of the few plains in the mountainous terrain of East Taiwan. Annals have it that this land is characterized by smooth terrain and rich soil, which is far better than the back slope of the mountains. During Japanese Occupation, Chialiwan become a praivie occupying a total area of 68,795 hectares, as shown in this picture depicting a scene of pasturage. Later, Hirano Natural Airport, an army airfield, was established here. In 1915, an air show was held at this airfield, and in 1936, an air terminal was established due to the initiation by the Japanese Aviation Society of air links between Taipei and Hualien Harbor (which ceased operation five years later as a result of fuel shortages). In July, 1961, after the retrocession of Taiwan, a project to build concrete asphalt airstrips for the airfield was launched, followed by the establishment of the Hualien Air Terminal under the Civil Aviation Bureau and by successive renovations and upgrading of facilities. This airport, which is currently used jointly by the military and civilians, is equipped with a nocturnal landing system. In addition, in the east of the airport lies the Meilun Industrial Zone, completed in 1976.

RH-009

日治時代的加禮宛曠野，現爲軍民合用之機場

Chialiwan Field during Japanese era is a military and commuter airport today.

花蓮地名沿革
Evolution of the Name "Hualien"

花蓮之溪水奔流入海，溪海波浪相激縈洄壯闊而有「洄瀾港」之稱，清咸豐七年，原先在宜蘭拓殖的漢人陸續移民至此，形成聚落，此時稱此地爲「花蓮」乃取「洄瀾」之諧音而成。於是後人均以「花蓮」爲統一的名稱。

Hualien is known for the splashing waves created as rivers in the region flow into the sea; it was formerly known as Huilan Harbor (literally, wave splashing). The region became known as Hualien after the 7th year of the reign of Hsien-feng Emperor in the Ching Dynasty (1857), when the Han people came to settle in the region.

RH-010

日治時代遠望花蓮港全景

A panorama of Hualien Harbor during the Japanese era

山與溪的故鄉
——通霄
Tunghsiao — Home of the Mountains and Rivers

通霄爲苗栗縣西部濱海的鄉鎮之一，原爲平埔族道卡斯族「屯消」社的聚居地。而後，漢人移墾於此，取其音譯，名爲呑霄。日人來會後，見境内的虎頭山聳立於雲霄之間，乃改名爲通霄。

通霄溪，舊名呑霄溪，或稱爲南勢溪，爲通霄鎮内最大的溪流，發源於鎮東的內湖、福興、南和（里名），昔日溪水深可停泊商船，因此，呑霄港爲苗栗一帶的貨物呑吐集散中心。後因呑霄溪的淤淺而逐漸沒落，現在是僅供小型漁船停泊的漁港。

虎頭山，位在通霄鎮東北方，僅高93公尺，但相較於四周的平原，便顯出其高聳，又因其山形似虎，所以名爲虎頭山。由於虎頭山地勢高，登頂眺望，通霄一帶秀麗景色，盡收眼底，如「虎嶼觀潮」、「呑霄漁艇」即被文人墨客列爲通霄勝景及苗栗八景之一。此外虎頭山上還有忠烈祠（原日治時期之神社）、台灣光復紀念碑、壽公祠等名勝。 註28、128

Tunghsiao, one of the coastal towns in western Miaoli, was formerly the dwelling place of plains aborigines. The place was named Tunhsiao by the Han people who moved into the region later. During the period of Japanese rule, the Japanese were fascinated by the spectacle of Mt. Hutou amidst the clouds, and called the place Tunghsiao (literally, "Through the Clouds").

Formerly known as both Tunhsiao River and Nanshih River, Tunghsiao River is the largest river in the Tunghsiao region. Originating from the Neihu, Fuhsing, and Nanho areas east of the region, the river was formerly deep enough to accommodate commercial boats, which made Tunghsiao harbor the commercial hub of the Miaoli area. However, prosperity in the area declined as the water level subsided.

Today, only small fishing boats can be accommodated in the harbor.

Mt. Hutou, located northeast of Tunghsiao town, stands out among the surrounding low lands despite a height of only 93 meters. Its name, literally meaning "Tiger Head Mountain, "was given because of its tiger-shaped contours. The mountain is one of the eight scenic attractions of Miaoli. Also found on the mountain are attractions such as the martyrs' shrine (formerly a Shinto shrine during the period of Japanese rule), a plaque commemorating the retrocession of Taiwan to Chinese rule, and the Shoukung Shrine.

RH-011

通霄溪昔日水深可停泊商船，現爲小漁港

Tunghsiao Creek, which used to accommodate commercial vessels due to its deep water, is a small fishing port today.

番子田

番子田，因有麻豆社的平埔族原住民遷入於此，而名爲番子田。光復後，改名爲隆田，爲今台南縣官田鄉鄉治所在處。縱貫鐵、公路均在此設站、交會，爲地方上的交通中心，附近尚有嘉南大圳的水道工事。 註93

RA-125

圖爲日治時代位於台南番子田的嘉南大圳水道

Chianan Aqueduct in Fan Tzu Tien, Tainan during the Japanese era.

Fan Tzu Tien

Fan Tzu Tien(the land of the aborigines) acquired its name from its inhabitants - the Pingfu Tribe aborigines who moved here from Madoshe. After the recovery of Taiwan, the place was renamed Lungtien where the present-day county Administrative Office of Kuantian County, Tainan County is located. It is also the local transportation center where the main north-south railway and highway of Taiwan intersect with stations established. Waterway works of the Chianan Canal is in the vicinity.

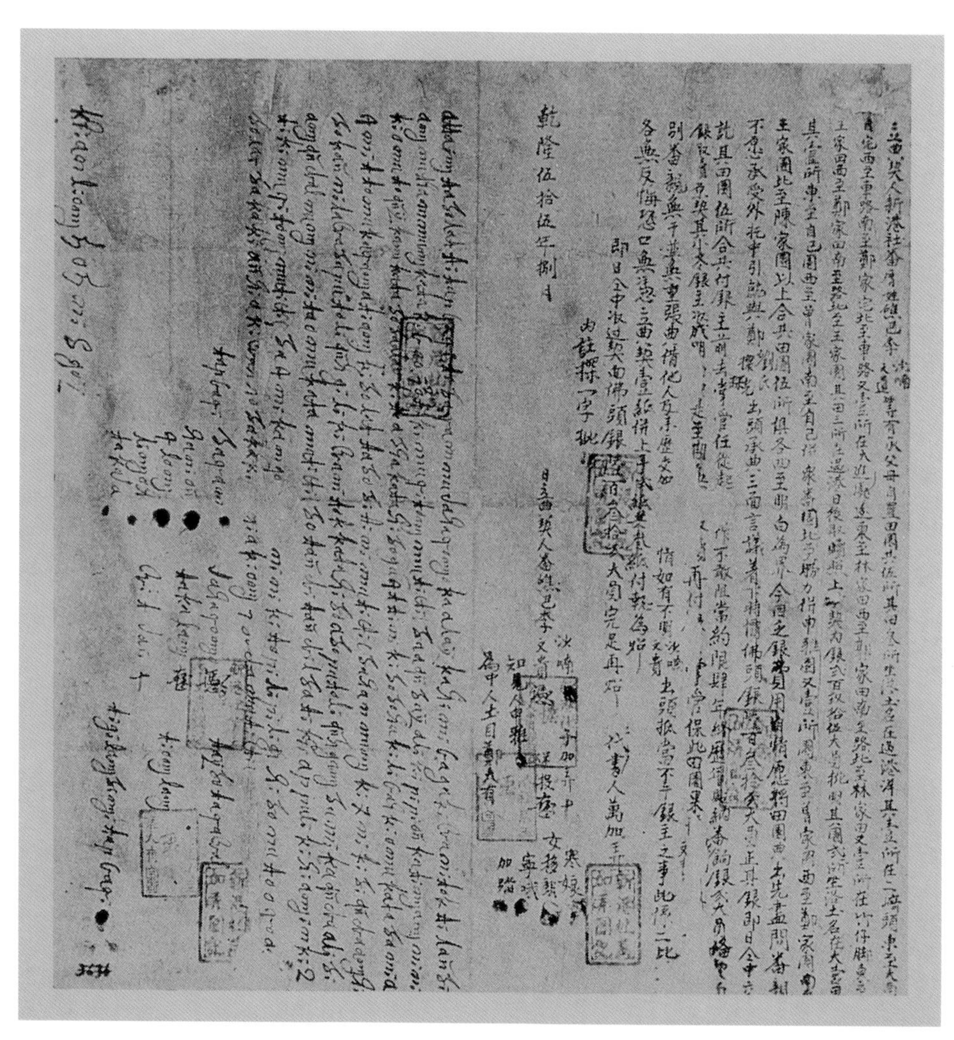

RB-156

圖為新港文書。乾隆 55 年 8 月（距今 140 年前）新港社原住民與漢人間所製作的契約書，除漢文外，同時記載著以羅馬字拼寫的原住民語譯文。本文書為漢語、原住民語對譯的文書，或者為以羅馬字拼寫原住民語為內容的文書記載，其中有不少為自康熙以至嘉慶年間的紀年，這些文書記載應是呈現在台之荷蘭人文化的最佳史料。

This picture shows the Hsinkang Document, which was an agreement between the indigenous people of Hsinkang Village and Han Chinese people. This document was written in Mandarin, Dutch, and a Romanized script of aboriginal language. In all three language the document specified a number of dates from the Kanghsi period to the Chiaching period of the Ching dynasty, and is therefore the best historical record for reflecting the Dutch culture in Taiwan.

RB-157

本圖爲台灣島古圖中，關於台南州附近的縮印，原圖爲距今約 230 年前的康熙中葉所描繪，寬 60 糎（公釐），長 5 米（公尺）47 糎的彩色大圖。圖中繪有今之台南的紅毛城、紅毛樓的外寧南坊、新街、大井頭等街路，台廈道、台灣府、縣、鎮、左右中營盤等文武官署，其他如天后宮、文廟、城隍廟、海會寺、山川台等。

This is a miniaturized version of the vicinity of Tainan in the archaic map of Taiwan. The original map was created in the middle of the Kanghsi period some 230 years ago. The color original was 60cm wide and 47cm long. The map depicts Forts Zeelandiu, Fort Provintia, Hsinchieh, Tachingten, Taihsiu Boulevard, governmental landmarks of prefectual, county and township adwinistions, and military in stallations as well an temples, such as Heaven Mother Temple, Wen Temple, Fortress God Temple, Haihui Temple and Shanchuantai.

湯匙山安平山墓地

安平墓地（今安平第一公墓地）位在湯匙山。荷人領台地時，稱爲 Uytrecht 要塞，是防護熱蘭遮城的第三座城堡。湯匙山的面前原是碼頭，後來成爲魚塭，今日魚塭已不復見。而關於安平的喪葬儀式中有一項特殊的風俗即爲，人在去世後的出殯行列必須由女婿來帶路，此項風俗流傳已久。 註 58、184

RH-012

Cemetery in Mt. Tanchih

Anping Cemetery (First Cemetery of Anping today) was located in Mt. Tanchih. During the rule of the Dutch, the cemetery was called Uytrecht Bastion, the third fortress established for the protection of Zeelandia. There used to be a pier, later turned into pisciculture ponds, in front of Mt. Tanchih. Today, the ponds have disappeared. In this area, there is a time-honored ritual for the burial of the Anping people. The funeral procession of the deceased must be led by the son-in-law.

蕃薯寮到旗山
From Sweet Potato Cottage to Chishan

旗山位在屏東平原西北方，羅漢外門里的中部。明萬曆年間已有西拉雅平埔族大傑嶺社人到此墾殖；清康熙年間，來自鳳山的漳州人招汀州佃農來此搭建寮舍種植蕃薯，因而稱作蕃薯寮。黃叔璥《台海使槎錄》中也記載，康熙年間在羅漢外門里新形成之山莊稱施里莊，即俗稱之蕃薯寮。

雍正 9 年（西元 1731 年），在此地設縣丞，屬鳳山縣；12 年改屬台灣縣；乾隆 54 年（西元 1789 年）改置巡檢。民國 9 年，改稱旗山，乃取其位在旗尾山之西南，故稱之。 註 94

Chishan is situated in the northwest of the Pingtung plain and in central Luohanweimen District. In Chishan, there had been settlements of aborigines from Tachiehling Village of the Hsilaya tribe during the Wanli reign of the Ming dynasty. During the Kanghsi reign of the Ching dynasty, the Changchou people from Fengshan recruited tenants to come here to establish cottages and grow sweet potatoes; therefore, this place was later called Sweet Potato Cottage. The Taihaishihcha Annals by Huang Shu-ying also indicates that the new village in Luohanweimen District was called Shihli Village, or nicknamed Sweet Potato Cottage.

In 1731, the 9th year of the Yungcheng reign of the Ching dynasty, a county magistrate was stationed here, administrating Fengshan County. In the 12th year of the Yungcheng reign, this village was put under the jurisdiction of Taiwan County. In 1789, the village became a Patrol and was later renamed as Chishan in 1920 because of its geographic location in the southwest of Chiwei Mountain.

蕃薯的故鄉——旗山

旗山鎮，原爲平埔族的聚落。清廷領台後，始有漢人移入，地屬台南縣羅漢門。旗山舊名蕃薯寮，相傳因有一位老婦人曾在此地蓋草寮賣蕃薯糊，不久過往休息的旅客漸多，蕃薯寮之名便不逕而走。日治後，日人以蕃薯寮之名不雅，乃取境內最高的旗尾山而命名爲旗山，時值大正 9 年（西元 1920 年），爲今高雄縣旗山鎮。照片中的建築物爲日治時期的蕃薯寮火車站，今已不存。

註 103、104、166

RF-073

旗山舊名爲蕃薯寮，圖爲日治時期的蕃薯寮

Chishan was originally called Sweet Potato Cottage. This picture depicts Sweet Potato Cottage during the Japanese era.

Chishan--Country of Sweet Potatoes

Chishan used to be a settlement of plains aborigines. During the rule of the Ching dynasty, the Han people began to move in, and this place was put under the jurisdiction of Luohanmen, Tainan County. The village was originally called Sweet Potato Cottage. Legend has it that an old woman built a cottage here and sold sweet potato gruel for a living, and soon news spread by travelers passing by the cottage. Gradually, the place became known as Sweet Potato Cottage. During the Japanese era, the Japanese considered the name to be vulgar, and in 1920 they renamed it Chishan, after Chiwei Mountain, the highest mountain in the vicinity. It remains Chishan of Kaohsiung County to this day. This picture portrays a building known as Sweet Potato Cottage Train Station during the Japanese era, which no longer exists.

旗後今非昔比

Chihou: Prosperous No More

旗後位於旗津北部，在打狗尚未築港之前，此地已有漁業發展。自從日人在打狗闢港之後更爲繁榮，洋行、商店、茶樓等林立街頭，但至日治末期已漸趨没落。光復後，受市區内移的影響，此地已繁華不再。如今想窺得往日光景，僅餘廟前路通山巷一帶的舊式建築供人緬懷。 註54、101

Located to the north of Chichin, Chihou long had a thriving fishing industry even before harbors were built in the Takou (Kaohsiung) area. Shops, stores, and tea shops greeted the more prosperous years after Takou Harbor was built during the Japanese period. Prosperity, however, went on a decline toward the end of the Japanese period and after World War II. Today, only the old architectures along Miaochien Road and Tungshan Alley stand as a reminder of past prosperity.

RF-109

日治時期的旗後街景

Street Scene of Chihou during the Japanese era.

不變的軍事地位——澎湖

Penghu — An Eternal Military Stronghold

澎湖歷來一直是台海軍事要地。元朝以澎湖爲兵站，對台灣用兵；明朝爲防倭寇而在此留有偏師駐防。自歸入清朝版圖後，清廷在澎湖設置巡檢司，之後更設廳、築城以爲防禦工事，並編制有澎湖水師左營鎮守，爾後改爲澎湖水師協標營、澎湖水師鎮標營，並設有砲台。日治時期，澎湖設有馬公機場，爲海空軍基地，馬公港充爲軍港，停泊軍艦，並有澎湖島要塞砲兵大隊駐守。光復後，澎湖負有保衛台海安全的重責，有國軍駐守。

註10、40、52

Penghu has always been a military stronghold in the Taiwan Strait. In the Yuan dynasty, military forces were stationed in Penghu, getting ready for any incursion into Taiwan. During the Ming dynasty, a troop was stationed in Penghu to discourage incursions by Japanese pirates. During the rule of the Ching dynasty, a garrison was established in Penghu. Later, Penghu was upgraded to the status of a prefecture, and a fortress was built. Later, a naval force was stationed there, and batteries established. During the Japanese era, an airport was built and served as a military base for the navy and air forces. Makung Harbor was reconstructed as a military harbor for the anchorage of military vessels and guarded by the Penghu Artillery Battalion. During the period of KMT rule, a military force was again stationed in Penghu to ensure the security of the Taiwan Strait.

RH-014

圖爲日治時代澎湖重砲兵本部

The Battalion Office of Heavy Artillery in Penghu during the Japanese era.

城堡舊事

Fortress Stories

台灣的第一座城堡，始於西元1625年荷蘭人於台南所建的普羅民遮城（即赤崁樓）。城堡可作爲防禦要塞，地理方位的標幟，通常爲一首善地區的中心，或扼守港口或平定亂事的重地。台灣的城堡建築形式歷經不斷拆毀、重建、或坍圮，還完整保留其建築美學者，已屈指可數，如今僅徒留其史蹟的形式……

The first fortress in Taiwan was Fort Provintia (or Chihkan Lou) established by the Dutch in Tainan in 1625. Fortresses, which served as a bastion and a landmark as well, typically became the center of major cities, or were strategic strongholds for the protection of harbors or the suppression of rebellions. Today, the aesthetic beauty of only a few fortresses has been preserved, as a result of changes to the architectural style of the fortress in the course of their demolition, reconstruction or dilapidation.

城門的功用？ Function of Fort Gates

早期台灣城市為了防止亂事而築城牆，牆高多在1丈5尺左右，上面築有雉堞，人車可行。大的城除了東西南北門外，另設小門，但在重要性上並沒有分別。且往往是出入頻繁的通道。城外設有半月形的附廓，以加強防禦功能。

In early times, ramparts were established for cities in Taiwan to prevent insurgence. Battlements were built on top of ramparts, mostly 15 feet in height, and accessible by pedestrians and vehicles. In addition to the main gates at the four sides, large forts had other small gates, which were no different from the main gates in terms of their importance, and which were often busy corridors. The forts had arc-shaped outer walls to enhance their defensive functions.

台灣著名城門沿革及現況

城　外	建造年代及構造	規　模	城　門　名	城樓形式	備　註
1嘉義城	1704年建木柵 1729年改土石 1788年改築磚城	744丈	東門（襟山） 西門（帶海） 南門（崇陽） 北門（拱辰）	重簷單脊歇山 不明 重簷單脊歇山 不明	被拆，有月城。 被拆 被拆 被拆
2臺南城	1725年建木柵 1788年改土石	2520丈	大東門（東安） 大西門（鎮海） 大南門（寧南） 大北門（拱辰） 小東門（迎春） 小西門（靖波） 小南門 小北門	重簷單脊歇山 重簷單脊歇山 重簷單脊歇山 重簷單脊歇山 單簷單脊歇山附軒 單簷單脊歇山 單簷單脊歇山附軒 單簷歇山馬背	近年重建 被拆 近年重建有月城 被拆，有月城。 被拆，有月城 近年遷建 被拆，有月城 被拆，有月城
3新竹城	1733年圍刺竹 1826年改石城	860丈	東門（迎曦） 西門（挹爽） 南門（歌薰） 北門（拱辰）	重簷單脊歇山 重簷單脊歇山 重簷單脊歇山 重簷單脊歇山	尚存 被拆 被拆 日據時毀於火災
4新竹外城	1840年建土石城	1495丈	東門（賓暘） 西門（告成） 南門（解阜） 北門（承恩） 小東門（卯耕） 小西門（觀海） 小南門（耀文） 小北門（天樞）	不明 不明 不明 不明 不明 不明 不明 不明	坍圮 坍圮 坍圮 坍圮 坍圮 坍圮 坍圮 坍圮
5彰化城	1734年植刺竹 1811年改築磚城	922丈	東門（樂耕） 西門（慶豐） 南門（宣平） 北門（拱辰）	重簷單脊歇山 不明 重簷單脊歇山 不明	被拆 被拆 被拆 被拆
6鳳山舊城 （左營）	1722年建 1823年改築土石	800丈	東門（鳳儀） 西門（奠海） 南門（啓文） 北門（拱辰）	單簷重脊歇山 不明 單簷單脊歇山 不明	已毀 已毀 尚存，似曾修改 尚存
7鳳山新城	1786年建 1805年重建	不詳	東門（朝陽） 西門（景華） 南門（安化） 北門（平朔） 小東門（同儀）	不明 不明 不明 不明 不明	不存 不存 不存 不存 尚存
8宜蘭城	1811年建	640丈	東門（震平） 西門（兌安） 南門（離順） 北門（坎興）	不明 不明 不明 不明	被拆 被拆 被拆 被拆
9大甲城	1881年建土石城	510丈	設4門	單簷單脊硬山	均不存
10里港城	1835年建土城		設4門	不明	尚存南門

城外	建造年代及構造	規模	城門名	城樓形式	備註
11後龍城	1834年建土城	300丈	設4門	不明	不存
12板橋城	1855年建磚城	2里許	設4門	不明	被拆
13桃園城	1839年建土城	4里許	設4門	不明	不存
14中壢城	1842年建土城	3里許	設4門	不明	不存
15房裏城	1855年建土城	3里許	設4門	不明	不存
16恆春城	1875年建土石城	972丈	東門 西門 南門（明都） 北門	單簷單脊歇山附軒 單簷單脊歇山附軒 單簷單脊歇山附軒 單簷單脊歇山附軒	城門存，城樓全倒 城門存，城樓全倒 城門存，城樓全倒 城門存，城樓全倒
17屏東城	1836年建土石城	不詳	東門（朝陽） 西門 南門 北門	不明 不明 不明 不明	尚存城門 不存 不存 不存
18馬公城	1889年建土石城	789丈	東門（朝陽） 西門 南門（敍門） 北門（拱辰） 小西門（順承） 小南門（迎薰）	單簷重脊歇山 無樓 不明 單簷重脊歇山 單簷單脊歇山 不明	不存 不存 不存 不存 尚存，略有修建 不存
19臺中城	1889年建	650丈	大東門（靈威） 大西門（兌悅） 大南日（離照） 大北門（坎孚） 小東門（艮安） 小西門（坤順） 小南門（巽正） 小北門（乾健）	不明 單簷單脊歇山 不明 不明 不明 不明 不明 單簷單脊歇山	城樓名朝陽樓 城樓名龍濤樓 城樓名鎮平樓 城樓名明遠樓 被拆 被拆 被拆 被拆
20雲林城（竹山）	1887年建土城	1300丈	設東西南北4門	不明	均不存
21斗六城	1893年建土城	1160丈	設東西南北4門	不明	均不存
22臺北城	1882年建石城	1506丈	東門（景福） 西門（寶成） 南門（麗正） 北門（承恩） 小南門（重熙）	單簷重脊歇山 重簷重脊歇山 重簷重脊歇山 單簷重脊歇山 單簷歇山	近年改樣重建，原有月城 被拆 近年改樣重建 尚存，原有月城 近年改樣重建
23大埔城（埔里）		二里許	設東西南北4門	不明	均被拆
24斗南城	約在乾隆年間	不詳	設南北二門	不明	不存
25鹽水城	不詳	不詳	設東西南北4門	不明	不存
26大溪城	約1820年	不詳	設東西南北門	重簷重脊歇山	被拆
27美濃城	不詳	不詳	不詳	不明	尚存南門

（註：取材自李乾朗著《台灣建築史》）

History and Current Status of Famous Forts in Taiwan

Name	Year of Establishment & Structure	Size	Gate Names	Type of Gate Towers	Remarks
1.Chiayi	1704/a palisade 1729/an earth and stone fort 1788/a brick fort	7,440 square feet	East Gate (Chinshan)	Multiple-Eaved Single-Ridged Half-Hip Roof	demolished/ with outer walls
			West Gate (Taihai)	unknown	demolished
			South Gate (Chungyang)	Multiple-Eaved Single-Ridged Half-Hip Roof	demolished
			North Gate (Kungchen)	unknown	demolished
2.Tainan	1725/a palisade 1788/an earth and stone fort	25,200 square feet	Large East Gate (Tungan)	Multiple-Eaved Single-Ridged Half-Hip Roof	rebuilt in recent years
			Large West Gate (Chenhai)	Multiple-Eaved Single-Ridged Half-Hip Roof	demolished
			Large South Gate (Ningnan)	Multiple-Eaved Single-Ridged Half-Hip Roof	rebuilt in recent years with outer walls
			Large North Gate (Kungchen)	Multiple-Eaved Single-Ridged Half-Hip Roof	demolished/ with outer walls
			Small East Gate (Yingchun)	Single-Eaved Single-Ridged Half-Hip Roof with Porches	demolished/ with outer walls
			Small West Gate (Chingpo)	Single-Eaved Single-Ridged Half-Hip Roof	relocated in recent years
			Small South Gate	Single-Eaved Single-Ridged Half-Hip Roof with Porches	demolished/ with outer walls
			Small North Gate	Single-Eaved Horse-Back Half-Hip Roof	demolished/ with outer walls
3.Hsinchu	1733/bamboo pickets 1826/an earth and stone fort	8,600 square feet	East Gate (Yinghsi)	Multiple-Eaved Single-Ridged Half-Hip Roof	still exist
			West Gate (Yishuang)	Multiple-Eaved Single-Ridged Gable Roof	demolished
			South Gate (Kohsun)	Multiple-Eaved Single-Ridged Half-Hip Roof	demolished
			North Gate (Kungchen)	Multiple-Eaved Single-Ridged Half-Hip Roof	burnt by fire during Japanese Era
4. Outer Ramparts of Hsinchu	1840/an earth and stone fort	14,950 square feet	East Gate (Pinyang)	unknown	collapsed
			West Gate (Kaocheng)	unknown	collapsed
			South Gate (Chiehfu)	unknown	collapsed
			North Gate (Cheng-en)	unknown	collapsed
			Small East Gate (Maokeng)	unknown	collapsed
			Small West Gate (Kuanhai)	unknown	collapsed
			Small South Gate (Yaowen)	unknown	collapsed
			Small North Gate (Tien Shu)	unknown	collapsed
5.Changhua	1734/bamboo pickets 1811/an earth and stone fort	9,220 square feet	East Gate (Lokeng)	Multiple-Eaved Single-Ridged Half-Hip Roof	demolished
			West Gate (Chingfeng)	unknown	demolished

Name	Year of Establishment & Structure	Size	Gate Names	Type of Gate Towers	Remarks
5.Changhua	1734／bamboo pickets 1811／an earth and stone fort	9,220 square feet	South Gate (Hsuenping)	Multiple-Eaved Single-Ridged Half-Hip Roof	demolished
			North Gate (Kungchen)	unknown	demolished
6.Fengshan Old Fort (Tsuying)	1722／built 1823／an earth and stone fort	8,000 square feet	East Gate (Fengyi)	Single-Eaves Multiple-Back Gable Roof	destroyed
			West Gate (Tienhai)	unknown	destroyed
			South Gate (Chiwen)	Single-Eaved Single-Ridged Half-Hip Roof	still exist, appear to have been modified
			North Gate (Kungchen)	unknown	still exist
7. Fengshan New Fort	1786／built 1805／rebuilt	unknown	East Gate (Chaoyang)	unknown	nonexistent
			West Gate (Chinghua)	unknown	nonexistent
			South Gate (Anhua)	unknown	nonexistent
			North Gate (Pingshu)	unknown	nonexistent
			Small East Gate (Tunging)	unknown	still exist
8.Ilan	1811／built	6,400 square feet	East Gate (Chenping)	unknown	demolished
			West Gate (Tui'an)	unknown	demolished
			South Gate (Lishun)	unknown	demolished
			North Gate (Kanhsing)	unknown	demolished
9.Tachia	1881／an earth and stone fort	5,100 square feet	four gates	Single-Eaved Single-Ridged Ying Roof (Similar to Half-Hip Roofs, but without Lateral Slopes)	nonexistent
10.Likang	1835／an earth fort		four gates	unknown	only South Gate exists
11.Holung	1834／an earth fort	3,000 square feet	four gates	unknown	nonexistent
12.Panchiao	1855／brick fort	2 square *li*	four gates	unknown	demolished
13.Taoyuan	1839／earth fort	4 square *li*	four gates	unknown	nonexistent
14.Chungli	1842／earth fort	3 square *li*	four gates	unknown	nonexistent
15.Fanli	1855／earth fort	3 square *li*	four gates	unknown	nonexistent
16.Hengchun	1875／earth and stone fort	9,720 square feet	East Gate	Single-Eaved Single-Ridged Half-Hip Roof with Porches	gate exists, gate tower completely down
			West Gate	Single-Eaved Single-Ridged Half-Hip Roof with Porches	gate exists, gate tower completely down
			South Gate (Mingtu)	Single-Eaved Single-Ridged Half-Hip Roof with Porches	gate exists, gate tower completely down
			North Gate	Single-Eaved Single-Ridged Half-Hip Roof with Porches	gate exists, gate tower completely down
17.Pingtung	1836／earth and stone fort	unknown	East Gate (Chaoyang)	unknown	gate still exists
			West Gate	unknown	nonexistent
			South Gate	unknown	nonexistent
			North Gate	unknown	nonexistent

Name	Year of Establishment & Structure	Size	Gate Names	Type of Gate Towers	Remarks
18.Makung	1889/earth and stone fort	7,890 square feet	East Gate (Chaoyang)	Single-Eaved Multiple-Ridged Half-Hip Roof	nonexistent
			West Gate	no gate tower	nonexistent
			South Gate (Hsumen)	unknown	nonexistent
			North Gate (Kungchen)	Single-Eaved Multiple-Ridged Half-Hip Roof	nonexistent
			Small West Gate (Shuncheng)	Single-Eaved Single-Ridged Half-Hip Roof	still exists, with some renovation
			Small South Gate (Yingsun)	unknown	nonexistent
19.Taichung	1889/built	6,500 square feet	Large East Gate (Ling-wei)	unknown	Gate tower name: Chaoyang Tower
			Large West Gate (Tuiyueh)	Single-Eaved Single-Ridged Half-Hip Roof	Gate tower name: Lungtao Tower
			Large South Gate (Lichao)	unknown	Gate tower name: Chenping Tower
			Large North Gate (Kanfu)	unknown	Gate tower name: Mingyuan Tower
			Small East Gate (Ken-an)	unknown	demolished
			Small West Gate (Kunshun)	unknown	demolished
			Small South Gate (Hsuncheng)	unknown	demolished
			Small North Gate (Chienchien)	Single-Eaved Single-Ridged Half-Hip Roof	demolished
20.Yunlin (Chushan)	1887/an earth fort	13,000 square feet	four gates	unknown	nonexistent
21.Touliou	1893/an earth fort	11,600 square feet	four gates	unknown	nonexistent
22.Taipei	1882/a stone fort	15,060 square feet			
			East Gate (Chingfu)	Single-Eaved Multiple-Ridged Half-Hip Roof	recently renovated and rebuilt
			West Gate (Paocheng)	Multiple-Eaved Multiple-Ridged Half-Hip Roof	original outer walls
			South Gate (Licheng)	Multiple-Eaved Multiple-Ridged Half-Hip Roof	demolished
			North Gate (Cheng-en)	Single-Eaved Multiple-Ridged Half-Hip Roof	recently renovated and rebuilt
			Small South Gate (Chunghsi)	Single-Eaved HalfHip Roof	original outer walls demolished, recently renovated and rebuilt
23.Tapu (Puli)		about 2 *li*	four gates	unknown	demolished
24.Tounan	roughly during the Chienlung Period	unknown	South Gate and North Gate	unknown	demolished
25.Yenshui	unknown	unknown	four gates	unknown	demolished
26.Tahsi	1820	unknown	four gates	Multiple-Eaved Multiple-Ridged Half-Hip Roof	demolished
27.Meinung	unknown	unknown	unknown	unknown	South Gate still exists

(Note: Adopted from *Taiwan's Architectural History* by *Li Chien-lang*)

臺北府城——重熙門(小南門)
Chunghsi Gate (Small South Gate) of Taipei Prefecture

重熙門——臺北府城的小南門(今愛國西路延平南路交叉口),據傳由板橋林家捐資興建,通艋舺、八甲一帶,亦是出入板橋的門户。臺北府城除東、西、南、北四門之外,另加設小南門。其城樓形式與其他城門不同,未採用封閉的碉堡,而似柱廊形式之亭閣,爲單簷歇山屋頂,雕樑畫棟、塗碧飛丹的外觀,顯得玲瓏秀麗,傳漳州匠派名匠陳應彬年輕時曾參與建造。正面有三座非常巨大的雉堞,但面對城內的一面則無雉堞,圍以輕巧的花磚欄杆。城樓在民國 55 年 (西元 1966 年)改建爲中國北方宮殿式。 註 53、65、66、72、115、118、120、125

Chunghsi Gate Small South Gate of Taipei Prefecture (the intersection of Aikuo West Road and Yenping South Road today), which was said to be built through the contribution of the Lin Family of Panchiao led to Mengka and Pachia and served as Panchiao s window to other cities. Taipei Prefecture consisted of East, West, South and North gates, with the additional Small South Gate, which was quite different from other gates in the style of its gate tower. The gate tower of Small South Gate, featuring a closed blockhouse and a gazebo built with colonnades, a single- eaved half-hip roof and artistically decorated and painted beams and pillars, appeared all the more ethereal and elegant. It was said that Chen Ying-pin, a renowned craftsman of Changchou School participated in the construction of the gate in his youth. The three huge battlements on the front side were used to ward off the enemies. In comparison, the inner side of the ramparts facing the interior of the fort had no battlements and was decorated with delicate flowery tiles and handrails. In 1966, the gate tower was remodeled into a palatial building typical of North China.

日治時代的重熙門

Chunghsi Gate during the Japanese era.

RH-015

臺北府城——麗正門(南門)

Licheng Gate (South Gate) of Taipei Prefecture

麗正門——臺北府城的南門（今愛國西路公園路交叉口），通往鼓亭（今古亭）、公館、景尾（景美）一帶。南門與西門極爲相似，採三川脊歇山重簷屋頂，但上簷類似硬山頂，爲華麗的歇山頂飛簷與厚重的碉堡混爲一體，樓上開口一圓二方的比例適中，面對城外的方洞開口較長，必要時供「吊城」（△）進出之用。按中國古代傳統，南門被視爲一城之主門，形制最大。日本領臺初期本城門曾爲砲火所毀，民國55年（西元1966年）改建爲中國北方宮殿式，僅臺座及圓拱門仍爲原物，雉堞新設，而城門額依舊。

註53、65、66、72、114、118、120、125

△：夜半遲歸者，由守城兵丁以竹籃吊上城樓方得入城。

Licheng Gate, or the South Gate of Taipei Prefectre (intersection of Aikuo West Road and Kungyuan Road of Taipei today), was open to the vicinity of Kuting, Kungkuan and Chingwei. Like the West Gate, South Gate featured a Sanchuan ridge (a typical ridge style of a temple) a multiple-eaved half-hip roof, with its upper eaves similar to Yinshan roofs, where a deluxe half-hip roof with up- turned eaves on the corners was perfectly integrated with the sturdy blockhouse. The windows of the gate tower, one round and two square, were appropriately placed, with windows on the exterior featuring a greater length, enabling passage through the fort by drawbridges, if necessary. In ancient Chinese tradition, the South Gate was the largest, and was regarded as the main gate of a fort. In early days of Japanese Occupation, this gate was destroyed by gunfire, but was remodeled in 1966 ito a palatial building typical of North China; the bedding and the round portals were the only original portions of the old gate that remained. The battlements were new establishments, and the gate sign was still in place.

RH-016

日治時代的麗正門

Licheng Gate during the Japanese era.

臺北府城——承恩門（北門）
Cheng-en Gate of Taipei Prefecture (North Gate)

承恩門——臺北府城的北門（今忠孝西路中華路等交叉口），是城內通往大稻埕之關口，爲三川脊單簷歇山屋頂之碉堡式城門樓。「承恩」意取朝北京承受皇恩而命名。其形式與東門相同，惟簷口下無通氣孔，牆體由石條與磚所砌成，樓上有一圓二方的開口。臺北府城的五座城門皆落款光緒壬午年（西元 1882 年）興建，如今西門早已拆除無存，而東門、大南門、小南門則皆經整修已失原貌；北門遂成爲臺北府城碩果僅存的清代原樣城門。現指定爲第一級古蹟。

註 53、65、66、114、118、120、121、125

Cheng-en Gate (the intersection of Chunghsiao West Road and Chunghua Road in Taipei today), which was a vital connection between the fort and Tataocheng, featured a blockhouse-style gate tower, with a Shanchuan-ridged, single-eaved half-hip roof. The name Cheng-en signified the receiving of royal kindness from the Emperor. This gate has the same style as the East Gate. However, there are no air holes below the eave openings, and the walls are bonded by stone bars and bricks. The gate tower has three windows, one round and two square. The five gates of Taipei Prefecture were all established in 1882. The West Gate was demolished a long time ago, and the East Gate, Large South Gate and Small South Gate all went through renovation which altered their original appearances. Thus, the North Gate is the only fort gate of Taipei whose appearance has remained unchanged since the Ching dynasty.

Currently, the gate is designated as a grade-one monument by the government.

日治時代的承恩門

Cheng En Gate during the Japanese era.

RH-017

淡水舊砲臺

淡水砲台位於淡水鎮外近淡水河口處，距紅毛城（前英國領事館）約半公里。砲台爲清光緒 10 年（1884）年所建，當年 6 月，劉銘傳赴滬尾督令孫開華所部趕造礮臺，藉以保護當時臺灣北部第一大港——淡水港。在中法戰爭爆發時，本砲台曾發揮嚇阻效果，使得法軍未自此登陸。中法戰後，又於澎湖、基隆、滬尾、安平、旗後各港口趕造砲臺，自光緒 14 年 6 月至 15 年 2 月底，新式後膛鋼礮才陸續抵台。「戍臺夕照」曾名列淡北八景之一。砲台現已頹圮，徒留石門、廢壘供遊人憑弔，而劉銘傳在堡門上所題「北門鎖鑰」亦已年久難識。註 95

RH-018

圖爲藉以保護淡水港的淡水舊砲台（日治時代所攝）
The old battery of Tanshui established for the protection of Tanshui Harbor (picture taken during the Japanese era).

Old Battery of Tanshui

Located outside of Tanshui near the mouth of Tanshui River, Tanshui Battery is only about half a kilometer from Red Hair Citadel (previously the British embassy). The battery was built by Liu Ming-chuan in 1876 to guard Tanshui Harbor the largest harbor in north Taiwan at that time. In the 10th year of the Kuanghsu reign (1884), the Sino-French War broke out, and the battery was used to discourage the French troops from landing. Later, the battery became one of the official Eight Vistas of Tanshui, thanks to its beautiful scene at dusk. The battery is now dilapidated, with only its stone gate and fortress ruins for its memory. The sign Key to North Gate by Liu Ming-chuan above the gate of the fortress has become illegible due to its long history.

獅球嶺砲台的歷史意義

Historical Significance of Shihchouling Battery

現爲三級古蹟的獅球嶺砲台，不但是扼守基隆港的咽喉亦爲防止外敵入侵台北盆地的重要據點。砲台於清光緒 10 年（西元 1884 年），由巡撫劉銘傳聘英國技師建造，在中法台灣之役中曾發揮莫大威力，遏阻了法軍入台北城的野心。乙未割台時，日軍自澳底登陸，當時守將提督張兆連、道員林朝棟、奧勇胡友勝駐防此地抗日。此時台灣島的政治中心，在劉銘傳治臺期間已完成北移的初步工作，全島砲台共十二處，北部佔七處，獅球嶺砲台爲位居台北、基隆之間唯一砲台，爲兩地之兵家必爭之地，台北城之門戶。 註 112、127

Currently a class-three historic site, Shihchouling Battery was a strategic position for the defense of Keelung Harbor and for the prevention of foreign invasion into Taipei Basin. Established by British engineers retained by then Ching dynasty Governor of Taiwan Liu Ming-chuan in 1884, the battery demonstrated formidable firepower during the Sino-French War by successfully frustrating the attempts of the French troops to invade Taipei. During Japan's offensive to take over Taiwan, the Japanese forces landed in Aoti. At that time, Chang Chao-lien, Lin Chao-tung and Hu Yung-sheng, all high-ranking officers of the Ching army, were based in Taiwan to counter Japan. By the time of Japan's invasion, preparation for relocating Taiwan's political center to northern Taiwan had been completed under the governorship of Liu Ming-chuan. During that time, there were 12 batteries in Taiwan, with seven in the north. Because Shihchouling Battery was the only battery guarding Keelung and Taipei, it was a vital position that had to be secured in times of warfare.

安平古堡的由來

熱蘭遮(Zeelandia)城，位在台南外海的「一鯤身」沙洲上。「一鯤身」的北方有北線尾島，其間相隔著一狹而長的水道，稱爲南口；北線尾島之北有加老灣島，兩島間相隔著一廣而淺的水道，是爲北口，因其形似鹿耳，所以又名爲鹿耳門；一鯤身的南方則相連羅列著二鯤身至七鯤身等 6 個沙洲島嶼，以達台灣的赤崁地方。

明朝天啓 4 年（西元 1624 年），原佔據澎湖島的荷蘭人被福建巡撫南居益所逐退，轉而往東來至此地，以一鯤身形勢險要，便在靠近港口的高地上修築砲壘。其間，砲壘曾被原住民所破壞，荷人便於明崇禎 3 年（西元 1630 年），把砲壘改築爲更牢固的磚造城堡，是爲內城。崇禎 13 年，外城亦告完工，至此，熱蘭遮城大致完成，因爲是荷蘭人所建，所以俗稱爲番仔城或紅毛城。

其城樓有三層，高三丈餘，周圍長 277 丈 6 尺，城牆厚 4 尺，形勢壯觀。明永曆 13 年（西元 1659 年）時，鄭成功北伐失敗，退守金門、廈門，但因金、廈爲彈丸之地，且沿海州縣多被清軍所佔領，所以決定東取台灣作爲反清復明的根據地。

永曆 15 年 3 月 30 日（陽曆），鄭自金門出發，航行一個月後，抵達鹿耳門，並由此地登陸，在與荷蘭人對峙達八個月後，荷蘭總督揆一自知不敵，於是交還熱蘭遮城投降。此後，鄭成功爲紀念其泉州安平故里，改「一鯤身」爲安平鎮，又因鄭氏居住於此，所以熱蘭遮又稱爲王城。

清康熙 23 年（西元 1684 年），台灣歸入清廷版圖時，台灣的政治中心亦轉移至台南赤崁地方即台南府城。康熙 61 年（西元 1722 年），清廷改安平爲效忠里，置水師協鎮署於熱蘭遮城，但此時的安平港已開始淤積。道光 3 年（西元 1823 年），颱風大作，使曾文溪改道向西南流，並挾帶大量泥沙而下，使日漸淤積的安平港更爲沒落。到光緒初年，安平港終於喪失其港口功能。

昔日，安平至台南府城間廣闊的內海，已成陸地，滄海桑田由此可見。至於熱蘭遮城則歷經多次改建，加上天災、人禍的摧殘，原貌已大失，至日治初期，內城多已傾毀，僅餘外城部份高牆。昭和 5 年（西元 1930 年），日人更剷平殘存的內城城垣，修砌成一方形階梯狀堡壘，其上並設有安平海關官舍，今所稱之安平古堡即爲此地。而今所見的瞭望塔則爲光復後駐軍時所修建的（民國 64 年時，已改建成尖頂瞭望塔）。

History of Old Anping Fort

Old Anping Fort sits on First Kunshen sandbar in the open sea off Tainan. In the north of First Kunshen lies Peihsienwei Isle, which is separated from First Kunshen by a narrow and long water channel called Nankou. The wide and shallow water channel between Peihsienwei Isle and Chialaowan Isle in its north is called Peikou, which is also known as Deer Ear Gate, thanks to its close resemblance to a deer ear. In the south of First Kunshen lies six sandbar isles, Second to Seventh Kunshen, leading all the way to Chihkan, Taiwan.

In 1624, the Dutch occupying Penghu were driven off the island by Nan Chu-yi, Governor of Fujian in the Ming dynasty. They then went eastward to this place. Because of First Kunshen's strategic advantages, the Dutch established a fortress with cannons in the highland near the harbor. Later, the fortress was once vandalized by indigenous people; therefore, in 1630 the Dutch reinforced the fortress by transforming it into a stronger brick fortress, which was the inner portion of the fort. With completion of the outer portion of the fort in 1640, development of the fort, called Zeelandia was generally concluded. Because the fort was built by the Dutch, it was commonly called Foreign Devil's Fort or Red Hair Fort.

The fort, which was 30 feet in height, 2,776 feet in circumference, and 4 feet in thickness, was a majestic construction. In 1659, Cheng Cheng-kung retreated to Kinmen and Hsiamen due to the failure of his expedition into northern China against the Ching government. However, because Kinmen and Hsiamen are small places and because most of the provinces along the coast of China had been taken by the Ching forces, Chen decided to move eastward and seize Taiwan, which became a base for his resistance against the Ching government in an attempt to restore the Ming dynasty.

On March 30, 1661, Cheng departed from Kinmen, arriving at Deer Ear Gate one month later. Cheng landed at Deer Ear Gate and faced off with the Dutch for eight months before Frederic Coyett, the Dutch Governor of Taiwan, who knew that he could not withstand the forces of Cheng, surrendered by turning over the control of Fort Zeelandia. Later, Cheng renamed First Kunshen as Anping, in commemoration of his hometown Anping in the Chunzhou area of Fujian in mainland China. Zeelandia was also called Imperial Fort because Cheng lived there.

In 1684 (the 23rd year of the Kanghsi reign), Taiwan became a territory of the Ching dynasty, and the political center in Taiwan was also shifted to Chihkan, Tainan, which was also known as Tainan Prefecture. In 1722(the 61st year of the Kanghsi reign), Anping was renamed as Hsiachung District, and a naval unit was stationed in Zeelandia. In the meantime, however, Anping Harbor had began to suffer from siltation. In 1823, a typhoon ravaged this place, causing Tsengwen Creek to change its course and flow in the direction of the southwest, with an enormous amount of silt. As a result, Anping Harbor suffered from siltation and gradually declined. In the early years of the Kuanghsu reign, Anping finally ceased to function as a harbor.

The vicissitudes of history are mightily demonstrated by the transformation of the spacious inland sea from Anping to Tainan Prefecture in the past into land areas in present times. Zeelandia has also lost its original facade as a result of a series of reconstruction and renovation, as well as damage from natural disasters and human chaos. Until the early years of Japanese Occupation, most of the inner portion of the fort had collapsed.

Only the outer walls of the fort remained. In 1930, the Japanese demolished the remainder of the inner walls and established a square steplike fortress where the Anping Customs were located. The fortress is known today as the Old Anping Fort. The watchtower of the fort (which was remodeled into a spire watchtower in 1975) today was established by the army stationed here after the retrocession of Taiwan.

RB-155

圖為熱蘭遮城之圖。原刊載於モンタヌス原著，オギルビー英譯，為西元1671年倫敦出版的「支那使槎錄」中熱蘭遮城圖的縮印。圖中呈現出城堡完成後，市街一片繁榮的景象，懸掛荷蘭國旗之處即為熱蘭遮城，其左為市街。曬網處旁的沙灘為北線尾，赤崁樓位於市街的左方，隔江的對岸已沒入圖中。

This picture depicts Zeelandia. This is a miniaturized version of the picture published in Atlas chinensis (Author: Montanus Arnold/Translator: I.C. Ogilby) released in London in 1671. This picture characterizes prosperity of the streets after the completion of the fortress. The spot where the national flag of Holland was hoisted was Zeelandia, with streets in its left. The beach adjacent to the drying ground of fishing nets was Peihsienwei. Chihkan Lou was located to the left of the streets, and the opposite bank simply faded away in the far distance.

安平赤崁城址
Old Anping Fort

台灣古蹟的龍頭老大

安平赤崁城址今稱「安平古堡」或「台灣城殘蹟」，爲荷蘭人在西元 1624 年至 1634 年間，賡續營建完成西方稜堡形式的海岸堡壘。今尚存「內城堡」之半圓堡和「外城堡」之南城壁、北城壁、西南稜堡等部份遺蹟。以建築年代而論，其他台灣古蹟未有出其右者，堪稱台灣古蹟的龍頭老大。

在低地沙洲中的城堡

安平赤崁城築於今台南市安平區國勝路 82 號。「安平」在荷據時期荷人依照平埔族西拉雅語音譯爲Tayouan，其後漢人以閩南語音譯爲「大員」或「台灣」(早期「台灣」地名一詞，僅指此沙洲，後漸擴及爲全島之地名)。安平爲台江內海被曾文溪泥沙沖積而成的沙洲。荷蘭原爲西班牙屬地的北尼德蘭(Nederland，意爲「低地」)，擅長在濱海之地建築，因而輕易在此處設立防禦堡壘，以保護其在遠東地區的商業活動。

註 143、144

Leading Monument of Taiwan

The Chihkan Fort of Anping is known as the Old Anping Fort or Remainder Fort of Taiwan today, which was a western-style coastal fortress established by the Dutch between 1624 and 1634. Today, only a semicircular fortress of the inner fort and the southern and northern walls of the outer fort survive. The fort has no equal in Taiwan in terms of age and is worthy of its status as the leading relic of Taiwan.

A Fort on a Lowland Sandbar

The current address of Chihkan Fort is No. 82, Kuosheng Road, Anping District, Tainan City. The name of the area known today as Anping was originally called Tayouan by the Dutch, who transliterated it from the Hsilaya dialect of the plains aborigines. Later, the Han people transliterated the Dutch expression into Fukienese as Tayuan or Taiwan(in early days Taiwan as a geographic name only referred to this sandbar and was gradually extended to cover the entire island). Originally an inland sea of Taichiang, Anping was a sandbar created out of the alluvia from the siltation of Tsengwen Creek. The Netherlands, which was originally a colony of Spain, was good at construction along coastal areas. Therefore, it was an easy task for them to establish a defensive fortress here on the sandbar to protect their commercial activities in the Far East.

安平赤崁城名稱更迭表

名　稱	命名時間	原　　　因
奧倫治城(Orange)	西元 1624 年	荷蘭人初建時命名。以紀念其對抗西班牙獨立戰爭之名將。
熱蘭遮城(Zeelandia)	西元 1627 年	荷人紀念獨立戰爭荷方七省聯盟之熱蘭遮省。
王城	西元 1662 年	鄭成功逐荷之後，居此城堡命名為郡王王府。
赤崁城、台灣城、紅毛城、安平城	清領時之後（西元 1683 年之後）	因對此城堡賦予不同意義故有此多項命名。
安平古堡	民國 53 年（西元 1964 年）	台南市政府重立石碑稱「安平古堡」，沿用迄今。

List of Erstwhile Names of the Old Anping Fort

Name	Year of Christening	Reason
Orange	1624	The name in memory of a well-known Dutch genreral during the Dutch's struggle for independence from Spain was given as the Dutch first established the fort.
Zeelandia	1627	The name was given in memory of Zeelandia of the Seven-State Confederation of the Netherlands during the Dutch's independence war.
King's Fortress	1662	The fort was renamed as Imperial Fortress after Cheng Cheng-kung ousted the Dutch.
Fort Chihkan, Fort Taiwan, Red Hair Citadel, Anping Fort	during the rule of the Ching dynasty (1683-)	A variety of names were given due to the different meanings attached to the fort.
Old Fort of Anping	1964	The Municipal Government of Tainan established a stele with the inscription Old Anping Fort, which is still in use today.

RH-019

RH-020

日治時代的赤崁城址。

Fort Chihkan during the Japanese era.

歷經滄桑——赤崁樓

17 世紀荷蘭人佔領台灣之後，陸續在台南、馬公築城。西元 1625 年初開始興建普羅民遮城（即赤崁樓）。郭懷一抗荷事件（△）時赤崁樓曾遭破壞，1653 年亂平後曾經整修。此地不但具有防禦的功能，也是商務及行政中心。

赤崁樓興建之初是一座荷蘭式的城堡，主體是一座四方形的三層樓建築物，其東北及西南角各有一單層建築，四隅建有寶塔形眺望亭，東南西北均設有砲座。城堡高約 10.5 公尺，外壁厚約 180 公分，內牆亦有 85 公分厚。城牆由紅磚堆砌，另加上糯汁、糖水、蚵殼灰攪拌物填充其間而成，地基很深，整座城可説是固若金湯。當時台江的潮水可湧至城下，城堡聳立浪濤之中，前方即是碼頭，景色壯觀。

明鄭時期改作承天府，仍是政治中心。至清同治年間發生大地震，致使荷式建築頹圮，僅餘台基部份，雖屢經整修，且又陸續興建蓬壺書院、文昌閣、海神廟、五子祠等閩式建築於其中，然昔日風光已難重現。

赤崁樓今僅存有文昌閣、海神廟與蓬壺書院之門廳，尤其前二者巍然聳峙在繁囂市區之間，兼以南側庭園置有九座造型特殊之乾隆皇御賜贔屭碑（彰表福康安平定林爽文事件的紀功碑），咸爲台灣古蹟鮮明之地標。

普羅民遮城被稱作赤崁樓有兩種説法：一説認爲是由於平埔族Saccam（赤崁社）的所在地。另一説係因爲早期潮水湧至城下，閩南人稱水涯高處爲「墈」，久傳訛誤爲「崁」，而紅磚在朝陽夕照之下，猶如蒸霞吐虹，故名之赤崁樓。又因爲是荷蘭人所建，亦有人稱其爲紅毛樓。

被喻爲觀光勝地的赤崁樓的外貌及功能雖然幾經更易，舊景全貌難尋，但其中陳列的史蹟卻紀錄著府城一步步走來的足跡。

△：**有關郭懷一抗荷事件**

郭懷一原爲鄭芝龍的手下，鄭芝龍受明朝招撫離台時，郭懷一和其部衆約 2、3 千人仍留在台灣二仁溪南岸一帶墾荒因而致富。幾年後，成爲地方領袖，荷人實施王田制度時，曾被委任爲大結首。

對於荷蘭人的欺壓，郭氏早有不滿，遂於西元 1652 年，見漢人勢力稍壯之後，召集舊部與有志人士計劃推翻荷人統治，該年 9 月 9 日郭氏等人於凌晨進攻普羅民遮城（即熱蘭遮城），無奈事前已有人向荷人密報；事發後傷亡慘重，不到 20 日就被平定了，郭懷一也在此役中喪生。

RH-021

日治時代赤崁樓群貌

Facade of Chikan Lou during the Japanese era.

The Vicissitudes of Fort Provintia

In the 17th century, the Dutch continued to build forts in Tainan and Makung (in Penghu) following their occupation of Taiwan. In early 1625, they established Fort Provintia (or Chihkan Lou), which was once damaged as a result of Kuo Huai-yi (△) insurgence against the Dutch. Later, the fort was renovated after the insurgence was quelled in 1653. The fort not only had defensive functions but also served as commercial and administrative centers.

In the beginning, Fort Provintia was a Dutch-style fort, its main structure being a square three-story building with a one-story building both in its northeast and southwest. At the four corners of the fort were pagoda-like watchtowers, and gun pits were established at the four sides of the fort. The fort was about 10.5 meters in height, with outer walls 180 meters thick and inner walls 85 meters thick. The walls consisted of red bricks mortared with a mixture of glutinous-rice paste, sugar water, and powder of ground clam shells. Together with a solid and deep base, the fort was a sturdy and strong structure. At that time, the water of Tai River could reach the fort during inundation, creating a magnificent view of a fort standing solitarily amid surging water with the front end of the fort resembling a pier.

During the rule of Cheng Cheng-kung of the Ming dynasty, the fort was renamed as Chengtien Prefecture, and it remained a political center. Major earthquakes during the Tungchih reign of the Ching dynasty ravaged the Dutch-style structures, with the fort base as the only remainder of the fort. Although several rounds of renovation took place, followed by the establishment of Penghu School, the Wenchang Hall, Haishen Temple and Five-son Shrine in the fort, the glory of its past could no longer be restored.

Today, Chihkan Lou merely consists of Wenchang Hall, Haishen Temple and the gate and reception buildings of Penghu School. The former two stand in a busy urban area. Chihkan Lou also features nine special tortoise steles bestowed by the Chienlung emperor (to honor the special achievement of Fu Kang-an, who crushed the rebellion of Lin Shuang-wen). The steles also serve as a conspicuous landmark among other relics in Taiwan.

There are two theories about why Fort Provintia was called Chihkan Lou. The first theory holds that the fort used to be the dwelling place of the Saccam plains aborigines. In the second theory, the Fukienese refer to high water as *kan*, and because in early days the tide could reach the fort, creating a beautiful scene in which the red bricks of the fort glistened at dusk, the fort was thus called Chihkan Lou (*chih* meaning red in Mandarin). The fort was also known as Red-hair Tower because it was built by the Dutch.

Although the facade as well as functions of Chihkan Lou, which is a popular scenic spot today, went through several changes and its original state has become untraceable, the history associated with the fort is closely linked with the development of Tainan.

△ : The Anio-Dutch Incidence of Huai-I Kuo

Kuo Huai, originally a subordinate of Cheng Chilung, stayed on in Taiwan with two to three thousand troops and cultivated around the south bank of Er-ren Creek when Cheng accepted the amnesty of Ming emperior and left for the mainland to serve his new ruler. Earning his fortune after a few years of hard work, Kuo Huai became a local leader and was appointed local head when the Dutch instituted the royal land policy.

However, long harboring dissatisfaction toward the suppression imposed by the Dutch on local people, Kuo Huai, seeing that the power of Han people(Chinese)had solidifed, organized his old troops and comrades with a common goal in 1652 to plot the overturn of the Dutch regime. On the morning of Sep 9 that year, Kuo and his followers launched an attack against the town of Proventia. Unfortunately, the Dutch was informed beforehand and the rebellion folded up in heavy casualty in merely 20 days. Kuo Huai lost his life in this incidence.

RH-022

圖爲荷蘭人所建的赤崁樓
，日治時代爲臺南衛戍病院

Chihkan Lou established by the Dutch was Weishu Military Hospital of Tainan during the Japanese era.

台南大南門 Large South Gate of Tainan

台灣唯一尙存外廓的城

大南門建於清雍正年間，原爲木柵門，乾隆年間將之改爲磚石門。台南大南門原爲「台灣府城」七座城門之一，位居清代台南府城通往屢生亂事的鳳山縣要道，因此在道光 16 年（西元 1836 年）另行增建有外廓，即在原城牆之外另增建半圓形城牆，形同城外城，以增加敵人攻城之難度，半圓形外廓形似月亮，因此別稱「月城」，城上有 6 座砲台。台灣府城大南門爲台灣現存舊城中唯一尙存外廓者，址在今台南市南門路 34 巷邊。

羅馬不是一天造成的

台灣府城爲前清首善之區，但康熙年間禁止建城，以防止叛亂發生時，城池遭叛軍攻陷佔據，不利官軍平服。雍正 3 年（西元 1725）始准「設險以守」以木柵圍城；乾隆元年（西元 1736 年）再以三合土夯土築城，大南門城樓用磚石改建爲「歇山重簷」之現貌；其後在道光 16 年（西元 1836 年）再添建月城，始成爲防務完備之城池。

城門城門幾丈高

台灣府城以大南門爲正門，營建比其他六座城門華麗壯觀，敵樓高逾八公尺，氣勢雄偉（如圖示）。中國一般鄉下人初次進城，未曾見過如此高的城門，難免生問「城門城門幾丈高？」，此爲童謠「城門城門雞蛋糕（諧音），衍生之背景。」

註 118

Taiwan's Only Extant Outer Wall Gate

One of the seven fort gates of Taiwan Prefecture, Large South Gate of Tainan was located in a strategic position controlling passage to Fengshan County, which was plagued with insurgencies. Thanks to its importance, outer walls, or moon walls, so named because of their semicircular, crescent shapes, were built as annexes to the original fort in 1836 to make it more difficult for the enemies to mount an effective attack against the fort. Located today near Lane 34, South Gate Road, Tainan, the Large South Gate of Taiwan Prefecture is the only outer wall still in existence among the remaining old forts in Taiwan.

The Long Process of Establishment

Taiwan Prefecture used to be the gem of Taiwan during the rule of the Ching dynasty. However, establishment of a fortress here was prohibited during the Kanghsi reign to prevent rebellion against the Ching dynasty by rebels overtaking the fortress, which would have been difficult for the government forces to recover. It was not until 1725 that palisades were permitted to be erected on strategically important locations to facilitate the defense. In 1736, a fortress made of pressed cement was established, and Large South Gate was remodeled into its current facade of half-hip roofs and multiple eaves by means of bricks. In 1836, Moon Walls were erected, putting a finishing touch to the fort with complete defensive capabilities.

How Tall is the Gate?

As the main gate of Taiwan Prefecture, Large South Gate, whose gate tower was eight meters high, appeared more majestic in comparison with the other six gates. Chinese peasants visiting this place for the first time used to be overawed by the high gate, which they had never seen in their lives. Naturally, they would ask, How tall is the gate? The query later became a nursery rhyme in Taiwan.

RH-023

台灣防務序幕——億載金城

Eternal Castle—Prelude of Taiwan's Defense

「億載金城」舊稱「安平大礮臺」，又稱二鯤鯓砲台。位在今台南市安平區南塭十六號。清同治13年（西元1874年）3月牡丹社事件發生後，清廷派沈葆禎來台交涉，並籌備防務。9月即在此扼守海口，營建新式礮台，光緒2年（西元1876年）8月竣工。此座礮台是當時沈葆禎延聘法國工程師帛爾陀(Berthault)設計監造，爲台灣地區第一座洋式礮臺，且首開先例配置有英國製阿姆斯壯前膛大礮五尊（日俄戰爭時爲日人變賣、破壞、僅存一尊），是台灣第一座現代化西式砲台。（圖中門額題字「億載金城」即爲沈葆禎墨寶）

其後此礮台在光緒10年（西元1884年）中法戰爭之際，曾扼制台南門户，其發礮轟擊海面逼近之法艦，保全了台南地區未遭兵戎之害，此爲當時中法雙方所始料未及。　註76

Originally called Anping Battery, Eternal Castle is located at No. 16, Nanwen, Anping District, Tainan City. In 1874 after the outbreak of Mutanshih Incident in March, the Ching dynasty sent Shen Pao-chen to Taiwan to handle negotiations and to prepare for Taiwan s defense. In September, troops were stationed here, and construction of a modern battery here began and was completed in August, 1876. The battery was designed by Berthault, a French engineer retained by Shen Pao-chen to also supervise the construction, and was the first western-style battery, with an unprecedented array of five British Armstrong muzzleloading cannons, which is quite historically significant. (The calligraphy, which reads Eternal Castle on the sign above the gate, was done by Shen Pao-chen.)

Incidentally, the battery, to the astonishment of both China and France, served as a strategic position guarding the entrance of Tainan later during the Sino-French War in 1884 and fired at the approaching French fleet, thus protecting Tainan from the ravages of war.

圖爲日治時代所攝之億載金城

Picture of Eternal Castle taken during the Japanese era.

RH-024

旗後砲台
Chihou Battery

清同治13年（西元1874年），沈葆楨來台處理牡丹社事件的善後事宜時，體認到海防的重要性，便命淮軍提督康定奎、副將王福祿，勘定打狗（高雄）港北岸（即哨船頭）、南岸（即旗後山頂），並分別興築「雄鎮北門」砲台、「威震天南」砲台，以爲海防要塞。清光緒21年（西元1896年），日本欲以武力接收台灣，抗日軍將領劉永福之義子劉成良，曾據此砲台與日軍相抗，砲台因遭受日軍砲擊而局部毀損。日治時期間與光復後，旗後砲台均受日軍與國軍重視，而派有軍隊駐守，然均未加以維護與管理，且任意改建，使之有如廢墟。至民國80年，高雄市政府與軍方有關單位協調後，進行整建及修護的工程，於民國83年完工並對外開放參觀。 註99、100

Sheng Pao-cheng, an official sent by the Ching government in 1874 to handle the aftermath of the Peony Village Incident, realized the importance of coastal defense for Taiwan. Therefore, he asked Kang Ting-kui and Wang Fu-lu, both generals of the Huai Regiments, to inspect the northern shore (Shaochuantou) and southern shore (top of Mt. Chihou) of Kaohsiung. Sheng then established a battery at each location as bastions for coastal defense. In 1896 when Japan attempted to overtake Taiwan by force, Liu Cheng-liang, leader of the resisting forces and foster son of Liu Yung-fu, used the batteries against the Japanese forces. The batteries were partially damaged as a result of shelling by the Japanese. During the Japanese era and after World War II, both the Japanese and KMT military paid special attention to the batteries by stationing forces there. However, they failed to maintain and manage the batteries properly. In addition, the military engaged in reconstruction at will, which almost ruined the batteries. Finally, in 1991, the Kaohsiung City Government negotiated with the military and other relevant government agencies for the renovation and maintenance of the batteries, which were reopened in 1994 following the completion of the renovation.

日治時代的旗後砲台門

Gate of Chihou Battery during the Japanese era.

RH-025

台灣最早的土城——鳳山縣舊城

Old Fort of Fengshan County Earliest Earth Fortress of Taiwan

台灣最早的城是建於康熙43年（西元1704年）的諸羅縣（今嘉義市）城，當時是以木柵圍築而成，並不算正式的城。到了康熙61年（西元1772年）土石築起鳳山縣城，台灣始出現正式的城池。

鳳山縣城在今高雄市左營區蓮池潭附近，乾隆51年（西元1786年），因林爽文事件被攻破，而將縣治移往陂頭街（今高雄縣鳳山市），另築有鳳山縣新城，而原在左營之縣城被稱爲鳳山縣舊城。

事隔20年之後，鳳山縣新城又遭嘉慶11年（1806年）時蔡牽之亂攻克，於是將縣治又遷返舊城，並擴建原城規模。

現存之鳳山縣舊城，修築於道光5年（1825年）中元節至次年中秋節，共花費番銀十二萬兩，經費則由當時之台灣各府、縣、廳捐銀，並發動地方紳商百姓踴躍捐輸擴建而成。城圍1224丈，建有東（鳳儀）、西（奠海）、南（起文）、北（拱辰）等四座城門。

The earliest fort in Taiwan was built in Chuluo County (Chiayi City today) in 1704. It is not officially regarded as a fort because it was essentially palisades. Not until the earth fort of Fengshan County was established in 1772 was there any formal fort in Taiwan. Located at the vicinity of Lienchih Basin in Chuying, Kaohsiung City today, the fort of Fengshan County was destroyed as a result of rebellion by Lin Shuang-wen. As a result, the county government was relocated to Potou Street (Fengshan City, Kaohsiung County today) and a new fort was established. The county fort in Chuying was called the old fort of Fengshan County.

Twenty years later in 1806, the new fort was seized by Tsai Chien. As a result, the county government moved back to the old fort, which was then expanded.

The old fort in existence today was built between the Ghost Festival in 1825 and the Lantern Festival the following year. The total construction cost of 120,000 silver *liang* came from the Prefecture, County and Township governments in Taiwan with contributions from local citizens and businessmen. Covering an area of 12,240 feet, the fort featured four gates, the East Gate (Fengyi), West Gate (Tienhai), South Gate (Chiwen), and North Gate (Kungchen).

RH-026

照片爲 1920 年代鳳山縣舊城東門外側景觀，可辨識者計有：城門樓、門洞、城牆、雉堞、護城河等。城牆高約 20 公尺，雉堞高約 5 尺半，城牆內外壁以硓砧石（珊瑚礁石，常見於澎湖）砌成，因材質講究，現仍存有牆體 350 多公尺，藉此可一窺台灣城池之最後面貌。

This picture shows the outside of East Gate of the old Fengshan County fort. Discernible in this picture are the gate tower, the gate, the wall, the battlements, and the moat. The wall was about 20 meters high, and the battlements 1.7 meters high. The exterior of the wall was bonded with coral commonly found in Penghu. Because of the fine quality of the materials employed in making the wall, over 350 meters of wall still exist today, providing a glimpse of Taiwan's old fortresses.

媽宮城

興築的背景

媽宮城又稱「澎湖城」，其城門建造的背景緣於建城前兩年（光緒 11 年，西元 1885 年）澎湖曾爲中法戰爭戰場，遭法將孤拔率領的「亞非利加兵團」攻陷（孤拔旋即病故並葬於馬公）。議和退兵之後，台灣巡撫劉銘傳有鑑於澎湖「島平近海，無險可守」，乃責成澎湖總兵吳宏洛率軍士築媽宮城，並另在西嶼等地築有「西嶼砲臺」等五礮臺，大力提昇澎湖防務。

城池之營建

媽宮城築於光緒 13 年 12 月至 15 年 10 月之間，費時近兩年。全城周長 789 丈，僅爲台北府城一 1506 丈之半；但築城經費 23537 兩，僅及台北府城所費九分之一，因陋就簡，可見一斑。城開六門：東門名朝陽、南門名即敍、小南門名迎薰、北門名拱辰、小西門名順承，西門未築門樓亦無別稱；今僅存小西門與西門。

台灣最後的長城

媽宮城爲清建十五座城池的第十四件作品，略早於光緒 19 年興築的「斗六城」，惟斗六城今已不存，以台灣建城史而言，媽宮城實爲本地區現存最後之作品，別具歷史意義。

媽宮城建成之後，雖在日治時期遭兩次（西元 1909、1934 年）拆除，但因西城牆一段（順承門至觀音亭之間）位在前日本澎湖島要塞司令部（今澎湖防衛司令部）範圍，倖獲保存約 700 公尺，爲台灣現存城牆（鳳山縣舊城、恆春縣城）中最長之一段，乃台灣建城史重要史料。 **註 9、18、42、76、77、81**

RH-027

目前媽宮城僅存的遺跡爲順承門、大西門（中興門）及殘存之西側城垣是，其中順承門上的敵樓是媽宮城遺構中最完整的部分。

Today, only Chengshun Gate, Large West Gate (Chunghsing Gate) and the western section of the Fort Makung survive. Among them, the gate tower above Chengshun Gate is the most complete structure left of Fort Makung.

Fort Makung

Historical Background

Two years before the establishment of Fort Makung, also called Fort Penghu, Penghu was a battlefield of Sino-French War in 1885 when the African Corps commanded by the French general Courbet seized Penghu. (Courbet subsequently died and was buried in Makung.) After the French invaders withdrew as a result of a peace settlement, Liu Ming-chuan, then governor of Taiwan who realized that there was no proper defense for a flat island like Makung, asked Wu Hung-luo, the Ching general stationed in Penghu, to build Fort Makung as well as five batteries, such as Hsiyuhsitai, to strengthen the defense for Penghu.

Construction

It was two years before construction of Fort Makung, which took place between December of the 12th year and October of the 15th year of the Kuanghsu reign, was completed. With a circumference of 7,890 feet, which was about half of that of Taipei Prefecture (15,060 feet), the fort was built at a total cost of 23,537 silver *liang*, only one-ninth of the money spent for the construction of the fort of Taipei Prefecture. The shoddiness of the fort is apparent. The fort had six gates: East Gate (Chaoyang), South Gate (Chihsu), Small South Gate (Yinghsun), North Gate (Kungchen), Small West Gate (Shuncheng) and West Gate (which, without a gate sign, did not have another name). Today, only Small West Gate and West Gate are extant.

The Last Great Wall in Taiwan

The 14th of the 15 forts established in the Ching dynasty, Fort Makung predated Fort Touliu established in the 19th year of the Kuanghsu reign, which is no longer in existence. In the fort- building history of Taiwan, Fort Makung carries special historical significance, as it is the last fort in existence in Makung.

Although Fort Makung were demolished twice during the years of Japanese occupation (in 1909 and 1934), a section of the west wall (between Chenghsun Gate and Kuanyi Tower) survived, thanks to its location within the perimeter of the former Japanese Garrison Headquarters of Penghu (Penghu Garrison Headquarters today). The wall, about 700 meters in length, is the longest among the surviving fort walls in Taiwan today (the other two being the Old Fort of Fengshan County and the Hengchung County Fort), and it provides a vital glimpse at the fort-building history of Taiwan.

日治時代的澎湖媽宮（馬公）拱辰門

Kungchen Gate of Fort Makung, Penghu during the Japanese era.

RH-028

RH-029

照片為即敘門（右）與水上派出所（左）。日治時期，為修築港灣而陸續拆除媽宮城。最初拆除東南臨海部份，僅留下即敘門及迎薰門未拆，接著朝陽門、拱辰門亦遭拆除，未幾，即敘及迎薰也被拆除。

This picture depicts Chihhsu Gate (on the right) and Shuishang Police Station (on the left). During the Japanese era, Fort Makung was demolished for harbor development. In the beginning, only the south-eastern section of the fort was torn down, with Chihhsu Gate and Ying-chun Gate untouched. Later, Chaoyang Gate and Kungchen Gate were also demolished. It was not long before Chihhsu Gate and Yingchun Gate were torn down as well.

老街紀行

Strolling on Old Streets

日人自 1899 年即公布市區計劃之土地與建物的相關規定，1900 年公布了家屋建築規則，開始一系列的街路改善計劃。舉凡街屋拆建、拓寬馬路、因災害而全部重建街區建築、因汽車之引進而拓路，因排水設施不良而重新規劃，甚至改造河道……，且讓我們跨越時空，領略昔日的地景與街情。

In 1899, the Japanese rulers of Taiwan promulgated regulations governing land and buildings under urban plans. In 1900, regulations governing the construction of family houses were enacted, kicking off a series of projects aimed at renovating the streets. The implementation of these projects was followed by demolition and reconstruction of street houses, expansion of roads, reconstruction and redesign of street houses as a result of natural disasters, expansion of roads for the introduction of automobiles, redesign of the drainage system, and even the rechanneling of waterways. Let's move beyond the constraint of time and space and witness the landscape and scenery of the past.

打造台灣都市三部曲
——日人對台的都市計劃

日本統治之下，開始有計劃的建制台灣的市街，引進西方的都市計劃理論，並視台灣爲其南進的基地，在日本國土計劃中，加重台灣各重要的港灣都市的都市規劃。日治時期台灣的都市計劃約可分爲下列三時期：

一、調查並整理台地資源時期（西元1895～1908）：西元1895年日本展開台灣大規模的人、地、物調查，並於此時完成基隆迄高雄全程247哩的縱貫鐵路，西元1899年公佈法63號，市區計劃之土地及建物相關規定後，鐵路沿線的市鎮也隨之發展。

二、市街整建改善期（西元1905～1935）：此時進入法制都市計劃作業，西元1900年8月律令4號，公佈台灣家屋建築規則，展開一系列市區街路改善計劃。西元1900年台中、台北首先公布市區計劃，1905至1911年公布九處，並於1912至1935又公布大溪等十幾處市區計劃，尤其以1935年中部震災之後，日本快速完成約20處鄉街計劃。

三、依都市計劃法令建設時期（西元1932～1945年）：此一時期是由總督府聘專業技師，擬制法令並於西元1936年以律令第二號公布「台灣都市計劃令」，並依此規劃擴大或新訂標準規劃大都市，「新高港都市計劃」爲此一時期之代表。

註179、187、188

Three Phases of Urban Development under the Japanese Rule

Under the rule of Japan, systematic efforts were made to draft urban development plans by introducing Western urban planning theories. Because Japan regarded Taiwan as a springboard for its southward incursion in Asia, urban planning for major harbor cities in Taiwan became a priority for policy implementation during the Japanese era. Urban development plans in Taiwan during that time evolved through three stages.

1. **Investigation and collection of information (1895-1908):** In 1895, the Japanese rulers launched large-scale investigations about the population, geography and resources of Taiwan. In the meantime, the north-south railway between Keelung and Kaohsiung, with a total length of 247 miles, was completed. After the promulgation of the Six-Three Law and other relevant regulations for the land and buildings required for urban development in 1899, the cities along the railway were gradually developed.

2. **Renovation and Improvement of City Streets (1905-1935):** At this stage, urban development plans were officially underway. A series of projects for improvement of downtown areas and streets were implemented as the Regulations for Family Buildings in Taiwan were promulgated through Edict 4 in August, 1900. In 1900, urban plans were announced in Taichung and Taipei. Between 1905 and 1911, nine urban plans were announced, along with similar plans for a dozen cities announced between 1912 and 1935. After the earthquake in central Taiwan in 1935, the Japanese rulers expedited the announcement of about 20 urban development plans.

3. **Development under urban development regulations (1932-1945):** At this stage, the Taiwan Governor's Office retained professional engineers for their plans and enacted regulations. In 1936, the Urban Planning Directive was promulgated through Edict 2. Under this directive, urban plans were expanded or revised for the planning of large cities, a good example being the Nigata Harbor Urban Project.

環山、臨灣的港城——日治時期的基隆港市

基隆港的修築爲日治時代最早的建設，日人的「北進主義」便以基隆作爲日本內地、朝鮮、滿洲及「北支」的發展根據地。

基隆港於西元 1899 年（明治 32 年）開始興工。其工程自西元 1899 年至 1936 年共分五期，耗資工程費達 46,185,000 日圓。基隆港建築完成後號稱東洋第一大港，設備新穎完善，西元 1925 年帶動基隆市由台北縣的支廳升格爲市。基隆市三面環山，本不利於市街發展，因此基隆可稱爲標準的「港市」，是依灣頭而發展、依港口所帶來的商業利益、漁業利益而生存的港市，同時，利用台北盆地作爲腹地，因此日治時期所建台灣縱貫鐵路便以基隆作爲起點。

基隆港最重要的碼頭（即第一碼頭）就位於車站前。西元 1920 年（大正 9 年）市街重劃，利用港東岸大沙灣背後山腹建石砇公園（新公園），並造兩小運河。

若以昭和 7 年的基隆市街圖來看，即可明顯的發現基隆市是一個連著港口呈帶狀發展的城市。 註 1、62

RH-030

日治時代的基隆港是依港而生的標準港市

Keelung Harbor during the Japanese era was a typical harbor city that depended for its development on the harbor.

Harbor City Surrounded by Mountains and Open to a Bay —

Keelung Harbor during Japanese Rule

The Keelung Harbor was the earliest development project by the Japanese, because, under Japan's Southward Policy, Keelung was designated as part of Japan's hinterland and as a springboard for Japan's incursions into Korea, Manchuria and northern China.

Construction of Keelung Harbor commenced in 1899. The development of the harbor between 1899 and 1936 can be divided into five stages, with a total construction cost at 46,185,000 yen. As the development was completed, Keelung Harbor was known to be the largest harbor in East Asia, with advanced facilities. Thanks to the harbor, Keelung City was upgraded from a subsidiary department of Taipei County to the status of a city in 1925. Surrounded by mountains on the three sides, to the detriment of the development of the city areas, Keelung is a standard harbor city, which depends for its development on the harbor, and on the commercial benefits derived from the harbor and fishing. In addition, Keelung, with Taipei Basin as its hinterland, was the starting point of the north-south railway in Taiwan in the Japanese era.

Pier No. 1, the most important pier in Keelung Harbor, was located right in front of the train station. In 1920, the city area was repartitioned, and Shihpan Park (New Park), along with two small canals, was built on the mountainside in back of Tashawan in the eastern section of the harbor.

Judging from an ancient map of Keelung City created in the 7th year of the Showa period (1932), it is quite obvious that the development of Keelung City began in the harbor area and gradually rippled outward into adjacent areas.

非常時期的非常計劃——日治時期的新高港市

新高港計劃與新高都市計劃（簡稱新高港都市計劃），代表日本統治台灣末期最具國際觀及殖民城市特色的代表作。

就建港的目的而言，西元 1940 年台灣南北兩大港口及都市發展的形態大致成形，隨港口完成亦促進台北及高雄二大都市的發展。然中部地區面積、人口均較上述二區廣大，但卻缺乏港口，因此，台灣中部大甲溪充沛的水力，除了可以作爲濱海工業發展之外，對日本的殖民政策考量而言，更可增加南進港口。

由於日本受納粹政權探討國土計劃的刺激。便在西元 1936～1945 年間採取了一系列的戰時國土計劃、區域計劃、大東亞國土計劃。西元 1942 年台灣總督府內部成立國土局，著手發展新高港，希望將台中區域建設爲台中市及新高市包圍的雙子城，建港地點爲今梧棲，計劃興建一個兼具漁港、工業港、商港特色的港口。西元 1940 年（昭和 15 年）合併大甲、清水、沙鹿、梧棲、龍井等地爲新高市，並成立「新高都市開發株式會社」。計劃預定面積 12,500 公頃，市街面積 3,600 公頃，然因戰爭的影響及經濟困難，除了部份建設（如鐵路）有進行外，均無實踐。

至 1960 年代，政府否定此一規劃理念，在聯合國規劃顧問的指導下，否決此一殖民時代流行的設計，重新計劃。

註 49、97、98、129、181、182、189、190

An Extreme Project for an Extreme Time —

Nigata Harbor during Japanese Rule

The Nigata Harbor Project, along with its associated urban plan (collectively referred to as Nigata Harbor Urban Project) was a project with the international perspective and characteristics of a colonial city, and was the best project implemented in the final days of Japan's rule of Taiwan.

With regard to the purpose of harbor development, the two major harbors in northern and southern Taiwan, as well as their associated urban development, were generally completed in 1940. The establishment of the harbors also facilitated the development of Taipei and Kaohsiung, two major cities in Taiwan. As for central Taiwan, with a larger land area and population in comparison with northern and southern Taiwan, its development was hampered for the lack of anchorage. For the Japanese rulers, the ample supply of water from Tachia Creek in central Taiwan could be utilized for the development of coastal industries. Also central Taiwan could be used as a springboard for the implementation of Japan's Southward Policy.

Influenced by the land development projects of the Nazis, Japan implemented a series of wartime projects, such as land development projects, regional projects and the Greater East Asian Land Project. In 1992, the Land Bureau under the Taiwan Governor's Office was established to undertake the development of Nigata Harbor, with the functions of a fishing port and of an industrial and commercial harbor, in an attempt to develop Taichung into a twin city consisting of Taichung City and Nigata City. The location for harbor development was present-day Wuchi. In 1940, Taichia, Chingshui, Shalu, Wuchi and Lungching together became Nigata City. Meanwhile, the Company for Urban Development of Nigata City was established. However, with the exception of some railway projects, only a portion of the urban project, which covered an area of 12,500 hectares, including 3600 hectares for the downtown area, was implemented, due to World War II and financial deficiency.

In the 1960s, the KMT government rejected the rationale behind the project and decided to launch a different project, with the consultation of the United Nations.

港口變遷與港街規劃
—日治時期的高雄港市
Street Planning for Kaohsiung Harbor during Japanese Rule

日治時期(西元 1895～1945 年)是高雄市行政區域沿革史上變動最激烈的時期，從台南縣鳳山支廳、台南廳到高雄州、高雄郡至高雄市共計有 11 次變動。日治時期台灣島即爲大東亞共榮圈計劃中海運、軍事上的基地，依「南進主義」的發展，高雄實爲「南支」、「南洋」的發展根據地，此外，更有應付南方戰場軍事需要的積極性角色。

日治時期的高雄港共分三期築港工程：早期是以作爲商港爲主要目的，運輸台灣南部的糖及農產品；至末期則以軍運爲主，設有「高雄造船株式會社」、「台灣船渠株式會社高雄工場」等軍需工業。港口功能及港區的擴大連帶影響了高雄市街的發展，西元 1932 年（昭和 7 年）的「大高雄都市計劃方案」（直至西元 1935 年才施行）爲成熟期都市計劃的代表。

西元 1908 年（明治 41 年）公布「打狗市區改正計劃」是以當時最繁榮的地區及旗後、哨船頭及湊町海埔新生地爲範圍。至西元 1921 年「打狗市區改正擴大計劃」乃爲擴大市區，向高雄川以西發展，設置「高雄街」，並於同年公布「高雄市街區擴大計劃」，預計西元 1945 年時之人口爲 116,000 人。擴及高雄川東之前金、苓雅寮。除了市區的擴大之外，更有因應街路、運河和港區結合發展的設施。

光復後深受日治時期的影響，除上述港口的基礎外另有：㈠左營軍區、軍港的規劃。㈡半屏山北側、萬壽山南麓、獻獅甲等地規劃爲工業區、「高雄工業地帶計劃」以高雄爲南部工業中心。㈢鹽埕因築港塡地成爲商業中心，更成爲市中心。三者均在日治時期定下基礎，直至光復後仍保留日治時期發展的軌跡。

註 32、48、56、60、102、105

The period between 1895 and 1945 in which Japan ruled Taiwan was an extremely tumultuous time, in which a number of changes were made to the administrative districts of Kaohsiung City. From the subsidiary department of Fengshan of Tainan County, Tainan Department, Kaohsiung Prefecture, Kaohsiung County, to Kaohsiung City, the city went through 11 administrative changes. During the era of Japanese rule, Taiwan was designated as a military springboard under Japan's Greater East Asian Co-Prosperity Plan. According to Japan's design, Kaohsiung was to be developed into a military springboard for Japan's incursion into southern China and South Asia. In addition, Kaohsiung could also play an active role for reinforcing Japan's military actions in South Asia.

During the Japanese era, the development project for Kaohsiung was carried out in three stages. Initially, Kaohsiung Harbor functioned mainly as a commercial harbor for the shipment of sugar and agricultural products in southern Taiwan. At the final stage, the harbor was used primarily for the transportation of military supplies, for which purpose two military suppliers, the Kaohsiung Shipping Company and the Kaohsiung Subsidiary of Taiwan Shipping Company, were established. The operations and the expansion of the harbor had an adverse impact on the development of Kaohsiung's city areas. The Kaohsiung Urban Development Project, proposed in 1932 (but not implemented until 1935), exemplified a mature urban plan during the Japanese era.

In 1908, the Project for Transformation of the Kaohsiung Urban Area was announced, covering the busiest districts of Kaohsiung, Chihou, Shaochuantou, and Chouting, an area reclaimed from the sea. In 1921, the project was expanded to enlarge the city areas, and the focus of development was extended to the west side of Kaohsiung River. For this purpose, Kaohsiung Chih (an administrative unit during the Japanese era) was established. In the same year, the Project for Expansion of the Kaohsiung Urban Area was promulgated, with the population of 1945 projected at 116,000. This project also covered the development of Chienchin and Lingyialiao in the east of Kaohsiung River. In addition to the expansion of the city areas, facilities which accommodated the development of roads, streets and the harbor area were also established.

After World War II, the Japanese influence on the development of Kaohsiung was apparent. In addition to the existing development for the harbor, the military zone at Tsuoying and a military harbor were planned, along with an industrial zone covering areas north of Mt. Panping, areas south of Mt. Wanshou and Hsienshihchia. In addition, the Kaohsiung Industrial Zone Project, aimed at developing Kaohsiung into an industrial center in southern Taiwan, was implemented. Yiencheng became Kaohsiung's commercial center and downtown area, thanks to harbor development and reclamation of land from the sea. These projects were successful, owing to the foundation laid during the Japanese era, which was directly discernible after World War II.

日治時代的打狗港，不但是商港，同時也爲南進發展的重要軍事基地。

Takou Harbor during the Japanese era was not only a commercial harbor but also an important military base for the implementation of Japan's Southward Policy.

RF-107

日治時期台北市的街道區域劃分説明

㈠台北市爲日治時代台北州三市之一，亦爲日人建設最力者。三市是指今宜蘭、基隆、台北三市。今日的內湖（內湖庄）、北投（北投街）、士林（士林街）屬七星郡；木柵、景美（深坑庄）屬文山郡；林口（林口庄）屬新莊郡，此爲昭和 20 年（西元 1945 年）的行政區域劃分。

㈡明治 42 年 8 月（西元 1909 年），實施都市計劃，將原本的台北城牆拆除築成下水道，將城內區、艋舺（萬華）、大稻埕三區合併，並將東門城外、南門城外及三板橋一帶廣大地區併入，預定納入 15 萬人，大正9年（西元1919年）正式改爲台北市。

㈢大正 11 年（西元 1922 年）4 月，廢市內原有街庄名，改用日式町名，分全市爲 64 町及 10 村落。

㈣日治時代之市區疆域以《台灣省通志》所載爲準，大字名（相當於今日之段）、小字名繁而未載只記町名。 註 130

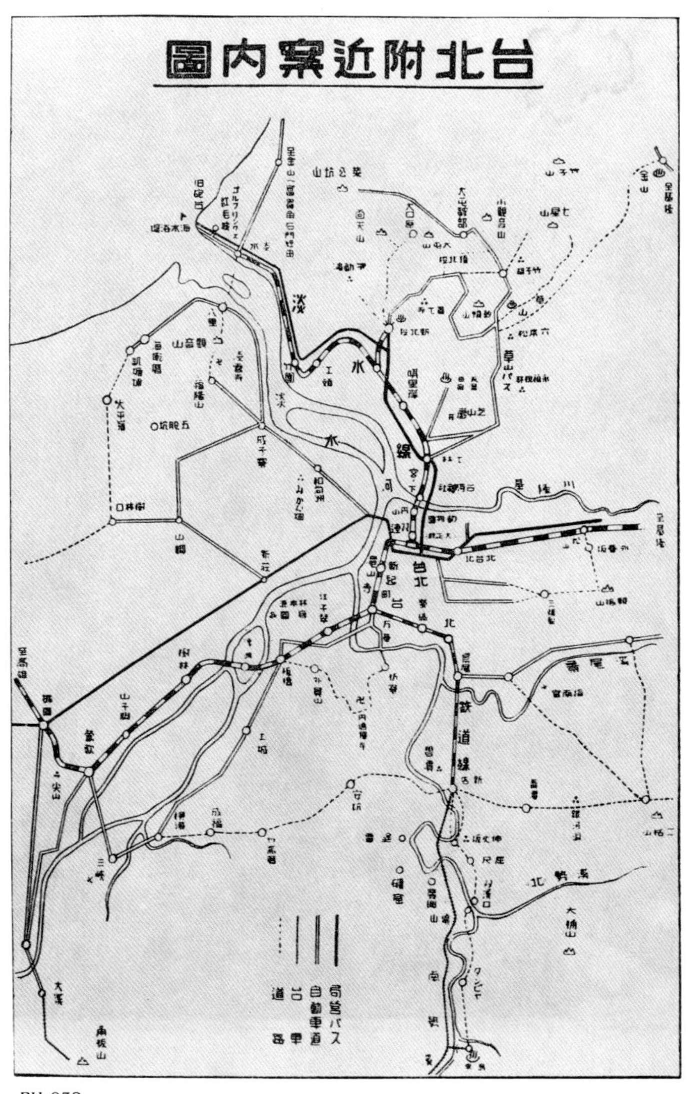

RH-032

Names of Districts in Taipei City during the Japanese Era

(1)During the Japanese era, Taipei City was one of the three cities under the supervision of the Taipei prefecture. The Japanese also spent the most effort in building the city. The other two cities were Ilan City and Keelung City. In 1945 during the 20th year of the Showa era, the administrative territories were divided as follows: the present-day districts of Neihu, Peitou, and Shihlin belonged to Chihsing County; Mucha and Chingmei were part of Wenshan County; Linkou was part of Hsinchuang County.

(2)Urban planning was implemented in August 1909 during the 42nd year of the Meiji era. Walls surrounding Taipei were torn down, and construction of the underground sewage system began. The three districts of Chengei, Mangka and Tataocheng were integrated, together with areas outside of the east gate and the south gate, as well as the Panchiao area. The resulting area had a population of 150,000 residents. In 1919 during the 9th year of the Taisho era, the region was formally renamed Taipei City.

(3)In 1922 existing names and districts in the city were given Japanese names, and the city was sub-divided into 64 *ting* (subdivisions) and 10 communities.

(4)The book *Taiwan Sheng Tung Chi*(*Taiwan Provincial Record)* contains an accurate list of the names of the different districts in Taipei City during the period of Japanese rule.

RH-031

日治時代台北市西區的街道鳥瞰圖

A bird's eye view of the streets in the western district of Taipei City during the Japanese era.

台北市區街道的軀幹——三線道路

清代臺北城的四面城牆址在今忠孝西路、中山南路、愛國西路、中華路一段。明治33年（西元1900年）起陸續拆除改闢爲三線道路，所謂三線道路是指中間爲快車道，兩側是慢車道。各路寬約40公尺，路面最初是鋪設煤脂，利用城牆石材鋪設下水溝，路間植榕、椰、茄苳等樹木，均具特色。北城牆之三線道路種植椰子樹；西城牆之三線道路有鐵路；東城牆之三線道路北望端景爲七星山；南城牆是茄苳樹景觀。構成寬闊的市區環路，綠蔭夾道，臺北市區的特色街道，日後以此爲核心發展市區各幹道。

據說臺北之三線道路仿自德國萊比錫市；亦有稱爲三線道路之園林環帶(Ring Garden)概念，主要源自奧地利首都維也納。三線道路是由北段首先完成，俾配合縱貫鐵路通車，明治44年（西元1911年）開始植樹，大正2年（西元1913年）遍植蒲葵綠化。圖爲臺北城牆舊址上的北段三線道路，中央建築物爲鐵道飯店，右側遠處高塔爲重慶南路轉角之消防單位（今消防隊址）。戰後初名中正路，民國59年（西元1970年）改名忠孝西路。

註65、66、67、68、72、108、114、115、117、125、126

RH-033

愛國西路安全島上的茄苳樹種植於大正2年（西元1913年），遠處是小南門，此圖係攝於今博愛路口西望小南門方向，闢設未久之景象。

The nightshade on the safety island of Aikuo West Road were planted in 1913, with Small South Gate in the distance. This picture, taken from the corner of Po-ai Road in the east and focusing on the Small South Gate, depicts a scene of new developments.

城中區沿革表

現行里名	日治時期町名
營邊里	東門町、旭町
忠勇里	東門町、旭町
東門里	東門町
文化里	東門町
文陽里	東門町
文祥里	東門町
文南里	東門町
華幸里	幸町、樺山町
桂花里	樺山町、幸町
玖橋里	樺山町、幸町
梅花里	樺山町
華山里	樺山町
杜聚里	幸町
幸福里	幸町
幸市里	幸町
北門里	北門町
府後里	表町、明石町
明光里	表町、明石町
府南里	京町、本町、榮町
府北里	京町、本町
光復里	京町、本町、榮町、大和町
撫臺里	大和町、京町
文武里	榮町、書院町、朵町、文武町
建國里	榮町、書院町、朵町
榮文里	榮町、文武町
文賓里	文武町
延華里	大和町、未廣町
龍華里	書院町
國際里	末廣町、壽町
福壽里	末廣町、壽町
公館里	末廣町、壽町
福星里	末廣町、壽町
慈雲里	壽町、濱町、築地町
長壽里	壽町、築地町
萬壽里	築地町、濱町
江濱里	濱町
築城里	濱町、築地町

建成區沿革表

現行里名	日治時期町名
興東里	上奎府町
興南里	上奎府町
建成里	建成町
建功里	建成町
建德里	建成町
建仁里	建成町
建文里	建成町
建明里	建成町
建泰里	建成町
建福里	建成町
建和里	下奎府町
文美里	下奎府町
文興里	下奎府町
文明里	下奎府町
文德里	下奎府町
文化里	下奎府町
文進里	下奎府町
星明里	下奎府町
星光里	下奎府町
星輝里	下奎府町
星華里	下奎府町
星拱里	下奎府町
光興里	下奎府町
光華里	下奎府町
光智里	下奎府町
光安里	下奎府町
光輝里	下奎府町
光能里	下奎府町
光躍里	下奎府町
光進里	下奎府町
復元里	下奎府町
復雙里	下奎府町
復連里	下奎府町
復康里	下奎府町
復益里	下奎府町
復壽里	下奎府町

延平區沿革表

現行里名	日治時期町名
江元里	太平町
稻元里	太平町
永興里	太平町
得興里	太平町
稻新里	太平町
永和里	太平町
新興里	太平町
得勝里	太平町
成德里	太平町
延樂里	太平町
南芳里	太平町
橋南里	太平町
延登里	太平町
延年里	太平町
延壽里	太平町
朝陽里	太平町、日新町
玉泉里	泉町
金泉里	泉町
維新里	日新町
建興里	日新町
維興里	日新町
井頭里	日新町
舊市里	日新町
慈聖里	日新町
長興里	日新町
興民里	日新町
良德里	永樂町
勝得里	永樂町
六館里	永樂町
劍窗里	永樂町
平樂里	永樂町
安樂里	永樂町
長樂里	永樂町
民和里	永樂町
中北里	永樂町
怡和里	永樂町
普願里	永樂町
大有里	港町、永樂町
建昌里	港町
千秋里	港町
元安里	大橋町
普安里	大橋町
光裕里	大橋町
光榮里	大橋町

大同區沿革表

現行里名	日治時期町名
仁和里	蓬萊町
新登里	蓬萊町
蓬萊里	蓬萊町
德鄰里	蓬萊町
聚英里	蓬萊町
石城里	蓬萊町
田寮里	蓬萊町
崇德里	蓬萊町
聚德里	蓬萊町
雙連里	蓬萊町
融和里	大龍峒町
福澤里	大龍峒町
金城里	大龍峒町
老師里	大龍峒町
保生里	大龍峒町
近聖里	大龍峒町
大同里	大龍峒町
龍塘里	大龍峒町
保安里	大龍峒町
楊雅里	大龍峒町
贍聖里	大龍峒町、圓山町
斯文里	大龍峒町、圓山町
鄰江里	大龍峒町、河合町
福環里	大龍峒町、河谷町
福境里	大龍峒町、河谷町
文昌里	大龍峒町、河谷町
國昌里	太平町
國隆里	太平町
國安里	太平町
國順里	太平町
國慶里	太平町
國殷里	大橋町
景星里	大橋町
國盛里	大橋町
橋北里	大橋町
依仁里	大橋町
聚仙里	大橋町
集華里	大橋町
星耀里	大橋町

中山區沿革表

現行里名	日治時期町名
正仁里	大正町
正宜里	大正町
正守里	大正町
正義里	大正町
正得里	大正町
正自里	大正町
正由里	三橋町
康樂里	三橋町
富強里	三橋町
正信里	三橋町
山河里	御成町
民安里	御成町
國泰里	御成町
中順里	御成町
中山里	御成町
安慶里	御成町
謙和里	宮前町
集英里	宮前町
明和里	宮前町
聚英里	宮前町
東興里	宮前町
南山里	宮前町
恆安里	宮前町
長安里	宮前町
寓褒里	宮前町
永靖里	宮前町
太唐里	宮前町
晴光里	宮前町
志新里	宮前町
圓山里	圓山町
劍潭里	大宮町
永安里	無(空地)
成功里	無(空地)
大佳里	無(空地)
新庄里	無(空地)
下埤里	無(空地)
中庄里	無(空地)
興中里	無(空地)
興亞里	無(空地)
一江里	無(空地)
中和里	無(空地)
朱崙里	無(空地)
朱園里	無(空地)
朱豐里	無(空地)
朱蘭里	無(空地)
朱馥里	無(空地)
龍江里	無(空地)
復華里	無(空地)
復國里	無(空地)
力行里	無(空地)
復興里	無(空地)
平和里	無(空地)
明德里	無(空地)
埤頭里	無(空地)

註1、46、95、139

台北市各區疆域沿革表（日治時期——光復後）

大安區沿革表

現行里名	日治時期町名
錦泰里	錦町
錦中里	錦町
錦華里	錦町
錦安里	錦町
師院里	錦町
龍池里	古亭町
古莊里	古亭町
龍泉里	古亭町
古風里	古亭町
龍坡里	無(空地)
靜龍里	昭和町
龍安里	昭和町
重光里	福住町
光明里	福住町
永康里	福住町
福住里	福住町
大安里	福住町、東門町
惠愛里	東門町
信愛里	東門町
普愛里	東門町
文光里	東門町
育才里	無(空地)
民輝里	無(空地)
民炤里	無(空地)
民榮里	無(空地)
建南里	無(空地)
仁愛里	無(空地)
濟南里	無(空地)
義安里	無(空地)
通安里	無(空地)
群英里	無(空地)
臥龍里	無(空地)
芳和里	無(空地)
黎和里	無(空地)
黎順里	無(空地)
通化里	無(空地)
萬安里	無(空地)
鳳雛里	無(空地)
義村里	無(空地)
建安里	無(空地)
龍圖里	無(空地)
龍崗里	無(空地)
新龍里	無(空地)
龍關里	無(空地)
龍飛里	無(空地)
龍淵里	無(空地)
龍門里	無(空地)
龍生里	無(空地)
龍陣里	無(空地)

古亭區沿革表

現行里名	日治時期町名
龍福里	兒玉町
華林里	兒玉町
南市里	兒玉町
自治里	兒玉町
向營里	千歲町
新隆里	新榮町
龍匣里	千歲町
龍津里	佐久間町
龍口里	龍口町
龍光里	龍口町
龍興里	龍口町
南門里	南門町
南興里	南門町、龍口町
永儀里	馬場町
永寶里	馬場町
永成里	馬場町
螢林里	川端町
營塘里	川端町
網溪里	川端町
板溪里	川端町
河堤里	川端町
螢圃里	川端町
螢光里	川端町
古亭里	古亭町
舊街里	古亭町
福興里	古亭町
亭東里	古亭町
頂東里	古亭町
杏林里	古亭町
新店里	古亭町
林口里	水道町
水源里	水道町
大學里	水道町
富田里	富田町
農場里	富田町
國校里	水道町
文盛里	水道町
健軍里	水道町
愛國里	龍口町、南門町
花圃里	南門町、龍口町
永昌里	馬場町
忠義里	馬場町
騰宵里	馬場町
久安里	馬場町
新和里	馬場町
永順里	馬場町
永功里	馬場町
螢雪里	川端町
龍潭里	千歲町
祿德里	西園町
福德里	西園町
保德里	西園町
惠德里	西園町
全德里	東園町
壽德里	東園町
興德里	東園町
美德里	東園町
廈安里	龍江町、堀江町
廈慶里	堀江町
頂碩里	堀江町
福益里	堀江町
勝利里	堀江町
新成里	堀江町
敦正里	堀江町
精華里	堀江町
大明里	堀江町
厚裕里	堀江町
重碩里	堀江町
廈碩里	堀江町
信義里	堀江町
博愛里	堀江町
和平里	堀江町
民生里	堀江町
信安里	堀江町
寺前里	新富町、龍山寺町
蓮池里	綠町、龍山寺町
石南里	綠町
石中里	綠町
石北里	綠町
滿花里	綠町
愛鄉里	綠町
糖廍里	綠町
綠柳里	綠町、柳町
楊柳里	柳町

龍山區沿革表

現行里名	日治時期町名
富裕里	新富町
富安里	新富町
富貴里	新富町
富民里	新富町
富福里	新富町
富榮里	新富町
萬安里	新富町
大衆里	新富町
蓮花里	新富町
福安里	新富町
新安里	八甲町
東寮里	八甲町
舊站里	八甲町
福地里	八甲町
公安里	若竹町、老松町
泰安里	老松町
仁德里	若竹町
福音里	若竹町
城西里	新起町
新起里	新起町
清水里	新起町
廟口里	新起町
西門里	西門町、築地町
寧南里	西門町、壽町
復榮里	西門町
頂新里	龍山寺町
龍山里	龍山寺町
育英里	龍山寺町
料館里	龍山寺町
蓮園里	龍山寺町
寶斗里	有明町
大竹里	有明町
新廈里	有明町
水山里	有明町
義倉里	有明町
直興里	入船町
歸仁里	入船町
溪口里	入船町
歡聚里	入船町
青山里	入船町
福祐里	入船町
祖師里	元園町
菜園里	元園町
復旦里	元園町
布埔里	元園町
路店里	元園町
帆寮里	元園町

Three-Lane Road Skeletons of Taipei City

The four walls of Fort Taipei in the Ching dynasty were where Chunghsiao West Road, Chungshan South Road, Aikuo West Road, and Section One of Chunghua Road are today. In 1900, the walls were gradually demolished and converted into three-lane roads, one lane for speedy vehicles and the other two for slow vehicles. About 40 meters wide, the roads were initially paved with pitch, and the gutters were constructed of stones from the demolished fort walls. Pagoda trees, coconut palms and morel trees were planted in the middle of the roads, carrying unique characteristics of their own. Coconut palms were planted along the three-lane roads where the North Wall of the fort used to be; the three-lane roads of the West Wall overlapped with a railway; the three-lane roads of the East Wall offered a view of Mt. Chihsing in the far north; and the South Wall was characterized by the scene of morel trees. Together, these roads constituted a spacious circular road system of Taipei with the decoration of green trees. It was based upon this road system that other arteries of Taipei were subsequently developed.

It is said that the three-lane roads of Taipei were copied from Leipzig. Another theory holds that the concept of "Ring Garden" with three-lane roads comes from Vienna, the capital of Austria. The three-lane road in the north section was the first to be completed to facilitate the operation of the north-south railway in Taiwan. In 1911, trees were planted along the roads and large- scale landscaping with the planting of the Chinese fan palms was instituted in 1913. This picture portrays the three-lane road in the northern section where the North Wall used to be. The building in the middle was the Railway Hotel, and the high tower on the far right was the fire department (a fire station today) at the bend of Chungching South Road. Originally named Chungcheng Road after World War II, the road was renamed Chunghsiao West Road in 1970.

RH-034

愛國西路三線道路東望，右方安全島上有一支高聳的路燈，道路前方遠處右側爲總督府專賣局高塔（今南昌路口臺灣省菸酒公賣局）。民國 58 年（西元 1969 年）道路拓寬、民國 80 年（西元 1991 年）因捷運系統施工，愛國西路上的四百多棵老樹被遷移至北投大度路。

A high street lamp was erected on the safety island to the right, as viewed eastward from three-laned Aikuo West Road. Ahead of the road in the distance to the right was the tower of the Monopoly Bureau of the Taiwan Governor's Office (Taiwan Tobacco& Wine Monopoly Bureau today on the corner of Nanchang Road). In 1969, the road was expanded, and in 1991, a total of over 400 old trees along Aikuo West Road were relocated to Tatu Road in Peitou, due to the construction of the mass rapid transit system.

辛亥暴風雨與災後重建

明治44（西元1911年）8月底，歷來少有的颱風造成臺北地區嚴重災情，臺北的災情以城內受災最爲慘重。市街淹水三尺高，房屋倒塌3400餘家，府前街（今重慶南路一段）、府中街（今懷寧街）、府後街（今館前路）、文武街（今衡陽路）均見災情，房屋不是全倒便是半塌，多數必需重建，到處一片泥海。府後街只剩「吾妻館」等兩三家外，全街無一倖免，災情最慘重。災後當局便藉此改正市區街道，拓寬路幅，多數歐洲風格立面的街屋即爲這次災後所改建。 註67、117、118

RH-036

府中街五丁目（今懷寧街在襄陽路口附近）房屋倒壞水深及膝，圖爲居民劫後餘生察看受災情形的情景。

In this picture, residents of the 5th section of Fuchung Street (near the intersection of Huaining Street and Hsiangyang Road today) are seen assessing the damage to their houses, which collapsed or were inundated with water to the depth of their knees.

Reconstruction after Tempest

At the end of August, 1911, a typhoon wreaked tremendous havoc on Taipei on a scale almost unequaled by its predecessors. The hardest hit was the downtown area, which was flooded with water as deep as three feet, flooding more than 3400 houses. Damage was reported on Fuchien Street (Section One of Chungching South Road today), Fuchung Street (Huaining Street today), Fuhou Street (Kuanchien Road today), and Wenwu Street (Hengyang Road today) where houses were either wiped out completely or partially tumbled down. Most of these houses had to be rebuilt amid a sea of mud. In Fuhou Street, the hardest hit area, almost all of the buildings were destroyed, except for a handfull, including Wuchi Hall. After the typhoon blew over, the government took this opportunity to rearrange the road and street system in the city and expand roads. Most of the European-style houses in Taipei today were part of this post- disaster reconstruction.

RH-035

位於府中街二丁目臺北廳浸水甚深，廳內的老榕樹也倒下，圖爲附近房屋浸水的情景。

The serious flooding in Taipei Department located in the 2nd section of Fuchung Street brought down the old pagoda tree within the department. This picture shows the flooding of houses in the vicinity.

台北最早的商店街——館前路

臺北市館前路，自臺北火車站通往新公園博物館前，即日治時期之「表町」。清光緒 4 年（西元 1878 年）艋舺人洪祥雲、李清琳等人在此闢路並興建店鋪，爲臺北城內最早的商店街，因位於臺北府衙正後方，故名府後街，臺北府衙址約爲今開封街（北）、漢口街（南）、重慶南路（西）、館前路（東）所圍成之街廓。日治時期將街道拓寬，改建歐洲風格的二、三層店鋪建築，因位於火車站附近，萬商雲集，如鐵道旅館（今新光摩天大樓、大亞百貨現址）、吾妻館、美人座等飯店，重要商業如日本勸業銀行支店、華南銀行、三井物產商社、日淸生命（壽險）、大成火災（產險）等金融機構皆在此處林立。

註 65、66、68、72、117、126

The Earliest Shopping Street of Taipei——Kuanchien Road

Kuanchien Road, connecting the Taipei Train Station with the museum in the New Park, was where Piao District used to be during Japanese Occupation. In 1878, Hung Hsiang-yun, Li Ching-ling and others from Mengka developed a road and set up stores here, which was the first shopping street in Taipei. It was called Fuhou Street (meaning behind the government), because of its location in back of Taipei's government offices, which occupied an area south of Kaifeng Street, north of Hankou Street, east of Chungching South Road west of and Kuanchien Road. During the era of Japanese rule, this street was expanded and the buildings were remodeled into European-style two- or three-story shop buildings. Because of its proximity to the train station, this area teemed with commercial enterprises, such as Railway Hotel (where Hsinkong Mitsukoshi Department Store and Asia World Department Store are today), hotels such as Wuchi Hall and Meijentsu, and financial institutions such as Dai-Ichi Kangyo Bank, Hua Nan Commercial Bank, Mitsui Fire& Marine Insurance Co., Nisse Life Insurance and Tacheng Insurance Co.

由中段漢口街路口一帶南望的街景，右側有圓頂之二層建築爲華南銀行，帶有西亞拜占庭建築風格，端景即博物館。華南銀行後來易主爲臺灣產物保險公司，民國 63 年（西元 1974 年）拆除改建。

This picture shows a scene viewed southward from the vicinity of the entrance to Hanku Street. The two-story building with a domed roof at the right is Huanan Bank. The building with Byzantine-style architecture was the museum. The Huanan Bank building later housed the Taiwan Marine& Fire Insurance Co., and was later demolished in 1974.

RH-037

RA-102

由博物館前的襄陽路口上北望，端景爲臺北火車站，左側前爲三井物產會社（今土地銀行）。

This picture portrays a scene viewed northward from the entrance of Hsienyang Road in front of the museum. The Taipei Train Station was located at the far end. On the left was the Mitsui Fire& Marine Insurance Co. (Taiwan Land Bank today).

RH-038

這是博愛路沅陵街口北望的早年街景，左側可見永綏街口，右爲沅陵街轉角，有花王石鹼及白粉等化妝品廣告，可看出博愛路東側街面在前方的武昌街口略向西轉折。

This is an old-time scene viewed northward from the entrance of Wanling Street. In the left is the entrance to Yungshui Street and in the right is a curve in Wanling Street, with conspicuous advertisements for cosmetics such as chalk and ceruse. In this picture, the eastern side of Po-ai Road skewed slightly westward upon the entrance to Wuchang Street up ahead.

RH-039

博愛路舊稱北門街，圖爲位於總督府後方長沙街口北側之臺灣電力株式會社（今臺電公司前身）一角，後方依次爲總督府圖書館（原彩票局、博物館，今國防部大樓）、帝國生命（人壽）保險會社臺北支店，盡頭朝北門而去。臺灣電力株式會社係大正8年（西元1919年）7月底成立，前身爲官營電力事業，而在新公園內之館舍落成以前，博物館係借彩票局爲臨時館址。 註65、66、67、118

In the past, Po-ai Road was called North Gate Street. This picture shows a corner of Taiwan Electricity Company (the predecessor of Taiwan Power Company today), located on the northern side of the intersection with Changsha Street, in the back of the Taiwan Governor's Office. Behind it are shown the library of the Taiwan Governor's Office (previously the Lottery Bureau, then a museum and currently the Ministry of National Defense), the Taipei branch of Imperial Life Insurance Co. further down, and all the way in the distance, the North Gate itself. Established in July 1919, Taiwan Electricity Company was restructured from a government-owned electricity business. Before the building of the museum was completed, the museum was temporarily housed in buildings borrowed from the Lottery Bureau.

臺北博愛路舊景（京町）

京町，位於今博愛路在衡陽路以北的路段，大正14年（西元1925年）10月起進行街屋改築，經七年才全部竣工，奠定博愛路今日的街肆規模。由於街道的建設年代較晚，街面式樣已隨新的潮流趨於簡化，是城內通往大稻埕臺灣人市街的道路，其熱鬧程度僅次於榮町（衡陽路）、本町（重慶南路）。

註66、68、114、117、118

Nostalgic View of Poai Road, Taipei (Ching District)

Located around the section of Poai Road north of Hengyang Road, the Ching District saw remodeling of street buildings beginning in October, 1925 and completed seven years later, a project which determined the scope of street buildings in Poai Road today. Because this street was developed later than others, it was characterized by a simple style, which was a popular trend at that time. The street was a major artery for Taiwanese moving from the city to Tataocheng, and was constantly bustling with traffic nearly as great as the Jung District (Hengyang Road) and Pen District (Chungching South Road).

由新公園側門西望街景，可見升川洋服（左側）、寫眞館、運動用具、江山樓支店（右側）等商店的招牌。

Looking west from the side gate of the New Park, we can see signs of Masukawa Costume Co. (left), a photo shop, a sportswear store and an outlet of Kang San Lao *(right).*

RH-040

臺北衡陽路舊景（榮町）

榮町，今衡陽路，爲當年臺北城最繁華的街道，有臺北的銀座之稱，是日本人採購回內地禮物的商店街，其前身爲清代之西門街（西段）、石坊街（東段）。西門街在光緒 6 年（西元 1880 年）闢建，光緒 11 年劉銘傳創設「興市公司」發展臺北城的商業，以石條與卵石鋪設路面，興建成排的兩層街屋，吸引富商紛紛在此設立商店；石坊街因豎有光緒 14 年所立表彰貢生洪騰雲之「急公好義石坊」（現移置新公園內）而得名。日治後日本人聚集於「城內」（臺北城），此即來臺第一批日人所居之處，大正 3 年（西元 1914 年），臺北城與府前街一起拓寬，將傳統的舊式店面改建成歐洲風格的建築，一直是熱鬧繁華的商業地帶，民國 84 年（西元 1995 年）7 月，一場火災燒燬十多棟具有歷史風貌的布莊、銀樓等老字號建築。

註 2、65、66、68、72、114、115、117、118、125、126

西門橢圓公園東望榮町街景，左側依次爲臺灣日日新報社（光復後改名台灣新生報，現今臺灣新生報業大樓）、電話交換局（交通銀行現址）。

This is an outlook of Sakimachi Street viewed from the Hsimen oval park in the west. Immediately to the left of Sakimachi Street was "Newspaper Building," the offices of Taiwan Daily News *(renamed* Taiwan Shin Sheng Daily News*), followed by the Telephone Exchange Bureau (currently the location of Chiao Tung Bank).*

RH-041

今衡陽路自重慶南路口西望的早期街景，左側是大倉商會本店（經營洋雜貨）、右側爲府前街郵便局（後改爲茶舖）

A long-passed scene of the entrance of the Chungching South Road intersection viewed from the east on Hengyang Road. To the left is the headquarters of the Okura Company (dealing in imported goods), and on the right corner is the Post Office (which later became a tea shop) on Fuchien Street.

RH-043

今衡陽路自博愛路口東望的早期街景，左側轉角爲盛進商行茶舖、右側轉角爲近江屋吳服店，路底是新公園。

This is an old-time scene viewed from the intersection of Hengyang Road and Po-ai Road in the west. On the corner in the left was Sheng Chin Tea Shop. On the corner in the right was the Omiya Costume Store, with the New Park at the end of the road.

RH-042

Nostalgic View of Hengyang Street, Taipei (Jung District)

Nicknamed the Ginza of Taipei, the Jung District, which is Hengyang Street today, used to be the busiest street in Taipei. This street, which was Hsimen Street (western section) and Shihfang Street (eastern section) in the Ching dynasty, was a street frequented by Japanese shoppers buying gifts to take home. Hsimen Street was developed in 1880. In 1885, Liu Ming-chuan set up the Hsingshih Company to develop business in Taipei. He attracted rich businessmen to establish stores here by paving the road with stone bars and pebbles and establishing rows of two-story buildings. Shihfang Street was known for its Stele of Generous Deed (which was later relocated to the New Park) erected in 1883 in honor of Hung Teng-yun. When Taiwan came under the rule of Japan, Japanese stayed in Fort Taipei, which was the first Japanese settlement in Taiwan. In 1914, Fort Taipei was expanded, together with Fuchien Street, where traditional stores were remodeled into European-style buildings, which were well-known for their busy commercial activities. However, a dozen of historic clothing and jewelry stores were burned to the ground by a fire in July, 1995.

臺北重慶南路一段舊景（本町）

本町，今重慶南路一段衡陽路以北的路段，前身爲清光緒 5 年（西元 1879 年）所闢的府前街，當年係臺北府衙前的街道。明治 44 年（西元 1911 年）8 月底的水災造成城內的房屋倒壞嚴重，府前街（本町，今重慶南路一段）、榮町（今衡陽路）等處房屋都因而必須全部重建，各戶原欲個別改建，當時臺北廳長井村大吉建議統籌興建，總督府營繕課設計，同年全面重建，先由東側開始，同時改正市區拓寬路幅。完成於大正 3 年（西元 1914 年）的沿街三層樓磚造建築，具有歐洲風格，造型各異變化豐富，呈現華麗的多樣面貌，市容煥然一新。大正 11 年府前街改稱本町，許多大商行、批發店、布料行均集中於此；光復後聚集數十家書店、出版商，因而以書店街著稱。

註 6、65、66、68、72、117、118、125、126

RH-044

圖爲衡陽路口北望的街景，以本町的東側街面爲主，右邊即現今路口轉角上的金石堂城中店。

This picture shows the eastern side of Pen District as viewed northward from the corner of Hengyang Road. To the right is the building which houses the Chengchung Branch of Kingstone Bookstore today.

本町的西側街面。圖中街道左側可見今沅陵街口轉角上的丸山吳服店（今中華書局），當時附近有日進商會、金庫（北側）、革工商森田商會、理髮店、金旭堂（南側）等店。

This picture shows the western section of, with the Maruyama Costume Store (Chunghua Bookstore Co. today) on the corner of Wanling Street (current name) on the left. In the vicinity at that time were Nissin Company, the Kinko (in the north), the Kakukoshomorida Company (dealing in leather products), a barber shop, (in the south), etc.

RA-100

RH-045

今漢口街路口南望所見的本町中段街景，右側為三和銀行支店。三和銀行前身為大阪中立銀行，明治28年（西元1895年）9月成立，為臺灣最早成立的銀行，次年改名日本中立銀行，明治32年由三十四銀行合併，至昭和8年（西元1933年）時與日本鴻池銀行及山口銀行合併，改稱三和銀行，戰後與臺灣儲蓄銀行歸併為臺灣銀行儲蓄部。

This picture shows the midsection of Pen District as viewed southward from the corner of Hanku Street today. To the right was the Branch Office of the Sanwa Bank, which was the predecessor of the Cyuritsu Bank of Osaka. Established in September of 1895, the bank, which was the earliest bank in Taiwan, was renamed the Nihoncyuritsu Bank the following year. The bank merged with Sanjuyon Bank in 1899, and became Sanwa Bank through a merger with Nihon Kochi Bank and Yamaguchi Bank. After the end of World War II, the bank merged with Taiwan Savings Bank and became the Savings Department of Taiwan Bank.

Nostalgic View of the Pen District (Chungching South Road, Section One, Taipei)

The Pen District was developed in 1879, in the area around Fuching Street, which today is Chungching South Road, Section One, north of Hengyang Road. Fuching Street ran in front of the Taipei government building. The flood of August 1911 caused serious damage to buildings in Taipei. As a result, houses on Fuching Street (Pen District) and the Jung District (Hengyang Road today) had to be rebuilt. The citizens had planned to rebuild the houses on their own. However, the mayor of Taipei, Imura Daikichi proposed that the reconstruction be undertaken collectively that year, based on the design of the Taiwan Governor's Office, starting with the eastern section of the buildings. In the meantime, expansion of streets and roads in Taipei commenced. The European-style three-story brick buildings were completed in 1914, with rich variations and diversified appearances, creating a new facade for Taipei. Renamed the Pen District in 1922, Fuchien Street had a large concentration of large houses, wholesale stores and clothing stores. When Taiwan came under KMT rule after World War II, the street became known as a bookstore street, lined with scores of bookstores and publishing houses.

新世界館

新世界館是臺北市西門町（今中華路西門圓環邊）日治時期的電影院，光復後改稱新世界戲院，後充爲華僑之家，改建七層大樓。附近原只有成都路之芳乃館（後來改建今國賓戲院）及昆明街之世界館（太平洋飯店舊址）兩家戲院，待新世界館落成後，世界館改稱爲第二世界館。1920年代，附近再增加國際館、大世界館（今大世界戲院）、臺灣劇場（今中國戲院）等電影院，電影街於焉形成。當時新世界館後面的巷子片倉通裡壽司、佃煮、蒲燒、燒鳥等日式小吃應有盡有。 註2、125

RH-047

圓弧形正面及挑高的騎樓是其建築特色，當時新世界館前方的圓環有水池及樹木，可見附近民衆洗滌物品。圖右樹幹後方的街道爲現今漢中街。

This building at the corner of Hanchung Street features a round facade and an arcade with high roofs, In former times, there were a water fountain and trees inside the traffic circle in front of New World Hall. In this picture, people in the neighborhood were seen washing things. The street behind the tree in the right of the picture is currently Hanchung Street.

New World Hall

During the Japanese era, New World Hall was a movie house in Taipei's Hsimenting district (near the traffic circle at West Gate on Chunghua Road today). Renamed the New World Theater during the KMT era, it was later rebuilt as a seven-story building for the reception of overseas Chinese. In its vicinity, there had been only two movies houses, such as Fanai Hall (which was reconstructed as the Ambassador Theater today) and World Hall (where Pacific Hotel used to be). When New World Hall was established, World Hall was renamed the Second World Hall. In the 1920s, International Hall, Great World Hall (the Great World Theater today), and Taiwan Theater (China Theater today) were built in this vicinity, turning this area into a movie street. In the alley behind the then New World Hall, Katakura Road offered a wide variety of sushi and other Japanese cuisine.

西元1895年的台北西門町市街

A 1895 street scene of Hsimendin, Taipei.

RB-031 ▲▼

西元1915年的台北西門町市街

A 1915 street scene of Hsimendin, Taipei.

西門町日治時代即爲娛樂場所

石坊街即今重慶南路與懷寧街間之衡陽路段。右上爲清代街景街上所立之急公好義坊，是爲了獎勵艋舺貢生洪騰雲捐地建考棚而建，後移至新公園內；左下爲日治街景，當時的西門町是日本人的娛樂場所，兩側街屋則爲歐洲式立面建築。圖爲日治初期和 20 年後的西門町街景。 註 72、125

Hsimendin – An Entertainment Establishment Since the Japanese Era

Shifong St. occupied the section of the present-day Hengyang Road between Chungking S. Road and Hwainin St. To its upper right side, in a Ching-styled street scene, sat an archway commending the zealous public spirits of Manka scholar Hong Ten-yun who donated a piece of land for the construction of an examination hall; the archway was later moved into the New Park. Its lower left side depicted a Japanese-styled street scene. Hsinmendin during those periods of time was the public place of entertainment for the Japanese; the architecture on both sides of the street was of European style. The picture shows the street scene of Hsinmendin at the very beginning of and 20 years after the Japanese occupation.

從租界、雜居到造街運動——淡水老街

Tanshui Old Street

—— From Concession, Mingled Habitation to Street Development Movement

咸豐11年（西元1861年）英國副領事於淡水辦公開始，洋商便進入淡水。自光緒6年（西元1880年），洋商得以合法租借土地。由於華洋雙方生活習慣不同，爲便於管理，清朝政府與外國協定設立租界，將洋人居所、教堂、洋行、醫院等集中於租界區。日本據台之後，淡水雖不再爲「條約港」，但日本當局仍公告淡水爲「港口外僑雜居地」。此後洋人在淡水的聚居地便分散在華人市街的兩頭，即今淡水車站以東及紅毛城、油車口一帶。洋人當時的洋房，許多至今尚存。

至於淡水鎮内的主街道（今中正路）則是在昭和4年（西元1929年）在市區改正運動中改建成現在的規模。而市區改正運動的緣起，則是由於台灣各地市鎮原本街道狹窄，僅容行人及手推車通行，自汽車於明治33年（西元1900年）引進台灣之後，甚爲不便；舊街道又乏排水溝，污水潴留，不利衛生。因而總督府依「台灣家屋建築規則」進行房屋徵收拆除、拓寬道路等工作。淡水的主街自四公尺拓寬爲九公尺，而在道路拓寬之後，路兩旁住户亦紛紛改建住户爲二層紅磚建築，臨街立面均披上當時流行的昭和式樣，構成今日所謂「淡水老街」的主體。

註123

Since the British vice-consul began operation in Tanshui in 1861, foreign businessmen found their way into Tanshui. Beginning in 1880, foreign businessmen were allowed to lease land. Because of the different lifestyle between the Chinese and foreigners, the Ching government entered into agreements with foreign governments and established concessions where residences, churches, stores owned by foreigners, and hospitals were located. Although Tanshui was no longer under such agreements during Japanese Occupation, the Japanese rulers still declared Tanshui a habitation for overseas nationals. From then on, foreign areas were intermingled with Chinese neighborhoods. These foreign enclaves were the vicinity east of Tanshui Train Station, Redhair Castle and Yuchekou. A great many Western-built houses still exist today.

The main street (Chungcheng Road today) of Tanshui was developed into its current scale in 1929 as a result of a street-building movement in the city. The movement was initiated because in those days, streets in cities and townships of Taiwan had been narrow and could only allow passage of pedestrians and handcarts. Their inconvenience was greatly felt, especially following the introduction of automobiles to Taiwan in 1900. In addition, old streets posed sanitary problems, because of a lack of drainage and sewage disposal facilities. Therefore, the Governor s Office demolished buildings by expropriation and expanded the streets under the Statute for Home Construction. The main street of Tanshui was expanded from four meters to nine meters, and following the expansion, citizens residing at the sides of the street remodeled their houses into two-story structures. Showa-style decorations were affixed to the side of the buildings facing the street. These buildings constitute the main body of so-called Tanshui Old Street.

日治時代的淡水景致

Scenery of Tanshui during the Japanese era.

RH-076

基隆市日治時期街町劃分圖與現今之對照表：

日據時期街町名	原轄區域	（約）現今位置
社寮町	社寮島一帶	和一、和二、三路；平一、二、三、四路
濱町	八尺門一帶	中正三路
眞砂町	大沙灣一帶	中正二路
八船町	鼻子頭一帶（二沙灣、三沙灣）	中正一路
日新町	日新橋通（今博愛橋）、通海岸通	信一、二、三、四、五、六、七路（部份）及義一路、港東街（全）
義重町	哨船頭本街，義重橋（今自由橋）附近	義二路（全）；義三路，信一、二、三、四、五、六、七路（部份）。
東町		東明路、仁一路（部份）
曙町	田寮港一部份	東明路（部份）
綠町	（原港東醫院附近）	東明路（部份）、仁一路（部份）
幸町	（自女學校至無線電信道下）	信一、二路（部份），義七、八、九、十路（全）
壽町	（自無線電信道下至基隆醫院前）	義三路（部份），義四路（全），信一、二路（部份），義五、六路（全）
田寮町		仁一路（部份）
天神町		仁一、二路（部份），愛八、九路（全）
雙葉町	田寮港之部份	仁一路（部份），愛五、六、七路（全）
玉田町	玉田街	仁一、二、三路（部份），愛四路（全）
元町	石碑街及草店尾一部	仁一、二、三、四路（部份），愛三路（全）
福德町	福德街及新興街	仁二、三、四路（部分），愛一、二路（全）
瀧川町	石硬港一帶	南榮路（全）
堀川町	獅球嶺一帶	精一路（全）
旭町	新店及媽祖宮口一帶	忠一、二路（全），孝一、二、三、四路（部分）
高砂町	高砂公園前（崁頂，媽祖宮後井子一帶）	忠三、四路（全），孝一、二、三、四路（部分）
觀音町	佛祖嶺一帶	樂路（全），安路（部分）
寶町	蚵殼港一帶	西定路、安路（部分）
西町	曾子寮山頂	西定路（部分）
明治町	曾子寮，牛稠港一帶、基隆車站及舊埠頭一帶	安路（部分）、港西街（全）、中山一路
大正町	牛稠港之部份	中山二路（全）
昭和町	仙洞之部分	中山三路（全）
仙洞町	仙洞窟以北	中山四路（全）

註171

Keelung City during the Japanese Era

Names of Districts during the Japanese Era	Area of Coverage	Approximate Present-day Location
Sheliao District	areas around Sheliao Island	Hoyi, Hoerh, Hosan Roads; Pingyi, Pinger, Ping-san, Pingshih Roads
Pin District	areas around Pachimen	Chungcheng San Road
Chensha District	areas around Tashawan	Chungcheng Er Road
Pachuan District	areas around Pitzetou (Erhshawan, Sansh-awan)	Chungcheng Yi Road
Chih-hsin District	Chih-hsin Bridge (present-day Po-ai Bridge), Tunghai coastal area	Hsinyi, Hsinerh, Hsinsan, Hsinshih, Hsinwu, and Hsinliu Roads, part of Hsinchi Road; Yiyi Road, Kangtung Street
Yichung District	Shaochuantou Street, near the Chungyi Bridge (present-day Tzuyu Bridge)	Yierh, Yisan Roads; Hsinyi, Hsinerh, Hsinsan, Hsinshih, Hsinwu, and Hsinliu Roads, part of Hsinchi Road
Tung District		Tungming Road and part of Jenyi Road
Shu District	part of Tienliao harbor	part of Tungming Road
Lyu District	near the former Kangtung Hospital	part of Tungming Road; part of Jenyi Road
Hsing District	from the Girls' School up to the radio station	Hsinyi and part of Hsinerh Road; Hsinchi, Hsinpa, Hsinchiu, and Hsinshih Roads
Shou District	from the radio station to the front of the Keelung Hospital	part of Yisan Road, Yishih Road; Hsinyi and part of Hsinerh Road; Hsinwu and Hsinliu Roads
Tienliao District		part of Jenyi Road
Tienshen District		Jenyi Road, part of Jenerh Road; Aipa and Aichiu Roads
Shuangyeh District	part of Tienliao harbor	part of Jenyi Road; Aiwu, Ailiu, and Aichi Roads
Yutien District	Yutien Street	Jenyi Road, Jenerh, and part of Jensan Road; Aishih Road
Yuan District	Shihpai Street	Jenyi Road, Jenerh, Jensan, and part of Jenshih Road; Aisan Road
Futeh District	Futeh and Hsinhsing Streets	Jenerh, Jensan, and part of Jenshih Road; Aiyi and Aierh Roads
Lungchou District	Shihying harbor	Nanjung Road
Chuechuan District	Shihchiu Hill	Chingyi Road
Hsu District	areas around Hsintien and Matzu Temple	Chungyi and Chungerh Roads; Hsiaoyi, Hsiaoerh, Hsiaosan, and part of Hsiaoshih Roads
Kaosha District	in front of Kaosha Park (Kanting, areas at the back of the Matzu Temple)	Chungshan and Chungshih Roads; Hsiaoyi, Hsiaoerh, Hsiaosan, and part of Hsiaoshih Roads
Kuanyin District	Fuotzu Hill	Le Road, An Road
Fu District	Heke harbor	Hsiting Road, part of An Road
Hsi District	Tsengtzu Liao Mountain	part of Hsiting Road
Meichin District	Tsengtzu Liao, Niutiao harbor; Keelung train station	part of An Road, Hsikang Street, Chung Shan Yi Road
Tacheng District	part of Niutiao harbor	Chungshan Erh Road
Chaohe District	part of Hsientung	Chungshan San Road
Hesientang District	north of Hsientung	Chungshan Shih Road

基隆郵便局及日新橋

基隆郵便局，建於1911年間，與基隆驛隔著港區東西遙遙相望。入口圓頂及高塔是港區明顯的地標，而極為壯觀的入口臺階亦為其建築一大特色，可惜在1962年即被拆除改建。圖中橫跨運河口的日新橋是稍後改建的第二代鋼筋水泥橋。橋邊的駁船港岸已經填平，圖中的景況已難追尋。

RA-139

Keelung post office and Bridge Jih-Shin

The Keelung post office was built in 1911, crossed to Keelung train station by the harbour. Round roof in the entrance and the high tower is the symbol of the area, the fabulous stairs in the entrance is one of the attractions for building, yet it was torn down in 1962. The Bridge Jih-Hsing which being rebuilt was the 2nd generation steel framed concrete. The shore beside the bridge was filled to land. The sight in the picture is no more seen.

基隆港與市街舊景

照片爲由基隆神社（今忠烈祠）向西南俯瞰港區景色。左爲義重橋通，大正 5 年（西元 1916 年）6 月落成的臺灣銀行基隆支店，其前面爲坐落小崗上的公會堂。圖中與街道呈 45 度角者爲基隆憲兵分隊。右前方向爲基隆驛、一號碼頭所在。

RH-048

Keelung Harbor and its Streets

This picture depicts a view of the harbor area overlooked from Keelung Shrine (Martyrs Shrine today) in the northeast. On the left was Chungyichiao Road and Taiwan Bank s Keelung branch established in June 1916, with the Community Center situated on a small hill in the foreground. The building forming a 45 degree angle with the street in the picture was the Keelung Military Police Division. In the right were the Keelung Post and Pier No. 1.

日治時期日新町的建築特色

日新町的範圍包括日新橋(博愛橋)至海岸通一帶，即今日中正區西南角，田寮河以北，信七路以南之地區。當時的日新町街道兩旁的房屋立面採用日人所盛行的風格，房屋實體則採閩式建築。 註25

RH-049

圖爲日治時期的日新町通，即今介於信一路至信七路間之義一路，自基隆憲兵分隊以北朝東北（街尾）方向所望見的街景。

This picture depicts the end section of Chihhsin District (which is the section of Yiyi Road between Hsinyi Road and Hsinchi Road today) during Japanese Occupation as viewed from the northern area of the Keelung MP Division in its southeast.

Architectural Highlights of the Chih-hsin District During the Japanese Era

The Chih-hsin district extended from Chih-hsin bridge (Po-ai Bridge) to Hai'an Boulevard covering the southwest areas of the present-day Chungcheng district, areas north of Tienliao River, and areas south of Hsinchi Road. During the Japanese era, the facades of the houses along the streets of Chih-hsin were designed according to popular Japanese architectural styles, while the buildings themselves were designed according to the Fukienese architectural styles.

基隆公會堂及日新橋

由基隆郵便局大門口北望所見日新橋與公會堂。左端公會堂背後可見港內大阪商船會社所屬輪船的船桅、煙囪。日新橋，位田寮運河河口，連接日新町（今義一路）與元町（今愛三路），為鋼筋混凝土橋，橋分三孔，總跨度 27.1 公尺，寬 14.1 公尺，橋下運河 27 公尺，深 1.2 公尺，可供小船通行及避風。二次大戰時曾被炸毀，民國 35 年（西元 1946 年）修復。 註 23、25、163

RH-052

日治時代的基隆公會堂及日新橋

Community Center and Chihhsin Bridge in Keelung during the Japanese era.

Community Center and Chihhsin Bridge, Keelung

Looking north from the gate of Keelung Post Office, Chihhsin Bridge and the Community Center are visible in the distance. In the left at the back of the Community Center, one can see the masts and chimneys of steamboats owned by the Osaka Maritime Society in Keelung Harbor. Chihhsin Bridge, which was located at the mouth of Tienliao Canal and connected Hsin District (Yiyi Road today) and Yuan District (Aisan Road today), was a reinforced concrete bridge, featuring three spans, a total length of 27.1 meters and a width of 14.1 meters. The bridge allowed passage of small vessels and served to protect vessels against wind. The bridge was destroyed in World War II and restored in 1946.

日治時期基隆新店街之建築

清朝之基隆新店街（今忠二路）是基隆的發展起源地「大基隆」的一部分。日治時，改名爲旭町，明治33年（西元1900年）起基隆陸續開始改正街道，並配合港岸規劃格子狀街道，所以街道顯得寬直，沿街建築整齊一致。

基隆在1907年（明治40年）時進行市區計畫，規劃幾何形式的街區，以期獲得寬廣筆直的馬路，並將立面改爲「大正型」、「昭和型」建築樣式；新店街即爲一例。其房屋立面多爲明治末至大正初期最流行的作法，一樓圓拱砌法工整，間以洗石子或白灰砂漿修飾紅磚立面；二樓則有三個拱窗或平拱窗，屋頂建有女兒牆，雖無華麗的氣息，卻建立起整齊清爽的視覺效果。　註117

RH-051

Keelung's Hsintien District During the Japanese Era

Hsintien Street (Hsintien and Wenchang areas of Jenai District today), which was part of Greater Keelung, the original focal point of Keelung s development, was mainly the residence of Taiwanese. Since 1900, efforts were made in Keelung to remodel the streets and accommodate the planning in which the streets were to be grid-like in conformity with the harbor plans. Thanks to the planning, the streets were made straight and wide, the buildings neat and coherent.

The urban-planning project of 1907 divided Keelung into districts with geometric shapes, in order to obtain wider roads. The fronts of houses facing the main streets were also designed according to architectural styles in the Taisho and Showa era. An example was the Hsintien area, where houses were designed using styles most popular between the latter years of the Meiji era and the early years of the Taisho era. A carefully laid brick arch at the first floor, a brick wall decorated with washed stones, and arched windows on the second floor made up the simple and yet eye-pleasing design.

基隆劉銘傳路舊景

Old-time View of Liu Ming-Chuan Road (Tienshen District), Keelung

劉銘傳路，在日治時期稱爲天神町，其形成因日本人印山氏爲解決住的問題，在此投資興建日式木造平民住宅 19 棟，容納日本人家 66 户，因而發展成一處日本人社區，故此地又有印山町之別稱。圖爲自田寮運河北岸(今上智橋，舊名天滿橋)頭所見劉銘傳路一帶仁愛區水錦、虹橋二里的景觀。天滿橋係鋼筋混凝土臺墩三孔木構橋面，長 28.3 公尺，寬 4.5 公尺，載重 10 噸。南岸街道東側的世界館（活動常設館）是一棟 1930 年代新穎的折衷主義風格建築，圖右端有昭和 6 年（西元 1931 年）3 月闢築的泊船場。 註 23、24、25

To resolve housing problems, Uyama, a Japanese, invested in the construction of 19 Japanese-style wooden bungalows, which could accommodate 66 Japanese families. Thus, this area became a Japanese community, which was known as Uyama District. This picture shows the Shuichin and Hungchiao areas of Jenai District in the vicinity of Liu Ming-chuan Road (called Aipa Road in the past), viewed from today's Shangchih Bridge (formerly called Tienman Bridge) on the north bank of Tienliao Canal. With a length of 28.3 meters, a width of 4.5 meters and a capacity of 10 tons, this bridge featured a wooden surface supported by reinforced concrete abutments with three spans. Along the eastern section of the street on the south bank was the World Hall activity center, a 1930 eclectic-style building. In the right side of the picture was a moorage established in March of 1931.

RH-050

日治時代的天神町，今爲劉銘傳路

Tienshen District during the Japanese era is Liu Ming-chuan Road today.

基隆市政府附近舊景

Old-time View of Keelung City Government Building

基隆市政府現址爲清代基隆通判署所在，日治後歷設基隆區長役場、街役場、市役所，在當時屬日新町（今義一路）。昭和4年（西元1929年）倡議改建，第二代基隆市役所爲鋼筋混凝土三層建築，由該市土木課長藤田爲次郎設計，昭和6年8月上樑，昭和7年3月落成。遭二次大戰炸損，於民國34年（西元1945年）12月修復。市役所北鄰係圖中二層磚造斜屋頂雙山牆立面之憲兵分隊，對街爲臺灣銀行基隆支店。

註2、25、115

The current address of the Keelung City Government is where the assistant magistrate of Keelung was based in the Ching dynasty. During the Japanese era, a number of local government offices were established in Chihhsin Street (Yiyi Road today). A proposal was put forward in 1929 for the reconstruction of the government building. The second Keelung Civil Affairs Office was a three-story concrete building designed by Hwita Tamejiro, Director of the Keelung Civil Engineering Department. The framework of the building was completed in August 1931, and the building completed in March 1932. In December of 1945, this building, which was damaged during World War II, was restored in December of 1945. Opposite the Civil Affairs Office in the north as indicated in this picture was a two-story brick structure with sloping roofs and a double-gable facade, where the military police Division was located. Across the street was the branch office of Taiwan Bank.

RH-075

基隆港哨船頭海岸通之現址

哨船頭的範圍包括今中正區正義里、義重里、信義里、港東里一帶，即信一路至信七路近東三碼頭、東五碼頭的地區，哨船頭海岸通之現址應爲今中正頭東五碼頭一帶地方。

註25、26

RH-053

Shaochuantou Harbor in Keelung

Shaochuantou Harbor included the Chengyi, Yichung, Hsinyi, and Kangtung communities in the present-day Chungcheng district, which includes the areas along Hsinyi Road to Hsinchi Road, near Tungshan and Tungwu harbors. The former Shaochuantou harbor also included areas near the present-day Tungwu harbor.

基隆義二路舊景（哨船頭義重橋通）

義重町，舊稱哨船頭街，該町南端跨田寮運河，即義重橋（今自由橋）。圖爲該町大正年間向南望之街景，此地主要爲日人集居地區，是官署、商社、公司等集中的行政、工商重心，一二層建築參差，右側轉角「岸田吳服店」即屬大正初期飾帶紅磚建築，與之相若的風格今仍可見於大溪老街。

註 65、66、114

RH-054

Old-time View of Yi-erh Road (Yichungchiao Road of Shaochuantou)

Yichung Street was once known as Shaochuantou Street, with its southern area (Yichung Bridge, or Freedom Bridge today) spanning Tienliao Canal. This picture portrays the outlook of the southern section of the street during the Taisho period. This street was mostly resided by the Japanese and was an administrative and commercial center, with a high concentration of government buildings, business societies and companies. The street buildings were a mixture of single- or double-story buildings. At the bend at the right was Antienwu Clothing Store, which was a brick building with band-like decorations typical of the Taisho period. Comparable styles can still be found in the old streets of Tahsi.

新竹市中正路（榮町）舊景

Nostalgic View of Chungcheng Road (Jung District), Hsinchu City

新竹市榮町（今中正路），又稱爲停車場通（站前大道）。沿街皆爲二層街屋，兩旁並種植樹木，圖爲靠火車站一段之街景，左側有「高等理髮館」，右側三層建築爲「新竹旅館」，路的端景（南望）即新竹火車站。　註65、66、114

Also known as Parking Road (Train Station Avenue), Jung District (Chungcheng Road today) of Hsinchu City was characterized by two- story street buildings, with trees lining both sides. This picture delineates a section of the street near the train station, with Kaoteng Barber Shop in the left and Hsinchu Hotel, a three-story building, in the right. On the south side of the road was Hsinchu Train Station.

RH-055

日治時期台中市街道規劃 Street Planning of Taichung City during the Japanese Era

日治時期台中市街道經過3次市區改正計畫，分別為1900年、1903年及1911年，其中以1911年的擴張改正計畫最為重要，奠定了今天的台中市火車站前核心區的都市構圖。

該項計畫的要點如下：(1)市區採棋盤型。(2)市區河道均以土填平，僅保留柳川、綠川，並將綠川截彎取直，其水源段移至計畫區之西側。(3)規定路寬（一等道路25.2公尺、二等道路12.6公尺、三等道路10.8公尺）。(4)限期拆除計畫道路所經之建築物。

台中市被日人規劃成住宅型都市，街道大致排列成整齊的格子狀，其街道圖案分為三種不同的格子狀組合：

1. 鐵路以西：成立時間最早，每一單元的格子小而密，且受河道方向影響，排列成東北向西南或西北向東南的街道走向。
2. 鐵路以東：格子較大且最為整齊，與鐵路並行或與之直交是其特色。
3. 公園以北：發展最遲，有許多非格子摻雜其間。

註29

During the Japanese era, the streets of Taichung City went through three correction projects, which took place in 1900, 1903 and 1911 respectively. Of the three projects, the project of 1911 was the most important, since it laid out the current design of the downtown area in front of the Taichung Train Station today.

Under the project, a grid pattern was adopted for the layout of the streets. Most waterways in the city areas were leveled, with the exception of Liu River and Green River. Green River was straightened and its Shuyuan section was rechanneled to the western section of the project area. In addition, the statutory road width was promulgated (25.2 meters for class-one roads, 12.6 meters for class-two roads and 10.8 meters for class-three roads.) Meanwhile, buildings standing in the way of the designated streets were to be torn down within a specified time period.

Under the plan of the Japanese, Taichung City was treated as a residential city, with streets in a tidy grid pattern. The streets had three different grid combinations:

1.Streets west of the railway: This pattern was formed earlier than the other two, with a small, dense grid pattern.

In addition, the grids were arranged in a northeast-southwest or northwest-southeast orientation.

2.Streets east of the railway: This pattern features the tidiest arrangement of grids, with thoroughfares parallel or perpendicular to the railway.

3.Streets north of Taichung Park: This area was developed later than the previous two, with many irregular sectors mingled right- angled streets.

RH-056

圖中的景象是由臺中廳舍（現市政府）屋頂陽台東望所見之市容：正中央建築即臺銀臺中出張所；右後側遠處煙囪係高砂町（今樂業里）在大正元年（西元 1912 年）所創設之帝國製糖會社（臺糖臺中的總廠）；左側爲雨淋板外牆木構造二層建築的臺中郵便局。 註 6、7、34、65、66

This picture depicts an outlook of the city from the porch on the rooftop of the Taichung Department (Taichung City Government today) in the west. The building in the middle was the Taichung branch of Taiwan Bank. The chimney in the distant right belonged to the Empire Sugar Society (Taichung branch of Taiwan Sugar Company today) established in the Kaosha District in 1912. In the left was the Taichung Post Office, a two-story structure with exterior weather boards.

日治時代都市空間的遺跡——台中綠川

Reminiscence of Urban Space during Japanese Era — Green River, Taichung

綠川本無名，其後有人稱之爲新盛溪，西元 1912 年台灣總督佐久間左馬太改名爲綠川。其發源於台中市東北方北屯區北興里及北區錦村里附近，向西南方流，與柳川平行，貫穿台中市東部。綠川之河道原多曲流，西元 1903 年及 1911 年實行市區改正計畫時，將綠川截彎取直。

圖中綠川兩岸栽植垂柳，卵石砌的河岸爬佈蔓草，綠意盎然，其上的短橋各具特色，增添都市景觀的生氣，頗具日本京都風味，是臺中市至今仍保有的都市空間特色。當時爲建設模範都市於台中，明治 33 年（西元 1900 年）臺中規劃了棋盤式街道，因此而有小京都之稱。 註 65、66、67、115、116

Originally known as Hsinsheng Creek, Lu Chuan was given its current name (meaning "Green River") by Taiwan governor Sakuma Samata in 1912. The river upstream is located near Peihsing community in Peitun district and Chinchun community in the northern district northeast of Taichung City. It cuts through eastern Taichung City, flowing southeast and parallel to the Liu River. The course of the river was straightened and redirected during urban reconstruction projects in 1903 and 1911.

In this picture, willows were planted on both banks of Green River. The river banks bonded with pebbles were covered with vines, with a pleasant sense of greenness. The unique short bridges straddling the river helped bring out the liveliness of the city, which was quite similar to Kyoto in style. Such were the urban characteristics that Taichung has enjoyed even to this day. Taichung was known as Little Kyoto during that time because it was intended to be developed as a model city. Thus, in 1900, gridlike streets in Taichung were planned.

RH-057

日人聚集台中榮町通

台中榮町為今公園路繼光里、繼榮里一帶，區域範圍為鐵路至五權路間及民權路至公園路間的商業區。區內以柳川東路為界，以東為日籍商人聚集地，以西則為本地商人的大本營。照片所示榮町街道兩側為日本洋式店舖，當時日商多聚集於此。 註29

RH-059

The Jungting District Gathering Place for Japanese Businessmen

The Jungting District in Taichung was located on present-day Kungyuan Road, in the vicinity of Chikuang and Chijung districts. The district once included the commercial area bounded by the length of the railroad to Wuchuan Road, and by the length of Minchuan Road to Kungyuan Road. Liuchuan East Road further subdivided the district into two: to the east was the gathering place of Japanese businessmen, while the west was where Taiwanese businessmen gathered. The picture shows the Japanese-style stores along the streets of Jungting.

台商聚集的台中干城橋通

日治時期的台中干城橋通是今日台中市成功路。干城橋通是當時台人聚集的地區，本地人經營的商店林立，此區隔著柳川車站與榮町通、櫻橋通等日籍商人聚集處爲鄰，恰成一對比。

註57、96

日治時期的干城橋通

Kanchengchiao Road during the Japanese era.

RH-060

Kanchengchiao Road in Taichung: Gathering Place for Taiwanese Businessmen

During the Japanese era, the Kanchengchiao Road (present-day Chengkung Road in Taichung) was the popular gathering place for Taiwanese businessmen, featuring stores and shops run by Taiwanese. The district was located on the opposite side of Liuchuan Bus Station from the Jungting Road and Yingchiao Road, which were the popular gathering places of Japanese businessmen.

嘉義街今址

嘉義街是日治時期嘉義郡郡役所的所在地。昭和 5 年（西元 1930 年），改升嘉義街爲市，而市區則稱爲街，即今日嘉義市政府所在地附近之區域。

註 192

RH-061

圖爲日治時代的嘉義街大道，今爲市政府附近

The street of Chiayi Community as depicted in this picture is where Chiayi County Government is located today.

Present-day Location of Chiayi Community

During the Japanese era, the Chiayi County Government Building was located in Chiayi Community. In 1930 (the fifth year of the Showa era), Chiayi Community was elevated to the status of a city, and the city limits (the area around the present-day Chiayi County Government Building) were still known as. *kai* ("block")

北港朝天宮廟前大街

北港媽祖廟，位於北港鎮中山路底，創建於康熙 39 年（西元 1700 年），歷經過多次整修。日治時期，廟前大街早已是車水馬龍，絲毫不遜於今日。

註 148

RH-062

圖爲日治時代北港媽祖廟前大街

This picture depicts the street in front of the Matzu Temple of Peikang during the Japanese era.

Chaotien Temple of Peikang

Located at the end of Chungshan Road in the town of Peikang, the Matzu Temple was erected in 1700 during the Kanghsi reign of the Ching Dynasty. Since the end of the Japanese era, the temple has undergone several renovations and has attracted multitudes of worshippers.

臺南的銀座——末廣町（中正路）

Mokuang District (Chungcheng Road) — The Ginza of Tainan

末廣町（今中正路、忠義路口一帶）爲鬧區所在，緊臨州廳（今臺南市政府），有臺南的銀座之稱。這是攝於昭和年間的街景，左側街道轉角三至五層的商店住宅建於昭和7年（西元1932年），是前衛的折衷主義現代建築街屋作品；右側日本勸業銀行臺南支店（現臺灣土地銀行臺南分行址）完成於昭和12年，形式與該行臺北支店相彷，亦有巨大的柱列，同爲該行建築課設計之姊妹作，由東京清水組所施工。

註65、117、118、183

Adjacent to the Prefecture Offices (Tainan City Government today), Mokuang District was a downtown area nicknamed the Ginza of Tainan. This is a street scene taken during the Showa period. Built in 1932, the three- to five-story residential and business buildings at the curve in the left section of the street were avant-garde eclectic street buildings of modern times. In the right was the Tainan branch of Dai-Ichi Kangyo Bank (currently where the Tainan branch of Land Bank of Taiwan is located) established in 1937. Similar to its Taipei branch in terms of style and the characteristically large columns, the building was also designed by the architectural department of the bank and constructed by Shimizu Kumi Construction Company of Tokyo.

RH-065

由今中正路、忠義路口西望之舊街景
位於路口之「林商號」是臺南第一家綜合性百貨公司，內部裝設有臺南地區的第一部電梯，外牆黃褐色面磚，一至四樓賣場，四樓一部及五樓是餐廳，頂樓爲機房。

Old-time Scene of Chungcheng and Chungyi Roads
Located at the entrance of the street, Linshanghao was the first integrated department store in Tainan. With the first elevator in Tainan and khaki tiles on its outer walls, the department store had shops from the first to the fourth floor; restaurants on a portion of the fourth and the fifth floor; and a penthouse on the top floor.

RH-063

RH-064

東望所見街景，街道兩側對稱一致的立面整齊劃一，是由技師梅澤捨次郎統一設計，爲臺南市第一批整體規劃的商業街，百貨、酒店、旅館一一興起，路樹與街燈相間排列顯得秩序整然，市容一新，路底端景爲臺南州廳。

The street scene as viewed from the west featured a symmetrical and uniform facade on the buildings on both sides of the streets. Designed by the technician Umezawa Syajiro, this street was the first business street ever designed on an integrated basis in Tainan City. In the street, emerging department stores, liquor stores, and hotels were orderly placed with street trees and streetlamps, contributing to the new appearance of the city. At the end of the street was the Tainan Prefecture Office.

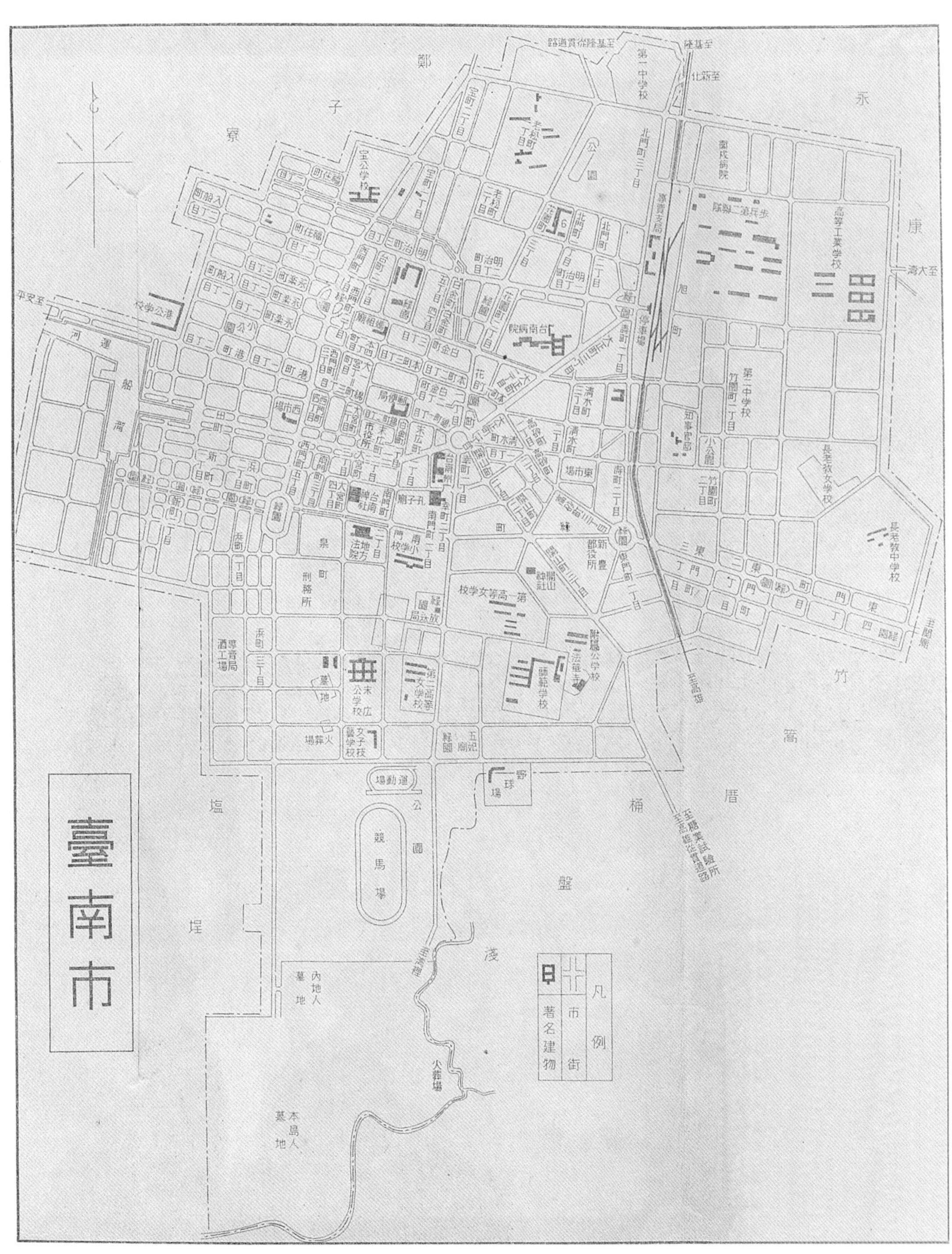

RH-066

台南市街道圖
昭和 10 年由台南市役所發行的台南市街道圖
It's street map of Tainan city issued in 1935.

台南銀座爲商業中心

日治時期台南的商業中心幾經轉移，而由本町(今民權路)，轉移至銀座。爾後又東移至末廣町，今日之中正路與忠義路交叉口。今日之中正路（即銀座），繁華依舊，但台南的商業中心已非限於一地。 註58

RH-067

Tainan Kinsha Commercial Center

After several relocation efforts, the Tainan commercial center during the Japanese era was moved from Penting (present-day Minchuan Road) to Kinsha. The center was subsequently moved to the Mokuang District before being relocated again to its present-day location at the intersection of Chungcheng Road and Chungyi Road. Today, despite being a busy and prosperous district, Chungcheng Road is no longer the sole commercial district in Tainan.

由來已久的台南鞋街、草花街

從台南市民權路、忠義路會口處，沿民權路西行，至 64 巷口爲止，北側爲清代及日治時期的鞋街；南側則爲草花街。鞋街、草花街、帽街、竹仔街是依經營行業分段命名的，曾是清代繁華一時的地帶，如今熱鬧依舊，舊名卻已不復存在。 註 133

日治時代的台南鞋街、花草街 RH-068

Shoe Street and Flower Street in Tainan during the Japanese era.

Tainan's Time-honored Shoe Street and Flower Street

During the Ching dynasty and Japanese era, Tainan City's " Shoe Street" was located in the area north of Minchuan Road, between the intersection of Minchuan and Chungyi Road and the entrance to Lane 64. South of this area was "Flower Street". Street names, such as Shoe Street, Flower Street, Hat Street and Bamboo Street, were given based on the type of business operated on a given street. Although these places, which were prosperous in the Ching dynasty, still have a lot of activity today, their old names are no longer in use.

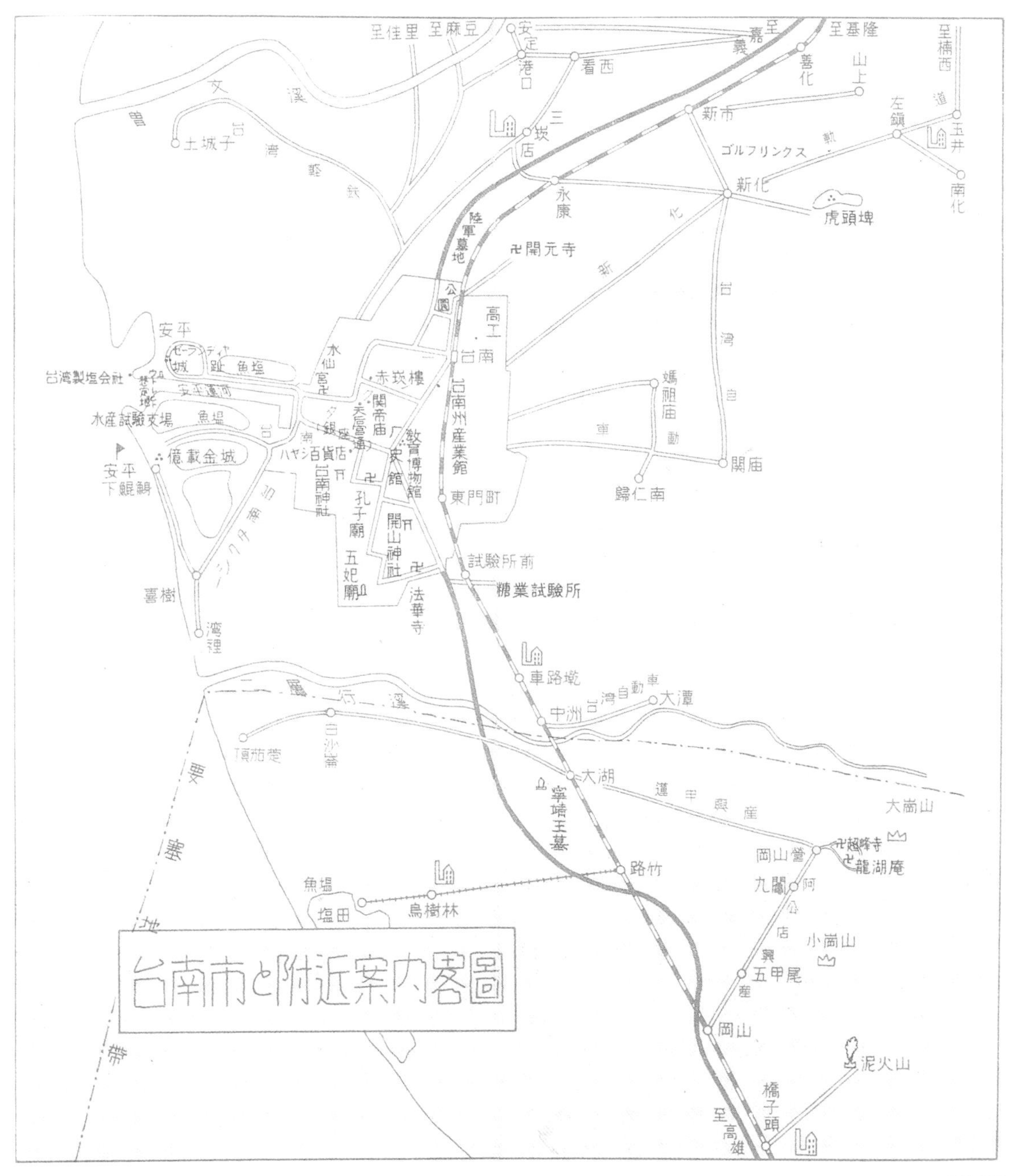

RH-069

台南市附近旅遊略圖

日治時期由鐵道部所發行的台南市旅遊圖

This traveling map issued by the Railroad Department of Transportation Bureau during Japanese era.

高雄鼓山一路舊景（山下町）

圖爲今鼓山區東南邊沿鼓山一路向西南望之舊景，日治時期稱「山下町」，每逢節日，沿街商家均插日本國旗。此街道爲當時高雄市街主要街道，也是縱貫道路終端的路段，路燈、電桿林立，沿路每幾戶即設一垃圾箱，左側路邊立有市內巴士的站牌。 註 65

RH-070

Old-time View of Kushan One Road (Shanhsia District), Kaohsiung

This picture depicts an old-time scene viewed westward along Kushan One Road from the southeast of Kushan District today. This was Shanhsia District during the Japanese era. Stores along the street erected national flags of Japan during festivals. This was not only one of the main streets in Kaohsiung in those days, but also the end section of the North-South Railway, with streetlamps and electric poles lining the street. A garbage can was set up near every few houses along the street. At the side of the road on the left can be seen a bus stop.

花蓮港市街發展大事紀要

年　　代	大 事 記
明治33年(西元1900年)	花蓮港市街自南濱海岸花蓮溪畔北遷。 建花蓮港出張所廳署於新港街(今舊市區)。 郵便局、國(日)語傳習所分教場(即後來的公學校)陸續移設。
明治35年(西元1902年)	移安平燈塔於花蓮港，稱花蓮港燈臺觀測站，兼司觀測氣象。
明治42年(西元1909年)	置花蓮港廳
明治43年(西元1910日)	燈塔與觀測站分立，原觀測站改稱花蓮港測候所。 公布花蓮港街市區計劃。 花蓮港尋常高等小學校建校。 花蓮港醫院成立
明治45年(西元1912年)	台灣銀行成立花蓮港出張所(辦事處)。
大正11年(西元1922年)	實施酒類專賣，宜蘭振拓株式會社花蓮港酒工場，由總督府收購改由官營。
昭和15年(西元1940年)	花蓮港升格爲市。
民國40年(西元1951年)	花蓮大地震，中華路(原高砂通)、中山路(原黑金通)鬧區毀損嚴重。

註 36、65、66、114、116、134

Stages of Development in Hualien Harbor

Year	Significant Events
1900	Streets of Hualien Harbor City moved north from the southern coast and the bank of Hualien Creek. Department of Hualien Harbor was established in Hsinkang Street(the old downtown today). Post offices and Japanese language schools(which later became public schools)were relocated.
1902	Anping Light Tower, which was relocated to Hualien Harbor, also served as a meteorological observation station named as Hualien Harbor Observation Post.
1909	Hualien Harbor Department was established.
1910	The light tower was separated from the observation post; the original observation post was renamed the Hualien Harbor Meteorological Observation Post. The Urban Plan of Hualien Harbor City was promulgated. The Ordinary High School of Hualien Harbor City was established. The Hualien Harbor Hospital was established.
1912	Bank of Taiwan set up its branch office in Hualien Harbor City.
1922	A monopoly of alcohol was imposted where the Alcoholic Factory of Yilan Sintaku Company in Hualien Harbor was acquired by the Governor's Office of Taiwan.
1940	Hualien Harbor was promoted to the status of a city under the jurisdiction of the Executive Yuan.
1951	A major earthquake hit Hualien, wreaking tremendous havoc on the downtown area around Chunghua Road(originally known as Kaoshatung)and Chungshan Road(originally Heichintung).

花蓮市街舊景

此景是昭和年間由位於花崗山的花蓮港測候所向西望所見，當時市區率爲木造平房，右側前方係昭和五年（西元1930年）4月遷設於筑紫橋通、黑金通交叉口（中正、中山路口）花蓮港郵便局之無線電鐵塔，亦爲市區的明顯地標。近前爲東臺寺之入母屋造（同中國的歇山頂）寺殿屋頂，該寺創建於大正7年（西元1918年），其北鄰淨光寺創建於大正3年，民國36年（西元1947年）2月兩寺合併改稱東淨寺，民國40年毀於大地震，次年4月底重建竣工。

註36、193

RF-081

An Old Street Scene of Hualien City

This was a view from the vantage point of the Hualien Harbor Meteorological Observation Post, located in Mt. Huakang, in eastern Taiwan during the Showa period. The urban area at that time was filled with wooden bungalows. In the foreground to the right was the radio electric tower of Hualien Post Office relocated to the intersection of Tzutsechiao Road and Heichin Road (intersection of Chungcheng and Chungshan Roads today) in April, 1930. The tower was a conspicuous landmark of downtown Hualien at that time. Also in the foreground was a Japanese-style roof of Tungtai Temple, built in 1918. In 1947, Tungtai Temple was merged with Chingkuang Temple immediately in its north, which was built in 1914, and became Tungching Temple, which was destroyed by an earthquake in 1951 and rebuilt in April the following year.

花蓮港市街近山舊景

此照片攝於深冬之際略帶薄霧的清晨，遠處中央山脈的山峰出現少有的降雪，前景樹木的樹葉凋零只剩光禿的枝幹，左下角近前的斜屋頂仿唐式日本建築爲東臺寺，圖面中央爲花蓮港廳廳舍，其右有小圓頂之建築爲臺灣銀行花蓮港支店，最右端爲小學校校舍（今花崗國中）一角，左方煙囪處爲專賣局工場。

RH-071

Nostalgic View of Hualien Harbor City Bordered by Mountains

Taken on a mid-winter's early morning, this picture depicts rare snowfall on the peaks of the Central Mountains in the distance and withered trees with naked twigs in the foreground. In the lower left of the picture was the building which housed the Hualien Harbor Department. In its right was a structure with a small dome, which was the branch office of the Taiwan Bank in Hualien Harbor. On the furthest right was a portion of a primary school (Hua-kang Junior High School today). The chimney in the left was the factory of the Monopoly Bureau.

自美崙山麓朝西南望花蓮港市街

圖中橫跨美崙溪的吊橋為菁華橋前身，在戰後不久改建。左上角花崗山臺地，海拔約 20 公尺，於大正 11 年（西元 1922 年）整平後開闢為公園，該地位於美崙溪南岸，北崖臨溪，東、西、南三面背緩坡，頂闊面坦，可極目滄海，眺望山川，其前方（西北緣）為昭和 4 年（西元 1929 年）設址的花蓮港高等女學校（今省立花蓮女中）校舍。

註 37、193

RH-072

View of Hualien Harbor City from the Piedmont of Mt. Meilun in the Northeast

The suspension bridge spanning Meilun Creek as depicted in this picture was the forerunner of Chinghua Bridge, which was rebuilt soon after World War II. The plateau of Mt. Huakang, about 20 meters in elevation, in the upper left of this picture was leveled and developed into a park in 1922. Situated on the south bank of Meilun Creek, the park overlooking the creek in its north was surrounded by mild slopes in the east, west and south. The park featured a flat surface and a nice view, enabling a beautiful outlook of mountains and rivers. In front of the park (or in its northwest) was a girls high school (Hualien Girls Senior High School today) established in Hualien Harbor in 1929.

RH-073

遠處海岸山脈山景依稀可見，左側地形緩起為花崗山臺地，對岸道路為筑紫橋通（今中正路），其左側係花蓮港醫院，右側為花蓮港公學校（今明禮國小）。

註 134

View of Hualien Harbor City from Mount Meilun in the North In this picture, Coastal Mountains are barely discernible in the distance. In the left is the plateau of Mt. Huakang with mild terrain. The road on the opposite bank was Tsutsechiao Road (Chungcheng Road today), with Hualien Harbor Hospital to its left and Hualien Harbor Public School (Ming Li Primary School today) to its right.

玉里街與羊羹

玉里，位於花蓮縣南部，爲八通關越橫斷道路東部起點，圖中即玉里市街街景，街上已有汽車通行。右側建築爲玉里郵便局，爲日式雨淋板木造建築。左下角小圖橋邊的商家立著「玉里羊羹」招牌，玉里羊羹是明治 38 年（西元 1905 年）日本人窪田引進此地生產製造，行銷至今已有 90 年歷史，成爲家喻戶曉的花蓮名產之一。羊羹原是中國的一道名菜，鐮倉時代由僧人傳入日本，日人喜愛吃甜食，乃加以研究改製，成爲今日大衆化的甜點。 註 35、66、74、114

RH-074

日治時代的玉里街

Yuli Street during the Japanese era.

Yangkeng of Yuli Street

Situated in the south of Hualien County, Yuli is the starting point of Patungkuan Highway in eastern Taiwan. The picture depicts the scene of Pentung Street (the main street) of Yuli, where automobiles could already be seen. The building at the right was Yuli Post Office, which was a Japanese-style wooden structure with weather boards. In the lower left by the bridge was a shop with a signboard which read Yuli Yangkeng. *Yuli yangkeng*, which has a history of 90 years, was introduced, manufactured and marketed here by a Japanese named Kubota in 1905, and has become a popular specialty of Hualien. Originally a popular Chinese dish, *yangkeng* was introduced to Japan by Buddhist monks during the Kamakura period. Because the Japanese relished sweets, research was undertaken to transform the dish into a popular dessert today.

古築物語

Antique Buildings

日治時代的台灣建築，各式風格羅列奔放，展現著前所未有的豐富建築語彙：蘊涵著歐洲古典、殖民色彩、日本和式、以及本土閩式建築等元素。與日本內地建築比較，顯得更爲繁瑣。隨著制度變遷，政治化的因素，建築的遞嬗、組織的沿革，如影隨形。

During the Japanese era, the buildings in Taiwan, which were characterized by a richness in architectural styles, including classic European elements, colonial, Japanese and traditional Fukienese styles, were more complicated that those in Japan. The transformation of social and political systems also contributed to the change of architectural styles.

台灣建築拼圖 RC-073

Taiwanese Architectural Jigsaw Puzzle

內、台
建築風格分析
Comparison of Taiwanese and Japanese Architectural Designs

臺灣的近代建築在19世紀中葉西方資本主義勢力的進入後產生變化，早期的洋行洋樓與傳教士建築充分顯現出陽臺殖民地建築樣式(Veranda Colonial Style)的英國殖民風格：磚造拱廊、拱圈及四坡屋頂大量採用。日治以後又逐漸變化，其所引進的建築風格，有延續自日本傳統木構造建築，有仿效法國之「帝國風格」，對西方古典建築元素的抄襲與模仿，強調形式的歷史主義。後者呈現出殖民地樣式的雨淋板 (Weather Board，日文稱下見板)、陽臺殖民地樣式的陽臺走廊、法國第二共和巴洛克式裝飾與馬薩屋頂以及辰野式的紅磚與特殊裝飾等特徵。東京大學建築史教授藤森照信認爲，臺灣這一段時期的樣式建築與日本本土作品相較顯得太過繁瑣。

註117、119、153、167、168、170、175、183

Traditional Taiwanese architecture underwent great changes under influence of Western capitalism during the middle of the 19th century. The Veranda colonial style was clearly evident in the business establishments and buildings, as well as other religious establishments during the period. This architectural style was characterized by arched brick passageways and sloped roofs spreading in four directions. During the Japanese era, traditional Japanese wooden architecture were greatly in use, together with imitations of French architectural styles. Imitation of Western architecture resulted in the wide use of weather boards, balconies with long passageways, Baroque-style decor, red bricks, and other special decorations. A professor at the Tokyo University College of Architectural History has noted that Taiwanese architecture at this time was far more complex than that in Japan.

閩、日
風格並存的
民間建築

日治時期除官方樣式的建築之外，臺灣民間的傳統閩南建築幾乎與日本傳統建築並存，而各自形成新舊社區。以日本人的移民村農家、各機構宿舍區而言，幾乎將日本本土和式的生活環境完全移植至台灣。例如，同樣種植菸葉的農村、功能相同的菸樓，卻在移民村的日本民家與美濃傳統民宅之間，由於文化差異而呈現不同的建築景觀。而都市內日本人與臺灣人集居地的街區風貌也各自擁有強烈的文化屬性。日本所引入的日本傳統木造建築，包括住宅、神社及廟宇等，也因日本建築源於中國唐代建築，所以在某種程度上，本地傳統工匠也就難以擺脫唐代建築風格，這種現象在當局灌輸西化即代表進步（現代化）的觀念及皇民化運動、同化政策的推動下逐漸改變，例如騎樓門窗面、室內居室空間的裝修等作品在日治後期即隨社會脈動已有所改造，只有傳統寺廟建築及格局仍維持閩南建築的原始風貌。

西方古典樣式與日本樣式是日治時期官方的正統建築語彙，其傳達的正是「日本的」與「進步的」象徵，具有本土意識的地方業主與匠師，僅能以局部或象徵性地使用本土元素來表達本土訊息。以臺北本町（今重慶南路一段）街屋建築而言，其在水患後由官方統一設計的災後復建，所自然流露濃厚的官方建築風格，非但形成新的街屋形式，亦爲各地匠師競相模仿且引以爲傲，而本土習慣的裝飾則仍持續使用，甚至更顯花俏繁複，故這種結合了西方建築語彙與臺灣傳統裝飾文樣於一身，既西化又本土的性格，成爲日治時期民間仿官方建築的特質。另外長老教會西方傳教士對本土文化的細膩觀察，表現的閩洋折衷樣式建築，更揉和了閩南樣式民居元素、西方歷史建築元素以及拱圈、拱廊等表徵。此外本地商紳模仿外籍買辦，興建中西合壁的洋樓也成了一種風氣時尚，爲建築樣式的另一支發展路線。

註 117、119、153、167、168、170、175、183

RB-039

現今植物園的林業展覽館，是台灣唯一以衙門形式尚存的建築。清朝的台灣布政使，相當於今副省長之職，衙門爲辦公兼住家合一，第三進爲住家。

The Forestry Museum located in the present Botanical Garden is the only existing building erected in the style of a government office in Taiwan. The Director General of Taiwan Civil And Financial Administration in the Ching Dynasty, a position which is equivalent to that of a Deputy Governor of the current provincial government, whose office was a complex to serve both as an office and resident. The area of the third courtyard served as a residence.

Co-existence of Fukienese and Japanese Architectural Styles in Private Buildings

Apart from the government buildings during the period of Japanese rule, private houses with their unique architectural styles also existed alongside traditional Japanese buildings. The Japanese lifestyle and living environment were almost duplicated in Taiwan, as evidenced by the dormitories of government organizations and houses of Japanese immigrants living in Taiwan's rural areas. As a result, stark contrasts may be seen between the style of houses of Japanese tobacco farmers and that of the Meinung people, who lived adjacent to the Japanese farmers. In the urban areas, residential neighborhoods of Japanese and Taiwanese also reflected the difference between the two cultures. Traditional Japanese wooden architecture was extensively used in building private houses, Shinto shrines, and temples. Since traditional Japanese architecture evolved from Chinese architecture during the Tang Dynasty, Tang influences were evident in works of local carpenters and craftsmen. However, architectural styles gradually changed, due to the efforts of the Japanese authorities to modernize and Westernize Taiwan, together with the movement toward imperial rule and the assimilation policy toward the Taiwanese people. The styles of doors, windows, inner decor and layout started to change during the Japanese era. In due time, the traditional Fukienese architectural styles could only be seen in traditional temples.

During the Japanese era, traditional Western architecture and Japanese-style architecture were characteristic of all government buildings. These buildings were uniquely Japanese and were symbols of progress. In their attempt to retain local flavor, local craftsmen and businessmen could only make partial use of local elements or use symbols depicting local flavor in their constructions. In the Taipei district (present-day Chungching South Road), for example, buildings erected after the massive flood were traditional of Japanese-style government buildings. Not only were the buildings popular during the time, their styles were also widely copied by local craftsmen from around the island. Decor of local flavor, however, continued to be in use, and eventually grew to become more complex. Buildings that integrated Western styles with traditional local decor thus became a distinct feature during the Japanese era. Western missionaries also contributed to the diversity of architectural styles during this period. Apart from these, some local business also imitated the office buildings of foreign purchasing agents, building their offices from a combination of Western and local styles and created a new route of development for local architectural designs.

日治時期
重要建築師介紹

日本近代建築的啓蒙是在19世紀末的明治維新。1868年德川慶喜還政於明治天皇，明治即位後一反過去江户時代的鎖國政策，採取積極開放路線，維新的文明開化風氣，極力吸收近代西方文明，擷取各國精華；建築界亦亟於吸收西歐建築精華，引入歐洲古典建築樣式。

英國建築家 Josiah Conder(西元1852-1920年)受日本工部省延攬，於西元1877年到工部大學校造家學科任教——該學科是日本近代建築教育的創始，他以歐式建築教育養成日本西化第一代建築師，所引進的英國風格古典建築樣式深深影響日本的近代建築。明治19年(西元1886年)工部大學校改併爲帝國大學工科大學，而造家學科主任教授便是由第一代建築師辰野金吾(西元1854-1919年)出任。先後畢業於該校的伊東忠太、長野宇平治、野村一郎、森山松之助等人，均爲辰野門生。

日本統治臺灣以後，除台灣神社(西元1901年)、台灣銀行本店(西元1937年)等極少數特定的建築物，是由日本本土的著名建築師設計，其他多數的建築多由臺灣總督府聘技師來臺，從事建設營繕工作。臺灣對他們的吸引力，主要是這塊日本新殖民地上，到處需要建設，有無限的發展空間與機會讓他們一展抱負，與北海道、朝鮮、中國東北（滿洲國）等其他日本殖民地建設有相似的條件。這些技師都是受過正統西方建築教育的日本第二代、第三代建築師，以所學去建構殖民地臺灣的建築樣式，台灣民間建築即多受其影響，且融合了本土建築風格。

Influential Architects during the Japanese Era

Modern architecture in Japan started to prosper at the end of the 19th century during the Meiji Restoration. After regaining power from Tokugawa in 1868, Emperor Meji initiated a more aggressive policy of liberalization and discarded the practices of the Bakufu era, which isolated Japan from the outside world. The openness and modernization process brought about by the Restoration encouraged the learning of contemporary Western cultures. The field of architecture welcomed the Western schools, as classical European architectural styles were introduced into Japan.

In 1877, the Japanese Ministry of Civil Works hired the services of English architect Josiah Conder (1852- 1920) to teach at the college of architecture in the university run by the ministry, whose efforts pioneered the teaching of architecture in Japan. Conder trained the first generation of Japanese architects in European architectural concepts, and the English-style traditional architects greatly influenced the contemporary and modern age Japanese architects. In 1886 during the 19th year of the Meiji era, the university was restructured to become the Imperial University, with the first generation Japanese architect Tatsuno Kingo (1854-1919) acting as head professor of the college of architecture. Subsequent graduates of the institution such as Ito Cyuta, Nagano Uheji and Moriyama Matsunosuke were all students of Tatsuno.

During the Japanese era, only the Taiwan Shinto Shrine (1901), the Bank of Taiwan (1937), and a few other designated establishments were designed by famous Japanese architects. For other projects, the Taiwan governor's office hired the services of Japanese engineers for building and construction. Taiwan provided an attractive opportunity for these engineers, for as a new colony of Japan, Taiwan offered the same opportunity for growth as in other Japanese colonies such as Hokkaido, Korea, and northeastern China. Trained in the school of traditional Western architecture, these engineers were considered the second and third generations of the Japanese architects. Many of Taiwan's private buildings during the period were influenced by their designs, which were also integrated into local architectural designs.

日治時期台灣重要的建築師如下：

建築師	簡介
福田東吾	歷任總督府技師、陸軍技師，作品有：總督官邸(1901)、台北步兵第一聯隊永久兵營(1903)、台中步兵第一聯隊第三大隊永久兵營、台南步兵第二聯隊永久兵營(1907)，並監造第一代台灣神社(1901)。
十川嘉太郎	總督府土木技師，擔任台灣北部水道工程、基隆築港及其它水利和土木工程工作，設計明治橋（今圓山中山橋）第一代鐵橋（1901）、第二代鋼筋混凝土拱橋(1932)。
伊東忠太 (1867-1954)	明治25年(1892)畢業於帝國大學工科大學造家學科(東京帝國大學建築學科前身)，在台作品為第一代台灣神社，被列為日本近代傳統樣式建築代表作品之一。伊東博士為日本傳統建築權威，曾擔任造神宮使廳技師，平安神宮(1895)、彌彥神社(1916)、明治神宮(1920)均為其作品。
長野宇平治 (1867-1937)	明治26年(1893)畢業於帝國大學工科大學造家學科，總督府競圖是他在台唯一作品，在日本作品甚多。
野村一郎	明治28年(1895)畢業於帝國大學工科大學造家學科，1902年出任台灣總督府土木局營繕課長。作品有：總督官邸(1901)、第一代台北火車站、第一代台灣銀行本店(1903)、總督府博物館(1915)。後來與中榮徹郎負責台北本町(重慶南路一段)街屋重建工作(1914)，堪稱台灣牌樓街面設計的鼻祖。
小野木孝治	明治32年(1899)畢業於東京帝大建築科，1904年來到台灣，作品有：桃園廳舍(1904)、中央研究所(1909)、台大醫院(1914-1924)等，後來隨後藤新平轉赴中國東北南滿鐵道任職。
近藤十郎	明治37年(1904)畢業於東京帝大建築科，作品有：總督府醫學校(1908)、台北新起街市場(1908)、台灣日日新報社(1908)、彩票局(1908)、台北第一中學(1908)、中央研究所擴建(1911)、台大醫院、監造總督府博物館。1920年出任總督府土木局營繕課長。
森山松之助 (1869-1949)	明治30年(1897)帝國大學工科大學造家學科畢業，1907年至台灣。作品如：台北電話交換室(1908)、台北水道唧筒室(1909)、台南郵便局(1910)、台中廳舍(1913)、總督府官邸改建(1913)、總督府專賣局(1913)、台北廳舍(1915)、台南廳舍(1916)、臨時台灣總督府工事部(電力會社)，皆為當時重要建築。作品年代前後涵蓋長達十年之久，並負責總督府(1919)實施設計，他的作品現今大多尚在使用中。其於大正初年回日本後，有別邸、醫院及齒科學校等多樣大小建築作品，展現他優秀的設計能力。
井手薰 (1879-1944)	明治39年(1906)畢業於東京帝大建築科，曾任職長野・葛西建築事務所。1910年來台，在台任職長達三十年之久，官至敕任技師高等官一等一級俸總督府官房營繕課長。昭和15年(1940)屆滿六十歲退休。主要作品包括：建功神社(1928)、台灣教育會館(1931)、台北警察會館(1931)、高等法院(1934)、台北公會堂(1936)，為折衷主義建築時期的主要設計者之一。昭和19年(1944)逝於台北。
栗山俊一	1919年任總督府土木局營繕課技師，作品包括：台北電信局板橋無線電送信所(1928)、淡水無線電受信所(1928)、台北郵便電信局(1929)、台北放送局演奏所(1931，現二二八和平紀念館)。
西村好時 (1886-1961)	西村曾長期擔任第一勸業銀行建築課長，該行各地支店行舍多出自其手，為銀行金融建築專家。後來自行開業，在台作品為第二代台灣銀行本店(1937)。另一代表作品是位於中國東北長春的滿洲中央銀行本店(1938)。
宇敷赳夫	任鐵道部技師，作品包括：第二代嘉義火車站(1933)、松山鐵道工場(1935)、第二代台南火車站(1936)、新營火車站(1936)、第二代台北火車站(1940)等折衷主義建築。
鈴置良一 (1893-)	大正4年(1915)畢業於名古屋高等工業學校建築科，1925年來台任台灣土地建物株式會社建築課技師，從事台北榮町共榮組合委託街廓設計。昭和4年(1929)轉任總督府交通局技師，設計基隆港合同廳舍(1934，現基隆港務大樓)，昭和9年(1934)轉任交通局遞信部技師，設計台北電話局(1937)、嘉義郵便電信局(1939)、民雄放送所(1940)等現代主義作品。昭和17年(1942)轉往台灣電力株式會社任營繕課長，負責天冷水力發電所(1944)等工程。戰後仍以顧問技師留用協助復舊，1946年返回日本。

The important architects during the Japanese era are as follows:

Hukuda Togo	Served as engineer at the governor's office and the army. Major projects included the Taiwan governor's residence (1901), the first Taipei army infantry building (1903), and the second Tainan army infantry building (1907). Also supervised the construction of the Taiwan Shinto Shrine (1901).
Sogo Kataro	Served as engineer at the governor's office, worked on the water- way project in northern Taiwan, the Keelung Harbor project, and other hydraulics and civil engineering projects. Other major projects included the Meiji Bridge (present-day Chungshan Bridge in Yuanshan), the first-generation steel bridge in Taiwan (1901), and the second-generation reinforced concrete arched bridge (1932).
Ito Cyuta (1867-1954)	Graduated from the Imperial University (later known as the Tokyo Imperial University) in 1892 during the 25th year of the Meiji era. Major projects included the Taiwan Shinto Shrine (1901), which was later regarded as the premier example of traditional Japanese architecture in the modern era. Served as an engineer in the Shinto shrine construction department. Other major projects included the Ping'an Shinto Shrine (1895), the Miyan Shinto Shrine (1916), and the Meiji Shinto Shrine (1920).
Nagano Uheji (1867-1937)	Graduated from the Imperial University in 1893. Despite having accomplished many other major projects in Japan, his plan for the Taiwan governor' s office, which was submitted in a design competition, was his only work in Taiwan.
Nomura Ichiro	Graduated from the Imperial University in 1895. Served as head of the Department of Building and Construction under the Taiwan governor's office in 1902. Major projects included the Taiwan governor residence (1901), the first-generation Taipei Train Station, the first-generation Bank of Taiwan (1903), and the Taiwan governor office's museum (1905). Later worked on the Taipei district (present-day Chungching South Road) reconstruction project (1914).
Ono Kitakaji	Graduated from the Tokyo Imperial University in 1899. Came to Taiwan in 1904. Major projects included the Taoyuan prefecture hall (1904), Central Research Institute (1901), and the University of Taiwan Hospital (1914- 1924). Later worked for the railroad department in northeastern China.
Kondo Juro	Graduated from the Tokyo Imperial University in 1904. Major projects included the Taiwan Provincial Medical College (1908), Taipei City's Hsinchi market (1908), the Lottery Bureau (1908), Taipei Number One High School (1908), the expansion of the Central Research Institute (1911), the University of Taiwan Hospital (1914- 1924), and the Taiwan governor office's museum (1915). Served as the head of the building and construction department under the Taiwan governor in 1920.

Moriyama Matsunosuke (1869-1949)	Graduated from the Imperial University in 1897. Came to Taiwan in 1907. Major projects included the Taipei Telephone Switching Office (1908), Tainan Postal Office (1901), Taichung prefecture hall (1913), reconstruction of the governor's residence and the Monopoly Bureau (1913), Taipei prefecture hall (1915), Tainan prefecture hall (1916), and the electric company building. Most of his works are still in existence today. Returned to Japan during the first year of the Taisho era, and continued to design several official residences, hospitals, and medical colleges.
Ide Kaoru (1879-1944)	Graduated from Tokyo Imperial University in 1906. Came to Taiwan in 1907 and worked for 30 years on the island. Retired in 1940 during the 15th year of the Showa era at the age of 60. Major projects included the Kento Shinto Shrine (1928), Taiwan Education Building (1931), Taipei Police Academy (1931), the supreme court building (1934), and Taipei Kunghui Hall (1936). Was one of the important architects during the era of modified architecture. Passed away in Taipei in 1944.
Nishimura Yoitok (1886-1961)	Specializing in the design of banks and financial buildings, he served as the chief engineer for the Nippon Dai-ichi Kangyo Bank and designed most of the bank's branch offices. Went to establish his own design house, and designed the second-generation Bank of Taiwan (1937) and the Central Bank in the northeastern China (1938).
Ushiki Takeo	Served as an engineer for the Railroad Bureau. Major projects included modified architectural designs such as the second-generation Chiayi Railroad Station (1933), the railroad factory at Sungshan (1934), the second-generation Tainan Railroad Station (1935), Hsinyin Railroad Station (1936), and the second-generation Taipei Railroad Station (1940).
Suzuoki Ryoichi	Came to Taiwan in 1925 to work as an engineer for the Land Construction Company, and engaged in the design of Taipei City streets. In 1929 during the 4th year of the Showa era, was transferred to the Bureau of Transportation under the Taiwan Governor's Office, and designed the Keelung prefecture hall (present-day Keelung Harbor office building). Served as an engineer in the Transportation and Postal Bureau in 1934. Designed the Taipei Telephone Bureau (1937) and Postal and Telecommunications Bureau in Chiayi (1939), both of which were modern-style architectural structures.

廳舍建築特色

Government Office-Building Architecture

日治時期，廳舍建築如總督府、各軍政部門、各州廳郡街政府辦公建築等，其設計幾乎全部出自於官方的營繕機構，尤其是總督府的營繕課，然而比較重大的設計亦有經過全國性競圖而選取的。廳舍建築多座落於城中重要位置，包括街角、端點、圓環或廣場旁，因此在設計上之考量也受限空間的特殊性。

最常見的廳舍建築特色是中央入口有寬敞的大廳或梯間；向左右伸長的兩翼有中央走道；或單邊走道的成列辦公室；高度多在二至五層樓之間；中央並常有高聳的塔狀突出建築，以強調其紀念性等。 註117

During the Japanese occupation, government offices such as the governor's office, the offices of the different military and administrative departments, the prefecture halls, and the provincial administrative office were mostly designed by the Department of Building and Construction. Nation-wide design competitions, however, were held for some major architectural designs, from which the winning design was selected. Most government offices were built in major locations around the city, such as street corners, a plaza or a square. Therefore, the designs of these buildings were also restricted to the building s predetermined location.

The most common government offices were two to five stories tall, with spacious main halls or stairways at the main entrances and long hallways extending to the left and right. In some cases, the hallways were flanked by offices extending to either side of the building. A prominent tower-like structure extended from the center of the building, making it more imposing and memorable.

花蓮港廳舍

明治 43 年(西元 1910 年)8 月落成的花蓮港廳舍，位在今花蓮市中華路與中山路口，爲明治時代建築特色之木構造雨淋板外牆二層建築，形式在當年的各廳舍建築中獨具一格。戰後作爲花蓮縣政府，然民國 40 年（西元 1951 年）10 月的大地震受損嚴重，縣府乃於民國 43 年 4 月遷至美崙府前路現址，此處便暫撥爲稅捐稽徵處、市公所辦公場所，今已改建爲商業區。圖中後方有圓頂塔樓者爲設立於大正元年（西元 1912 年）7 月之臺灣銀行花蓮港出張所（今臺灣銀行花蓮分行現址）。

註 2、38、65、117、134

RH-077

Hualien Prefecture Government Building

The Hualien Prefecture Government Building, constructed in August 1910, now stands at the intersection of Chunghua Road and Chungshan Road in Hualien City. This two-story wooden building was unique among contemporary department office buildings. It served as the Hualien County government office building after World War II, and was severely damaged during an earthquake in October 1951. After the county government office building relocated to its present address at Meilun Fuchien Road in April 1954, the building served temporarily as the tax collection office and office of the city government. Today, the building has been reconstructed into a commercial center. Pictured is the Hualien branch of the Bank of Taiwan, which was constructed in 1912.

臺中州廳 Taichung Prefecture Hall

爲今臺中市政府所在，初建於大正 2 年（西元 1913 年），現有格局係分數次擴建而成：入口門廳及左翼建築（臨民權路）最早完工，右翼的建築（臨市府路）則遲至大正 13 年才完成。整體式樣爲入口正面朝東之二層建築，與臺北（州）廳、臺南（州）廳等建築同爲森山松之助所設計。

註 65、114、115、116、117、118

Constructed in 1913, the Taichung Prefecture Hall now houses the Taichung City government. The current building layout, however, was constructed in different stages. The main hall at the entrance and the left wing of the building (close to Minchuan Road) were the first to be built, while the right wing building (near Shihfu Road) was not completed until 1924. As with the Taipei and Tainan Prefecture Halls, the two-story Taichung Prefecture Hall was designed by Moriyama Matsunosuke, with its entrance facing due east.

RH-078

宜蘭廳舍

宜蘭廳舍建於本世紀初，在宜蘭市坤門（南門「離順門」）外（舊城南路縣政府舊址），爲磚造木屋架瓦頂建築，坐南向北，外圍以牆，占地 1.4288 甲（合 4174.49 坪），建築面積 1181 坪，係日本明治初期風格，結合法國第二共和及明治時期日本國內的建築手法，正面圓拱入口、山形牆、四披屋坡尖頂是其特徵；當時宜蘭、桃園、苗栗、阿緱（屏東）等處廳舍建築及規模均相似，前三者表門前方均有溝渠，以橋銜接對外道路。宜蘭廳舍於大正 9 年（西元 1920）因地方制度廢廳，改設宜蘭郡役所，圖中大門及橋並非初建原貌，整建後較爲寬闊氣派。戰後初爲宜蘭區署，民國 39 年（西元 1950 元）10 月成立宜蘭縣，改爲縣政府所在地。

註 2、65、73、117、137

RH-079

Ilan Prefecture Government Building

The Ilan Prefecture Government Building, constructed at the turn of the century, was located outside of the kun-men (South Gate) in Ilan City (the past address of the county government along Old Chengnan Road).

Made of wood and bricks with tiled rooftops, thebuilding is aligned in a north-south axis with the entrance facing due north. Surrounded by walls, the 658 square meterbuilding sits on a 1.385-hectare landarea. The building was constructed according to the architecture of the early Meiji era, which also incorporated architectural designs from France. It is characterized by an arched entrance gate, a succession of surrounding walls, and a sloped and pointed roof. Contemporary government office building in Ilan, Taoyuan, Miaoli, and Aho (present-day Pingtung) were similar in size and architecture, and except for the office building in Aho, the rest had waterways around the building using bridges to connect the building to external passag eways. It served as the prefecture government office building after *ting* level of prefecture administration was abolished in Taiwan's governmental system. The picture shows the front gate and the bridge, which were both widened after reconstruction. The building served as the Ilan district (chu) office building after the World War II, and later as the county government office building after Ilan County was established in October 1950.

RH-080

宜蘭街役場址在巽門街，昭和 15 年（西元 1940 年）10 月宜蘭街陞格為市，改宜蘭市役所，戰後充作宜蘭農田水利會址。

The governmental administrative center of Ilan Town was located on Hsunmen Street. In 1940, Ilan Town was promoted to the status of a city, and the administrative center was renamed as the Ilan City Administrative Bureau. After World War II, the place was used as the Ilan Agricultural and Water Conservancy.

高雄州廳今爲地方法院

高雄州廳建於昭和 6 年（西元 1931 年），爲今日之高雄地方法院所在地，位於前金區河東路上，面向仁愛河（又稱愛河）。民國 77 年時，曾經一度修建，但大致仍維持原建築之架構。　註 55

RA-038

Kaohsiung Prefecture Hall

Built in 1931, the Kaohsiung prefecture hall today houses the Kaohsiung district court. The building is located along Hetung Road in the Chienchin district with its front facing Jenai River (also known as Ai River). Although the bridge was rebuilt in 1988, the original architectural structure was still maintained.

RH-081 日治時期的新莊郡役所
Hsinchung County Office during the Japanese era.

RH-082 日治時期的新莊街役場
Hsinchung Precinct Office during the Japanese era.

新莊街役場及郡役所

新莊街役場位在慈祐宮南側後方，爲一棟二層樓磚造建築。郡役所與街役場相距不遠，二者所在地爲日治時期新莊之核心區域。光復後，建物多已頹圮或遭改建，今該地區已爲新莊之商業區，高樓林立，往日街景已不復見。

註85、86

Hsinchuang Precinct and Hsinchuang County Office

Buildings The two-story Hsinchuang Chieh Precinct office building, located at the south and to the back of the Tzuyou Temple, was built in close proximity to Hsinchuang County Office Building. Both buildings were situated in the central district of Hsinchuang during the Japanese era. After World War II, however, most buildings in the area were either too damaged or were reconstructed for other purposes. Today, the area is one of Hsinchuang s commercial districts, lined with tall buildings and shops.

媽宮城內的澎湖廳

清康熙 23 年（西元 1684 年）澎湖置巡檢，駐劄於文澳；雍正 5 年（西元 1727 年）改置通判（臺灣府糧捕海防通判），海防廳就巡檢舊署略加式廓；光緒 15 年（西元 1889 年）通判移廳署於媽宮（今馬公）城內，城隍廟西側附近。裁缺水師副將之舊署修建爲通判衙門，掌司法、行政、船政，此廳舍是清季中國傳統官署建築，二披水的屋頂兩端築以封火山牆爲其特色。明治 28 年（西元 1895 年）6 月設澎湖島廳，越兩年復改稱澎湖廳，仍沿前清澎湖廳署爲廳舍。昭和 8 年（西元 1933 年）新建的廳舍落成後，改爲公會堂，其後又充爲馬公高等女學校臨時校舍，戰爭末期毀於盟軍空襲。 註 2

RH-083

Penghu Department Office Building in Makung Town

In 1684, Penghu was placed under the supervision of an imperial representative, who was stationed in Wenau. The representative was replaced by an assistant prefecture magistrate in 1727. The former representative's office building was also reconstructed to become the new assistant magistrate's building. In 1899, the assistant magistrate moved to a new building in Makung Town, located near the Cheng Huang Temple, which was reconstructed from an old navy office. The assistant magistrate was then in charge of judicial, administrative, and shipping matters, and the building was typical of government offices during the Ching Dynasty. When the Japanese took over in 1895, they renamed it the Penghu Island Prefecture; two years later, it was renamed Penghu Prefecture. The Prefecture continued to use the old building constructed during the Ching Dynasty as its office building. After the new office building was completed in 1933, the old building became the meeting place of different business societies, and later served as the temporary dormitory of the Makung Girls Senior High School. The old building was destroyed by Allied bombings toward the end of World War II.

新竹郡役所
Hsinchu County Office Building

新竹郡役所址在東門町二丁目（今中正里，現臺灣土地銀行新竹分行址），明治39年（西元1906年）將原前清巡檢署改建爲當時新竹廳舍，爲日治所建第一代官署建築物。大正9年（西元1920年）將桃園、新竹、苗栗三廳合併改制新竹州，轄有新竹、竹東、竹南、苗栗、大湖、中壢、桃園、大溪等八郡，新竹郡役所的管轄區域則包括新竹街及舊港、紅毛、湖口、新埔、關西、六家、香山等一街七庄。 註1、88、137

In 1906, the Ching Dynasty military building was reconstructed to serve as the Hsinchu county office building, considered the first government building during the Japanese occupation. The building was located at the present address of the Hsinchu branch of the Land Bank of Taiwan. In 1920, Taoyuan, Hsinchu, and Miaoli Prefectures were combined to form Hsinchu Prefecture, which included eight counties--Hsinchu, Chutung, Chunan, Miaoli, Tahu, Chungli, Taoyuan, and Tahsi. On the other hand, areas under the administration of Hsinchu County included Hsinchu Community and seven other villages, namely, Chiukang, Hungmao, Hukou, Hsinpu, Kuanhsi, Liuchia, and Hsiangshan.

RH-084

竹東郡役所現址

竹東昔稱樹圯林。日治時期設有竹東郡，其街庄廳設於林順昌宅（即今商華里朝陽醫院院址）。民國 17 年，新郡役所落成（於今竹東里鎮公所所在地），故遷址於此。民國 22 年，竹東莊升格爲竹東街。 註 27

RH-085

Chutung County Office Building

Chutung was once known as Shuyilin. Chutung county, which was created during the Japanese occupation, used the residence of Lin Shun-chang as its office building (the present location of the Chaoyang Hospital in Shanghua district). The county office was moved to a new building (the present location of the district office of Chutung community) after its completion in 1928. In 1933, Chutung was elevated in status from community to precinct.

臺中縣知事官舍
Taichung County Magistrate's Building

位於小北門街（即後來臺中廳的左後方，今三民路民權路口），爲日治初期二層磚造之舊臺中縣知事官邸，庭園爲純日式造景。廢縣置廳後，大正初年興建臺中廳之時此處復經整建，完工後的設計風格及細部處理與廳舍、市役所相似，且仍爲台中廳官舍，後改爲臺中俱樂部，由臺中廳管理。

註 65、114、115、117、137

The Taichung County Magistrate's Building was a two-story brick structure located at Hsiao Peimen Street (at the back and to the left of the Taichung Prefectural government building, the present- day intersection of Sanmin and Min-chuan Streets). Built with a Japanese-style garden, it was reconstructed to serve as a prefectural office during the first year of the Taisho era, when the county was abolished in the local administration system and the prefectures created. After reconstruction was completed, the architectural and interior design of the building became similar to other prefectural and municipal government buildings. The building later became the Taichung Club, which was under the supervision of the Taichung Prefecture.

RH-086

潛園爽吟閣
Shuangyin Pavilion in the Chien Garden

潛園，地址在新竹城西門內（今潛園里中山路），爲清道光29年（西元1849年）竹塹（新竹）富紳林占梅所建，俗稱內公館，以別於北門城外開臺進士鄭用錫所建之「北郭園」。潛園面積包括宅邸在內約10000平方公尺，一直延伸到城牆下，號稱新竹舊時的八景之一。爽吟閣是潛園精華所在，乃十六項重要景物之一，爲歇山頂之二層閣，在日本領臺之初曾充當北白川宮能久親王之宿營，大正7年（西元1918年）遷於松嶺的新竹神社內供人憑弔，遷建後的側立面曾稍作修改。潛園因林家家道中衰，光復後已遭拆除。 註65、66、115、118

Located at Hsinchu's West Gate (present-day Chungshan Road in the Chienyuan community), the Chien Garden was built in 1849 by Lin Chan-mei, a wealthy resident of Hsinchu. The garden was popularly known as the Inner Mansion, to distinguish it from the Peikuo Garden, which was built by the mandarin Cheng Yung-hsi and was located outside of the North Gate. The Chien Garden, which covered an area of 10,000 square meters, extended all the way to the west gate, and was then considered one of the eight scenic attractions of Hsinchu. The main attraction within the garden was the two-story Shuangyin Pavilion, which once served as the residence of Japan's Prince Yoshihisa (Kitashira Kawanomiya) during the early days of Japanese occupation. In 1918 during the Taisho era, the pavilion was relocated to the Hsinchu Shinto Shrine in Sunglin. The sides of the pavilion were also slightly modified and renovated after the relocation. The Chien Garden was demolished after World War II, as the Lin family started to loose its prominence and wealth.
Temple Architecture

圖爲1918年拆遷之後的爽吟閣，光復後已拆除

This picture depicts Shuangyin Pavilion in 1918 after its relocation. It was demolished after the retrocession of Taiwan.

RH-087

清代
台灣中部考棚
──湧泉閣
Yungchuen Pavilion ── Central Taiwan's Ching Dynasty Examination Houses

此樓閣爲清代臺灣省城（臺中）考棚建築的一部分，光緒16年（西元1890年）完成，乃主試官坐鎮監考之處，考棚建築群原在小北門內（今臺中市政府西側），其大木結構迥異於臺灣各地所見的漳泉或潮汕、客家風格，而是帶有福州以北的建築特色。臺中考棚是清季臺灣北、中、南三處考棚之一，其餘兩處分別位於臺北府城東北角（今臺北市議會舊址）以及今臺南憲兵隊附近。大正13年（西元1924年）爲進行臺中州廳（今市政府）後方的道路工程，將造型優美的台中考棚主樓拆遷至北郊的水源地（今雙十路孔廟以北一帶），當時的臺中州知事（州長官）本山文平將之取名「湧泉閣」，戰後因年久失修，木構朽壞，民國40年前後已被拆除。

註66、118

The Yungchuan Pavilion was one of the Ching Dynasty examination houses in central Taiwan, where the chief examiner supervised the imperial examinations. Originally located in Hsiao Peimen (today, east of the Taichung City Government Building), the examination houses were built in 1890. The liberal use of wooden frames, which differed from contemporary Changchuen, Chaoshan and Hakka architectural styles, was typical of the styles used north of Fuzhou in Fujian Province. The Taichung examination house was one of three examination houses on the island during the Ching Dynasty. The other two were located northeast of Taipei (old site of the present-day Taipei city council), and near the Tainan military police headquarters. During the Taisho era in 1924, the main hall of the examination house was relocated to the northern outskirts of Shuiyuan (presently north of the Confucian Temple on Shuangshih Road), to give way for the road construction project at the back of the Taichung Prefectural Government Building (the present-day municipal government office). The main hall was named the Yungchuan Pavilion by the prefectural magistrate of the day. Due to neglect after World War II, the wooden structures of the pavilion became severely damaged; the pavilion was subsequently demolished around 1951.

RH-089

圖爲1924年拆遷後的湧泉閣，民國40年代已被拆除

This picture depicts Yungchuan Pavilion in 1924 after its relocation. it was demolished in the 1950s.

日治時期的法制階段

日治時期台灣的法制可分爲以下三期。

一、軍政時期：此時期以軍令作爲法律，目的在於以軍力建立秩序。實行期間自明治28年(西元1895年)6月至明治29年(西元1896年)3月。民事審判方面，對本島人及大陸人依台灣舊慣；對日本人及外國人則採用內地之法律。刑事方面，另立嚴刑峻罰、威嚇的報復主義，但仍依國籍差異而採不同的法律條文。

二、律令立法時期：日本政府依當時台灣治安狀況，採納台灣總督府的意見，採取特別法主義，亦即明治29年(西元1896年)4月1日施行由日本政府「六三法」，賦予台灣總督府立法權，後於明治40年(西元1907年)1月1日施行「三一法」，兩法自西元1896年至1921年底共施行達25年，原則上仍延續了軍政時期的嚴刑峻罰、威嚇報復主義。

三、勅令立法時期：本時期是以「法三號」作爲治台之法源基礎，選定部分條文實行於台灣本土，有時更採用勅立之特定法律。除在少數特定情況下，台灣總督府直至戰後可說是已失去立法權。本期實行期間自大正11年(西元1922年)1月至1945年，其特色在於立法上標榜「內地延長主義」，但之前台灣總督府所立的各種律令，仍選擇性的施行，以利統治。

註91、140、156

Evolution of the Legal System under Japanese Rule

The legal systems of Taiwan under the Japanese rule evolved through three stages. The first stage was military rule, when the martial codes were the law. The purpose of this stage was to establish order by military force. In this period, between June of 1895 and March of 1896, the traditional legal practice in Taiwan was maintained in civil cases involving the Taiwanese and mainland Chinese, and the Japanese law applied to the Japanese and aliens. Strict punishment was effected for criminal offenses, and the principle of eye-for-an-eye was adopted. Nevertheless, separate laws and regulations were applied depending on the nationality of the offenders.

In the second stage, legislation was introduced. The government of Japan followed the recommendation of the Taiwan Governor's Office and enacted a special law to cater to the social conditions of Taiwan. Under the Six-Three Law, the special law enacted on April 1, 1896, the Taiwan Governor's Office was endowed with legislative power. Later on, on January 1, 1907, the Three-One Law was promulgated. Together, the two laws were in effect for 35 years between 1896 and 1921, perpetuating the spirit of severe punishment and revenge underlined in the military stage.

In the third stage, Code Three was the legal basis for the administration of Taiwan. In this period between 1922 and 1945, certain provisions were selected and applied in Taiwan, and sometimes special laws were followed. Except for a few separate cases, the Taiwan Governor's Office in effect lost its legislative power during this period. This period was characterized by the principle of extended application of the Japanese law in Taiwan, even though the laws and regulations previously enacted by the Taiwan Governor's Office remained selectively effective to facilitate Japan's rule over Taiwan.

司法大廈建築 The Judicial Building

在書院町（今重慶南路），昭和4年（西元1929年）開始改建，樓高三層，中間高塔五層，昭和9年（西元1934年）4月竣工。本建築以圓拱的廊道、門窗爲特色；外牆貼淺綠面磚；石材爲產自花蓮之大理石。其施工精細考究，建築莊嚴大方，是屬於折衷主義的風格。為高等法院、檢察局、臺北地方法院所在。光復後增建一層，改稱司法大廈，爲司法院、最高法院、高等法院等機關辦公場所。

註66、68、72、117、118、125、126

Located along Chungching South Road, the Judicial Building was a three-story building with a five-story tower in the middle. The building's construction began in 1929 and was completed in 1934. It is unique for its arched passageways, doors and windows. The exterior walls were pasted with light-colored green tiles, and marble from Hualien was used in the building material. The majestic building was typical of a modified architectural design, which was a transitional style popular in the 1930s. Another story was added to the building after World War II, and the building was renamed the Judicial Building. Currently it serves as the office building for the Judicial Yuan, the supreme court, and the high courts.

RH-088

圖爲日治時代的台北地方法院、高等法院建築物

Buildings of Taipei District Court and Taipei High Court during the Japanese era.

日治時期的警察組織

The Japanese - Era Police System

日治時期台灣總督府民政的推展實際上即依靠警政爲後援，警察制度的規劃爲事權專一、體系完整的組織，再加上本島原有的保甲制度配合、「試用合一」的人事及教育制度，使原來的政治民風得到改善。一般說來，台地的警察組織在日本的警政體系中，屬於特種警察官廳，直屬於總督府，警察組織主要依(1)民政（即一般行政）(2)警察業務(3)山地行政（即蕃務）分類，分爲中央、州、廳三級。田健治郎任總督府時期（西元1920～1937），轄下有警務局、警察官練習所，州轄下最大的爲警務部，其下轄有二大類：一類是五課（刑事、保安、衛生、理蕃、高等警察、警務）；另一類是平行的警察分署（市爲警察署）、郡守，此二類下則分爲基層的派出所以及駐在所。至於廳的組織也大約相同，只是二級組織分爲支廳、開導所，組織也較爲簡單。

註 176、177、178、185、186

During the Japanese era, the civil affairs of the Taiwan Governor's Office were basically implemented with the support of the police. The Japanese rulers designed a comprehensive police structure, with a sophisticated division of labor. In addition to the existing militia system in Taiwan, practical personnel policies, together with a sound training system for the police, contributed to stable political and social order. Generally speaking, the police force in Taiwan was a special police department in Japan's police system. Under the direct jurisdiction of the Taiwan Governor's Office, the police system in Taiwan had a hierarchy of three levels- central, prefectural, and departmental levels--in charge of civil affairs (or general administrative affairs), police operations, and administration of mountains (and the indigenous people). Under the governorship of Den Kenziro (1920-1937), the Police Bureau and the Police Academy were established under the jurisdiction of the Governor's Office. On the prefectural level, the police departments were the highest police authorities in charge of affairs in two categories. The first category of police dealt with criminal cases, security, sanitation and aboriginal affairs, as well as high-ranking and rank-and-file police matters. The other category of police were police agencies on the city and county levels, which were parallel to the other category of police in terms of organizational level. Under these categories of police were local police stations. The police force on the departmental level had basically the same structure, with a two-tier hierarchy and a simpler organization.

警察組織——台中武德殿
A Branch of the Police Organization —— Wute Hall in Taichung

隸屬大日本武德會臺中支部，該支部係置於臺中州警察部內之警察附屬組織。武德殿占地2738坪，屋頂形式是採用入母屋造（中國建築歇山頂）正面帶千鳥破風、縋破風、入口階梯向拜柱，側面唐破風及迴緣高欄等建築元素之木構造日本建築，昭和初年改建爲鋼筋混凝土建築，並有俱樂部、游泳池，另南投、鹿港等地演武場亦該支部所屬。 註65、79、80

A branch of the Wute Society in Japan, the Wute Hall in Taichung was an affiliated organization of the Taichung prefecture police department. Occupying an area of 1,526 square meters, the hall was surrounded by Japanese-style wooden fences, had a Chinese- style roof, and an entrance stairway facing the pillars. The hall was rebuilt as a reinforced concrete structure during the first year of the Showa era, complete with officers club and swimming pool. The Nantou and Lukang academies also belonged to the Wute Hall in Taichung.

RH-090

圖爲日治時代的台中武德殿

Wute Hall in Taichung during the Japanese era.

日治時期的美日關係

日治時期的美、日關係必須從日俄戰爭談起。日俄戰爭前英、美二國均有扶植日本以對抗俄國在中國東北發展的想法，西元1904年2月10日，日皇遂下令向俄宣戰，美、日關係此時十分良好。美國更企圖充作日、俄中的調停人，並聯合英人欲維持「門户開放」政策，以防止任何一國獨佔中國及東北利益，但卻也種下日、美交惡的種子，原來日本此時亦企圖走向帝國主義，乃以東北「北進」、台灣「南進」和列強爭利，因此遂有日、美東北鐵路競爭，美國鐵路大王哈利曼欲合作經營南滿鐵路，遂於西元1905年10月12日和日訂草約，日本中途拒絕，後來並反與俄合作瓜分東北利益，這又造成日美關係的矛盾之重大轉折點。

日俄戰爭後，日本開始發展自己強大的海軍，又威脅到美國太平洋之海權，中國貿易又爲日貨排擠，美國國内排日情緒大增，舊金山禁止日童入學，於是日美戰爭論、太平洋艦隊建設論遂日漸產生。此外，此時最明顯的表現在中國和美國的親善如庚子賠款的退回。日本有感於此，擬與美國意表親善，甚至一度建議美日條約的訂定，雖不成功卻仍有西元1908年1月30日的對華行政之日美照會，其中關於太平洋的政策主要有二點：一、保障並維護此區的商業及中國利益均等。二、互相尊重兩國在太平洋上的領土不得侵害，但與此時美日的外交方針基本上是相左的。

第一次世界大戰後，日本一躍而爲亞洲第一大國，在亞洲更形成與美對立的局面，美、日關係在20年代成爲軍事對敵。巴黎和會中未能解決的中國問題，引起各國不安，造成美、日、英三國的海軍造艦競賽，遂有西元1921年7月10日華盛頓會議（處理中國山東問題，軍備限制條約），並於西元1921年12月13日的英、美、日、法訂定「四國協約」，此一協約實有英、美、法牽制日本在太平洋之發展並防止日美戰爭之效力，此後美國陷入孤立主義，與世界各國和日本均無積極外交關係，然日本反自濱口内閣「協調外交」（西元1926-1931）之溫和做法轉向「焦土外交」以軍部爲主的激進手法，遂有退出國聯及918事變之舉。此時美國政府雖有關注（如曾於西元1929年向日發出對關東軍之警告，日亦取消計劃），然而隨著經濟大恐慌的腳步美自顧不暇，日本亦有了對英美及歐洲帝國主義的反彈，法西斯主義抬頭，此時表現在日、美關係上爲三：一、日本的外務省（文官）爲軍部（226事件）取代之成爲外交主力。二、德、義、日三國同盟企圖牽制美國，並有日美關係調整方針。三、美國由企圖調停中、日兩國，簽定「美日諒解」到全力支持中國抗戰。由此看來，此時可說是日美關係的另一個轉捩點，日本此時的近衛内閣原有機會停止太平洋戰爭的開啓，因外相松岡的親德反美日妥協，其間三次近衛均以内閣總辭企圖完成談判，然日軍方以駐兵問題無法讓步，遂有主戰的陸相東條代起，美日關係遂以珍珠港事變爲引爆點，走向戰爭。

註141、142、151、152、172、173

US-Japan Relations during Japanese Rule

Any discussion about US-Japan relations should begin with the Russo-Japanese War. Before the war broke out, both Britain and the U.S. supported Japan to counter Russia's expansion in the northeast of China. When the emperor of Japan declared war against Russia on February 10, 1904, relations between Japan and the United States were quite intimate. The U.S. even attempted to mediate between Russia and Japan, and advocated an"open-door"policy in alliance with Britain to prevent any single country from monopolizing the benefits in China and China's northeast. However, such a policy planted a seed of confrontation between Japan and the U.S. thereafter. There were several reasons. Japan was becoming an imperialistic state and was vying with other powers by implementing their"Northern Excursion"policy in northeast China and their"Southern Excursion"policy in Taiwan. As a result, Japan competed with the U.S. for operation of railways in China's northeastern provinces. The U.S. entered into a draft agreement with Japan on October 12, 1905, because the American railway tycoon Edward Harriman sought to operate South Manchuria Railway in cooperation with Japan. Japan turned down the agreement and worked, instead, with Russia in sharing the benefits in northeast China. This was a major turning point for the accelerating friction between the two countries.

After the Russo-Japanese War, Japan became a sea power, again threatening U.S. interests in the Pacific Ocean. As a result, there was a surge of anti-Japan sentiment in the U.S., followed by a ban on admission of Japanese children into schools in San Francisco, theories of warfare between Japan and the U.S. and of the establishment of America's Pacific Fleet. In addition, the relations between China and the U.S. were greatly improved, as exemplified by the United States' friendly gesture of returning payments made by China for damages incurred during the Boxer Rebellion. Confronted with this development, Japan attempted to improve relations with the U.S., even to the extent of seeking a treaty with the U.S. Although the treaty never materialized, the two countries reached an understanding on January 30, 1908 that the following guidelines would be followed in implementing Pacific policies. First, both countries would guarantee and ensure equitable benefits derived from business activities in this region and in China. Second, the countries would respect each other and refrain from aggression against the other's territories in the Pacific Ocean. At this juncture, however, the two countries had basically incompatible diplomatic policies.

After the end of World War I, Japan became the most powerful nation in Asia, creating an atmosphere of rivalry between the U.S. and Japan in the region. The 1920s saw a military standoff between the two countries. The Paris Convention, which failed to resolve the China issue, invoked a sense of insecurity among nations and caused an naval arms race among the U.S., Japan and Britain. As a result, the Washington Convention was convened on July 10, 1921 to discuss the issue of China's Shandong Province and a treaty for armament restriction. On December 13, 1921, Britain, America, Japan and France entered into a treaty through which Britain, the United States and France sought to check Japan's expansion in the Pacific Ocean. The treaty prevented the outbreak of the warfare between the U.S. and Japan. Later, the U.S. adopted an isolationist attitude and became passive on the diplomatic front. In contrast, Japan, which was dominated by the military, began to adopt aggressive diplomatic policies, departing from the moderate diplomatic policies of the cabinet(1926-1931). As a result, Japan withdrew from the League of Nations and initiated the Mukden Incident of September 18, 1931. Although the U.S. expressed her"concern"about Japan's aggression(e.g., the U.S. issued a warning to the Japanese forces occupying China's northeast in 1929 and discouraged them from further military actions), the Depression compelled the U.S. to focus on domestic issues. In Japan, there was a strong sentiment against the European imperialism represented by Britain and the United States, along with the emergence of fascism. The implications for the relations between Japan and the U.S. can be interpreted in three ways. First, the Ministry of Foreign Affairs of Japan gave way to the military in foreign affairs. Second, Germany, Italy and Japan formed an alliance to counter the U.S., causing Japan to adjust her relations with the U.S. Third, the position of the U.S. underwent a transition from the original"understanding" with Japan to assisting China in her fight against Japanese aggression. This was another turning point in Japan's relations with the U.S. Although the Konoe cabinet might have been able to prevent the outbreak of war in the Pacific, the cabinet resigned three times during the process of trying to negotiate with the U.S., and policy-making was eventually dominated by the belligerent, Japan's Minister of War.

Finally, the U.S. plunged into full-scale warfare against Japan as triggered off by Japan's attack on Pearl Harbor.

前美國駐臺北領事館

在御成町四丁目（今中山北路二段西側），館址占地375坪，爲二層四坡屋頂建築，正面爲三間多立克雙柱門廊。係美國政府向臺灣土地建築公司租用，大正15年（西元1926年）10月，領事館由大正町二丁目遷此辦公。次年美方原擬購下該址，但臺灣總督府以明治33年(西元1900年)1月律令第一號規定，未准其請。昭和16年（西元1941年）12月，太平洋戰爭爆發後，美方停止一切館務，關閉領事館。

註4

RH-091

Former U.S. Consulate Building

Leased from the Taiwan Land and Construction Company, the former U.S. consulate office was relocated to the west of present-day Chungshan North Road Section 2 in October 1926. The two-story building occupied an area of 209 square meters, with three double-pillar front doorways in the Doric style. The United States planned to purchase the site the following year, but the Taiwan Governor 's Office rejected this proposition, citing as reason Ordinance 1 issued in January 1900 (the 33rd year of Meiji era). In December 1941, the United States closed the consulate office after the outbreak of the war in the Pacific.

舊式風格——商品陳列館（史博館前身）

商品陳列館，在今植物園內歷史博物館址，爲總督府殖產局之附屬機關。大正 6 年（西元 1917 年）6 月開館，爲木造日式之二層建築，採千鳥破風屋頂搭配唐破風入口，有雲形鬼瓦（脊瓦）、狐格子（側面山牆）等日本建築構造特徵，用以展示臺灣商品。戰後暫充林務局員工宿舍，民國 44 年（西元 1955 年）12 月初設歷史文物美術館，民國 46 年改名國立歷史博物館，民國 64 年進行改建。

註 68、125、169

RH-092

Commodity Display House

Located at the present site of the Museum of History in Taipei's Botanical Garden, the Commodity Display House was an affiliated museum of the Manu facturing Bureau under the Taiwan Governor's Office. Inaugurated in June 1917 during the Taisho era, the museum was a two-story Japanese-style structure used to display goods made in Taiwan. The museum building was temporarily used as the dormitory for the Forestry Bureau employees after World War II, and was converted to the Museum of History and Art in December 1955. It was renamed the National Historical Museum in 1957, and reconstructed in 1975.

新公園博物館

博物館位於新公園北側，此建築正面朝北，與舊臺北火車站相對，爲清代天后宮原址，明治 39 年（西元 1906 年）爲紀念前任總督兒玉源太郎及民政長官後藤新平，將天后宮拆毀而建。大正 2 年（西元 1913 年）興工，大正 4 年 4 月竣工。建築形式屬希臘多力克(Doric Order)柱式文藝復興風格之地上二層、地下一層之白色建築。整體建築爲橫向長型對稱平面，兩翼爲主要展示空間，正背立面對等，造型莊重典雅。其中央入口大廳上方有圓頂，內爲彩色玻璃採光天窗；基座甚高爲地下室；壁面使用人造石，室內裝修材料爲大理石，細部裝飾考究，爲日治時期優秀建築之一。

博物館日治時期的全名爲臺灣總督府民政部殖產局附屬紀念博物館，前身係明治 33 年殖產局所設之商品陳列館；明治 41 年 10 月殖產局附屬博物館曾借用舊彩票局之建築，嗣新館落成乃遷現址，以收集、研究本省及華南、南洋資料爲主，館內收藏各地的地質、土產、礦物、動物標本及本省早期史料文物，分歷史、南洋、礦物、動物、蕃族五類，共四個陳列室，爲自然歷史博物館，戰後改名臺灣省立博物館。

註 2、66、67、69、72、114、115、118、125、126

New Park Museum

Situated to the north of the New Garden at the former location of the Ching Dynasty Tienhou Temple, the museum stood right in front of the entrance to the old Taipei Railway Station, with its entrance facing due north. To commemorate the achievements of Kodama Gentaro, the forth colonial governor, and Goto Shinbei, the head of the department of civil affairs, the old Tienhou Temple was torn down to give way to the museum. Construction started in 1913 and was completed in April 1915.

An example of cultural renaissance architecture in the Doric style, the museum consisted of two stories and a basement. The rounded dome at the main hall was adorned with colored glass windows to provide natural lighting. Walls were made of artificial stone, while marbles were used for interior decoration. Accented by exquisite interior design, the museum was one of the best architectural designs during the era of Japanese rule.

During the Japanese period, the museum was known as the "Affiliated Museum of the Manufacturing Bureau under the Civil Affairs Department of the Taiwan Governor's Office." It was originally built by the Manufacturing Bureau in 1900. In October 1907, the museum was housed temporarily in the old building of the defunct Lottery Bureau, and was later moved to its present address after construction at the new site was completed. The museum focused on the collection and research of information related to Taiwan, southern China, and the South Pacific. The museum's property included information on the geology, produce, and mineral products of different regions, as well as preserved animal specimens. Displayed in four separate rooms, it also had a compilation of early Taiwan history and artifacts, which were classified according to the categories of history, the South Pacific, mineral products, zoology, and aborigines. The museum was renamed Taiwan Provincial Museum after World War II.

RH-093

日治時代的台灣省立博物館

Taiwan Provincial Museum during the Japanese era.

新竹州商品陳列館

新竹州商品陳列館（後改稱商工獎勵館）在榮町二丁目，昭和 4 年（西元 1929 年）12 月落成開館，該館正門位於L形對稱平面之轉角，兩端各有側門，為造型簡練之二層建築，供物產商品陳列展示，並舉辦各相關活動，藉以促進工商產品銷路之開拓。當時全島五州均設有功能相當的商品展示場所，即總督府（殖產局）商品陳列館（設於臺北植物園內）、新竹州立商品陳列館、臺中州立物產陳列館（位於臺中公園內）、臺南州立商品陳列館、高雄州立物產陳列場（昭和 11 年改商工獎勵館）等。該館於戰後撥充憲兵隊隊址，迨新竹市升格為省轄市，新竹憲兵隊移駐麗池後，縣政府將建物拆除拍賣土地。

註 34、51、164

RH-094

The Commodity Display House of Hsinchu Prefecture

The Commodity Display House of Hsinchu Prefecture (later renamed the Center for the Advancement of Commerce and Industry) was situated the # 2 section of Jung distict In December 1929, the display house began operation. The front door of the hall was built in a right-angled corner of two walls. Each of these walls also had side doors. It was a two-story structure built in a simple design which was for the display of products and commodities. It also took charge of holding activities related to promoting sales and expanding sales channels. At the time, the five prefectures of the island each had a similar commodity display house: The Taiwan Governor's Office Commodity Display House (set up in Taipei's Botanical Gardens); the Commodity Display House of Hsinchu Prefecture; the Commodity Display House of Taichung Prefecture; the Commodity Display House of Tainan Prefecture; and the Commodity Display House of Kaohsiung Prefecture (later renamed the Center for the Advancement of Commerce and Industry in 1936). After World War II, the Hsinchu Commodity Display House was used as a barracks for military police. After Hsinchu City was upgraded in status to be directly administered by the provincial government, the Hsinchu Military Police Corps moved to Lichih, and then the county government demolished the house and auctioned the land.

日治時期台灣通信中樞

Japanese - Era Telecommunications Center of Taiwan

日治時期總督府交通局遞信部，位於書院町總督府後方（今博愛路長沙街一段路口南側轉角），與臺灣電力株式會社隔街相對，乃日治時期掌理郵政、電報、電話之機構，爲全島通信機關管理中樞。此建築於大正 14 年（西元 1925 年）動工，昭和 3 年（西元 1928 年）落成啓用，樓高三層，平面呈U字形。一樓爲仿石構造基座；正面中央入口設計爲圓拱形；上方爲希臘建築複合柱列（Composite Order），建築側面有愛奧尼克柱列（Ionic Order）；外牆可見外露之落水明管。戰爭末期盟機轟炸略有波及，光復後修復並加建一層，初充爲郵政電訊管理局，國民政府遷臺後，交通部所屬機構均集此辦公，稱爲交通大樓。

註 2、5、65、66、68、118

During the Japanese era, the Postal Department of the Transportation Bureau under the Taiwan Governor's Office was located right behind the Taiwan Governor's Office(or on the southern corner at the intersection of Poai Road and Section One of Changsha Street today). Across the street on the opposite side of the road was Taiwan Electricity Company. The Postal Department was in charge of postal services, telecommunications and telephone services, and it was the administrative center for telecommunications all over Taiwan. Construction of the office building commenced in 1925 and was completed in 1928. This was a three-story U-shaped structure on a foundation that was part stone, with an arched central entrance. The upper section of the building featured Composite-style columns and entablature, borrowed from Greek architecture, with Ionic-style columns on the sides. The pipelines of the building were exposed and could be seen from the outside. In the final days of World War II, the building was slightly damaged by the bombing of the Allied Forces.

After Taiwan fell under KMT rule, the building was repaired and an extra story added, and it was initially used to house the Bureau of Posts and Telecommunications. Since the Nationalist Government moved to Taiwan, affiliated agencies of the Ministry of Transportation and Communications have been located here.

RH-095

台灣第一座鋼筋混凝土建築

First Steel Concrete Structure in Taiwan

圖爲臺北市日治早期電話交換機房，另稱臺北電話交換所，原址在今衡陽路交通銀行，落成於明治41年（西元1908年），建築設計者爲森山松之助，並由得見常雄作結構設計，爲臺灣第一座採用鋼筋混凝土結構設計之建築，僅比日本本土第一棟鋼筋混凝土建築（位於佐世保鎮守府港）晚三年，在當時是相當先進的構造技術，具有拱廊、圓拱窗的古典歐式風格建築特色。

註66、68、69、117、168

The building in this picture was a telephone exchange in Taipei during the early days of Japan's rule. Also called Taipei Telephone Exchange and established in 1908, the exchange was located at the address of today's Chiao Tung Bank. The building, whose construction was designed by Moriyama Matsunosuke and whose structure was built by Tokumi Tsuneo, was the first steel- and-concrete structure in Taiwan, predated by the first steel- and-concrete structure in Japan (located in Saseho Chinjuhu) by only three years. The building was a product of the state-of-the-art construction techniques of the time, with characteristics typical of classic European architectural styles, such as arched windows.

RH-096

現代主義建築——台北電話局

臺北電話局在今博愛路貴陽街口，與遞信部爲鄰，昭和 12 年（西元 1937 年） 7 月，臺北實施自動式交換電話業務，遂脫離臺北郵便局，另行成立台北電話局。日治晚期市內自動電話容量達 8000 門；戰後爲擴充電話容量，另覓地遷建。圖片是由總督府後側鳥瞰博愛路的街景，對街爲電話局與遞信部，時爲日治晚期日本在臺灣實施志願兵募集，路上有歡送出征的遊行隊伍。電話局現爲臺灣北區電信管理局博愛路營業處，民國 85 年 7 月已改組爲中華電信公司。

註 5、65、66、67、117、183

RH-097

Architecture of Modernism -- Taipei Telephone Office

Located at the intersection of Poai Road and Kuiyang Street and next to the Postal Department, the Taipei Telephone Office was made independent from the Taipei Post Office in July of 1937, because of the implementation of automatic telephone exchange operation in Taipei. In the final days of Japan's rule, Taipei had a capacity of 8000 automatic telephones.

After the end of World War II, the office was relocated, due to the need to expand its exchange capacity. This picture presents a bird's-eye view of Poai Road from behind the Taiwan Governor's Office. Across the street were the telephone office and the Postal Department. At that time, Japan was recruiting volunteers in Taiwan, and on the road was a parade in honor of volunteers joining the forces. Today, the telephone office has become the Business Department of the Northern Telecommunications Administration of Taiwan(which was restructured as China Telecommunications Company in July 1996) on Poai Road.

第一代新竹郵局

新竹郵局，前身係陸軍野戰郵局。明治28年（西元1895年）軍方在新竹成立第三野戰郵局；翌年即改爲新竹郵便電信局，二等局；大正10年（西元1921年）升一等局；昭和16年（西元1941年）下設郵便、電信、會計三課。圖爲新竹郵局明治年間的單層斜屋頂雨淋板外牆木構建築，簷口有飛檐垂木（椽木），正面雙塔屋頂造型特別，兼有日本與歐洲之風格。民國84年（西元1995年）適値創局屆滿一百年，當地郵局曾舉辦慶祝活動。清光緒14年（西元1888年）巡撫劉銘傳即在臺北府創設臺灣郵政總局，日本領臺後亦隨即在臺灣設置郵政機構，均較創辦於光緒22年（西元1896年）之中華郵政的歷史還要早。

註5、66、118

RH-098

First-generation Hsinchu Post Office

Previously an army field post office, the Hsinchu Post Office was established as the third field post office in Hsinchu by the military in 1895. The office was renamed the second-grade Hsinchu Post and Telecommunications Office, which was upgraded to first-grade status in 1921. In 1941, the office set up departments of postal service, telecommunications and accounting. This picture depicts the wooden structure of the Hsinchu Post Office with a single-tiered, sloping roof and exterior weather boards. The structure, which exhibited both Japanese and European characteristics, was also unique for the cornices and principals of the eaves, as well as for the special design of the tower roofs on both sides of the structure. In 1995 during the centennial of the post office, a festival was held to celebrate its establishment. In 1888, Liu Ming-Chuan, Governor of Taiwan during the Ching dynasty, established the Directorate General of Posts in Taipei. Later on, right after Japan's takeover, postal agencies were established in Taiwan earlier than the establishment of the China Postal Service in 1896.

新莊郵便局變遷

——明治 31 年（西元 1898 年）日本人在新莊設郵便受取所。

——次年改爲台北郵便電信局新莊出張所。

——明治 39 年一度廢所，將業務交由板橋出張所辦理，但不久又重新設立。

——大正 9 年改爲新莊郵便局。

——光復後稱新莊郵局。

註 21

RH-006

圖爲大正時代的新莊郵便局

Hsinchuang Post Office during the Taisho period.

The Hsinchuang Post Office

In 1898, the Japanese established Hsinchuang Postal Service. The entity was renamed the Hsinchuang branch of Taipei Post and Telecommunications Bureau.

In 1906, the branch was closed down and its operation was transferred to the Panchiao branch. It was not long before the branch office resumed operation.

In 1920(the 9th year of the Taisho period), the branch was renamed the Hsinchuang Post Office.

After the KMT began to rule Taiwan, the Hsinchuang Post Office was restructured into its current status.

日治時代台灣體制外的教育機構

宗教學校

日本領台初期所設立的私立學校，除外國傳教士所設立的學校類型外，又多了一種日本佛教從軍佈教師所設立的型態。外國傳教士設立的學校，一般而言是教授神學、漢學、算學，或是教授相當於中學校、小學校程度的課程；而日本從軍佈教師所設之學校則又多了日語、歌唱。明治31年(西元1898年)，日本總督府訂定「私立學校廢止規則」，明治38年(西元1905年)訂定私立學校規則，又經大正年間兩次教育令及私立學校規則訂定。外國宣教師所設的學校，因不符規定而沒落。

書房私塾

書房私塾乃延續清領時期而來。教師頗多是科舉出身的學者，教授內容乃以傳統漢學爲主。書房經營者自任教師，修業年限、教授科目、學生年齡並無一定。日治初期，公學校之新式教育尚未發達，書房頗爲普遍，嗣後日益減少，所存者其教授科目，亦多與公學校相同，如：算術、日語、修身、唱歌、漢文等科目。教科書則使用台灣總督府發行之公學校用圖書，漢文科目採三字經、千字文、四書五經之一種或尺牘等課程。大正11年(西元1922年)教育令修正後，書房即依同年6月公布之私立學校規則規範管理之。

國語傳習所

明治29年(西元1896年)，日本總督府在全台各地設立「國語傳習所」，針對未受初等普通教育之本島青少年，施以日語爲主的簡易國民教育，屬於一種社會教育。修業年限爲一年，教育期間爲百日以上。除了日語外，又有幻燈會和理化實驗課程。昭和8年(西元1933年)以後，日本以國庫補助經費，又選擇農閒期間或其他適當時期，設立「簡易國語講習所」，以3個月到4個月期間，在夜間教授生活常規及國民禮儀。

台灣文化協會

台灣文化協會於大正10年(西元1921年)10月17日，由千餘台人在台北組成。推林獻堂爲總理，楊吉臣爲協理，蔣渭水爲專務理事。主要目的在敦促台灣議會支持請願運動外，也推行各項文化活動，以啓迪民智、喚醒民族意識及加強社會觀念。日治時期由台灣文化協會推動的民間社團及活動，主要有：

一、讀報社：

此社是爲打破言論管制和服務民衆而設，社中陳列台灣、日本的各種報紙雜誌及中國報紙十餘種，並以紅筆圈點有關殖民地解放運動或主要記事之文章。

二、講習會

大正 12 年(西元 1923 年)起，兩年間舉辦了各種講習會，傳授中外歷史文化及現代法律、醫葯衛生新知。

三、夏季學校

大正 13 年(西元 1924 年)起，連續 3 年在霧峰林家開辦。講習期間兩星期，以傳播現代知識爲主，課程密集而廣泛，包括經濟學、憲法、西洋文明史、科學概念、衛生常識、哲學、宗教等。

四、文化講演會

爲每週六、日定期於各城市中舉行，又組織講演隊到各地巡迴演講。講題涵蓋面極廣，主要在灌輸新知，並對殖民政治及社會不良風俗等面向作批判和檢討。

其他社會教育

日治時期的體制外教育，除上述幾種之外，其他尚有諸如原住民教育中的部落教化團體、教化委員部落集會所等；屬青年教育之男女青年團(青年會、處女會)；並爲初等教育出身者所開辦之補習教育——青年教育所、公民講習所及畢業生指導講習會、青年訓練所等；成人教育則有家長會、主婦會等。

註 59、82、89、109、149、150

RH-099

圖爲日治時代位於關子嶺的國語講習所

National Language Institute in Kuantzuling during the Japanese era.

Educational Institutions Outside the Regular School System during the Japanese Era

Religious Schools

In addition to schools set up by foreign missionaries, private schools during the Japanese era also included those set up by Japanese Buddhists. Curricula of schools set up by foreign missionaries were mostly theology, Chinese language and literature, and arithmetic, or other regular subjects equivalent to those taught in elementary or middle schools. For schools established by Japanese Buddhists, the curricula contained additional subjects, such as Japanese and music. In 1898, the Taiwan Governor's Office enacted the Regulation for Abolishment of Private Schools, and in 1905 promulgated the Regulations for Private Schools. During the Taisho period, new educational edicts or regulations governing private schools were promulgated. Schools established by foreign missionaries were gradually phased out for nonconformity with the edicts or regulations.

Seshu (Private Schools of the Ching dynasty)

Seshus were an extension of Ching dynasty tradition. The teachers were scholars who had participated in examinations for government offices. The curricula were primarily traditional studies of the Chinese humanities. In a seshu, there were no definite years of study, nor any fixed curricula, nor age limitation for the students, and the owner was also the teacher. In the early days of Japan's rule of Taiwan, seshus were quite popular for lack of public school education. Later, the number of seshus declined, and the remaining seshus also offered regular courses similar to those of public schools, such as arithmetic, Japanese, civics, music and Chinese language and literature. The textbooks used in seshus were published by the Taiwan Governor's Office. Chinese language and literature were taught with classical scripts and analects. In 1922 when the Education Edict was announced, seshus became subject to the Regulations for Private Schools enacted in June the same year.

National (Japanese) Language Academies

In 1896, the Taiwan Governor's Office established national language academies all over Taiwan, with an aim to providing simple civic education in Japanese for young Taiwanese. This was a type of social education, lasting for one school year with over 100 days of study. In addition to Japanese, the curricula also included slide presentations about chemistry chemistry and physics. Since 1933, simple national language centers, with subsidies from the government of Japan, were set up when farm land was in fallow or at appropriate times. The centers offered three to four months of training in the evenings, in etiquette and civic behavior.

Taiwan Cultural Association

The Taiwan Cultural Association was founded in Taipei on October 17, 1921 by well over 1000 Taiwanese. During the initiation of the association, Lin Hsien-tang was elected President, Yang Chi-chen Vice President, and Chiang Wei-shui Executive Director. The rationale behind the association was enlisting support from Taiwan's Parliament for its causes. The association also organized cultural activities to cultivate the awareness of the citizens and to inspire nationalism and social solidarity. During the Japanese era, the Taiwan Cultural Association sponsored and organized the following organizations and activities:

1.Newspaper Club:

This club was established to lift restriction on freedom of press and to serve the people. In the club, over a dozen Taiwanese and Japanese magazines and newspapers were displayed. In these magazines or newspapers, articles about colonial liberalization movements or major events were highlighted in red.

2.Seminars

A number of seminars were held between 1923 and 1925 to disseminate new knowledge, both domestic and overseas, about history, culture, law or medicine.

3.Summer School

A summer school was set up for three successive years at the residence of the Lin family of Wufeng. The school sessions lasted for two weeks in an effort to disseminate modern knowledge. The intensive sessions included economics, constitutional studies, Western civilization, principles of science, hygiene, philosophy, religion.

4.Cultural Lectures

Cultural lectures were held on Saturdays and Sundays in the major cities of Taiwan. In addition, teams of lecturers were organized to give lectures in different places. The topics of the lectures ran the gamut from new knowledge to criticism and reflection about colonialism and inappropriate social mores.

Other Social Education

In addition to the above-mentioned non-institutional forms of education, there were also centers for education of the indigenous people, assemblies of educators in aboriginal villages, and agencies for the education of the youth (such as youth clubs and women's clubs) during the Japanese era. There were also supplementary training institutes for citizens who had finished elementary education only, such as educational institutes for the youth, civic session institutes, graduate workshops, and training institutes for the youth. For adult education, there were organizations such as parents' clubs and mothers' clubs.

文石書院

體制外的教育

書院在前清時期係有別於一般官學的另類教育系統，以「導進人才，廣學校所不及」爲宗旨。台灣自康熙22年（西元1683年），施琅創建西定坊書院以來，共建有60座書院。文石書院建於乾隆31年（西元1766年），是台灣第廿五座書院，屬早期之書院形制，亦爲澎湖唯一之書院。

以地方特產命名的書院

「文石」爲澎湖與義大利西西里島之特產，其質地細緻密實，紋彩多變。文石書院創建者澎湖通判胡建偉以此特產命名，即期許書院諸生成就能如文石之秀美。圖示右側二樓之建築爲魁星閣，係道光9年（西元1829年）改建至巽方（東南方，主文運），以應「大啓文明」風水之說，屋頂形制爲「硬山廡殿」，全台殊爲少見。

註41、118、146

RH-100

日治時代所攝文石書院

Wenshih Academy during the Japanese era.

Wenshih Academy

Alternative Education

In the early Ching era, an academy was an educational system providing an alternative to the usual official schools. Its mandate was to cultivate human talent, and broaden what schools cannot reach. From 1683, when Shih Lang founded Hsitingfang Academy, Taiwan saw the founding of 60 academies. Wenshih Academy was founded in 1766; it was the 25th academy in Taiwan. Its form and organization is of the early type of academy. It is also the only academy in Penghu.

An Academy Taking its Name from Local Products

Wenshih means patterned rocks, a local product of both Penghu and Sicily, Italy. They have fine, intricate, closely spaced, and colorful line patterns. Rock Pattern Academy was founded by Penghu Assistant Prefectural Magistrate, Hu Chienwei, who named the school after this local product, hoping that the students of this academy would achieve accomplishments as beautiful as these patterned rocks. It was a deeply significant gesture. At the right of the illustration can be seen a two-story building, the Kui Star Building, which was rebuilt in 1829 in a southeasterly orientation, which according to the theories of Chinese architectural siting was lucky for cultural cultivation; also according to this geomantic theory about the great arising culture, the rooftop was reshaped in the motif known as the unyielding mountain and palace of corridors. Such an architectural form is very rarely seen in Taiwan.

本土科學研究的先河——中央研究所

日治時期，台灣總督府為了研究調查台灣本島的產業及衛生狀況，決定成立一所屬於應用科學的研究所。其於明治 40 年（西元 1907 年）始，支出 55 萬圓作為籌設研究所的經費，同時開始建築廳舍，擇定教育部現址作為中央研究所的所在地。明治 42 年部分建築完工，同年 3 月發布官制，研究所正式成立。然直到大正 10 年（西元 1921 年）8 月 2 日，台灣總督府中央研究所官制才公布，合併既設的糖業試驗場、種畜場、茶樹栽培試驗場及園藝試驗場，以避免研究調查領域的重覆。至此，中央研究所的組織及功能確定，直屬台灣總督府。中央研究所在於從事有關農業、糖業、林業、工業、其他產業及衛生的研究、調查、試驗、分析、鑑定與講習等事項；並進行有關種苗、種畜傳染病之防治藥品的研究調查與製造配給等事項。然而日治時期的中央研究所，與日後隨國府遷台的中央研究院之間並無多大的直接關係，兩者為完全不同性質的研究機構。

有關日治時期中央研究所的組織如下：

中央研究所組織一覽表

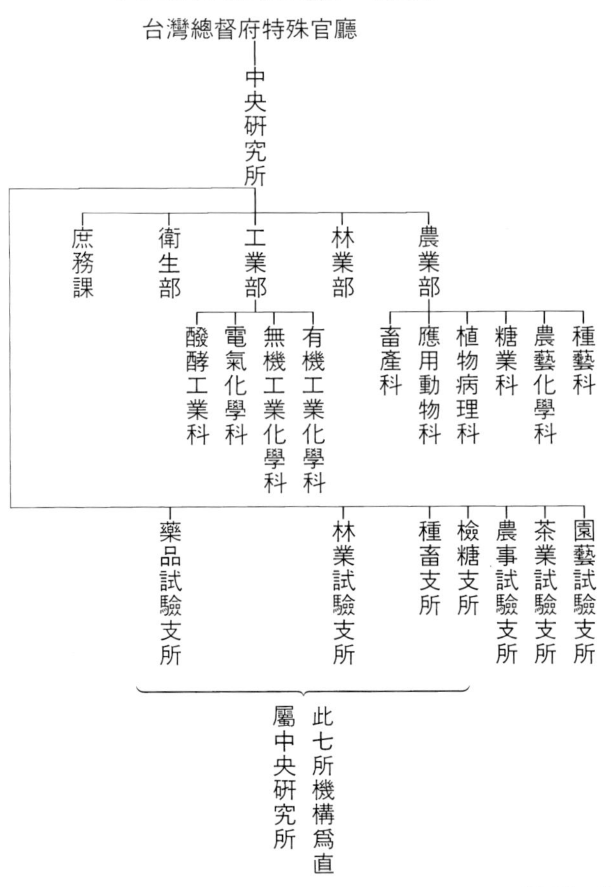

註 87、136、155、157

Central Research Institute—

Pioneer in Local Scientific Research

During the era of Japanese rule, in order to survey and study conditions of production and hygiene on the island of Taiwan, the Taiwan General Government decided to establish a research institute which would be a center of applied science. In 1907, 550,000 yen were allocated to fund the expenses of the research institute. At the same time, they began to construct an office building, located at the present site of the Bureau of Education. In 1909, a portion of the construction work was complete; in March of that year the bureaucratic structure was announced, and the Research Institute was officially established. The bureaucratic structure of the Central Research Institute of the Taiwan General Government was not announced until August 2, 1921: it was merged with the Sugar Industry Experimental Station, the Agriculture and Husbandry Station, the Experimental Station for Tea and Forestry Cultivation, and the Park Experimental Station. In this way overlap between research and survey areas was to be avoided. At this point the organization and function of the Central Research Institute was confirmed; it was directly affiliated with the Taiwan General Government. In this way, the Central Research Institute was devoted to research, surveys, experimentation, analysis, inspections, teaching and training, etc., related to agriculture, sugar production, forestry, industry, other areas of production, and health and sanitation. In addition, it handled matters concerning research, survey, production and distribution of preventative medicines against diseases contaminating seeds and husbandry industries. However, the Central Research Institute of the Japanese period does not have a great deal of direct connection with Academia Sinica, which came to Taiwan with the new government after the Japanese departed. These two were research agencies of quite different characters.

The organization of the Central Research Institute during the Japanese occupation is summarized in the following chart:

Schematic Chart of the Organization of the Central Research Institute

Special Office of the General Research Institute

Central Research Institute

- Agriculture Office
  - Horticulture Department
  - Agrochemical Department
  - Sugar Industry Department
  - Department of Botanical Medicine
  - Applied Animal Husbandry Department
  - Husbandry Roduction Department
- Forestry Office
- Industry Office
  - Organic Chemical Industries Department
  - Inorganic Chemical Industries Department
  - Electro-Chemistry Department
  - Fermentation Department
- Health Office
- Office of General Affairs
- Park Experimentation Branch
- Tea Cultivation Experimentation Branch
- Agriculture Experimentation Branch
- Sugar Refinery Banch
- Husbandry Branch
- Forestry Experimentation Branch
- Medical Experimentation Branch

中央研究所之建築特色

臺灣總督府研究所，是日治時期臺灣及南洋研究的重鎮，其址在今中山南路教育部、中央聯合辦公大樓現址。明治 38 年（西元 1905 年）由總督府的建築技師小野木孝志著手設計，明治 42 年落成，爲仿法國文藝復興式樣二層建築，斜屋頂有圓型老虎窗，屋脊有華麗的鐵柵裝飾，此建築爲臺灣本地首度嘗試鋼筋混凝土樓板構造之實驗性建築。其研究組織分工業、衛生二部，大正 10 年（西元 1921 年）改稱中央研究所，日治後期改組爲工業研究所，光復初仍沿舊制。

註 2、65、117、118、119

圖爲日治時期之中央研究所

Academia Sinica during the Japanese era.

RH-101

Architectural Characteristics at the Central Research Institute

The Central Research Institute of the Taiwan General Government was a major establishment in research in Taiwan and the Southern Pacific during the Japanese period. This site is located at the place where the Bureau of Education and the Central Allied Office Building are present found, on Chungshan South Road. Designed in 1905 by General Government Architect Shono Bokukoshi and completed in 1909, it was a two story building imitating a French Renaissance style, with the rounded, tiger windows on its sloping roof, and an elaborate ironwork balustrade along the ridge. This was an adventurous design, inasmuch as it was the first building in Taiwan to experiment with using reinforced concrete structures. The organization of research was divided in two divisions: Industry and Health. In 1921 it was renamed the Central Research Institute. In the late stages of the Japanese era it was reorganized to be the Industrial Research Institute, and in years immediately following Retrocession it continued on in this capacity.

辦學理念百年變遷——淡江中學

Tanchiang High School — A Century of Transformation

淡江中學，爲西元1914年馬偕博士之子偕叡廉先生，奉加拿大母教之命，爲提高台灣神學院學生素質而創立的教會學校。昭和11年（西元1936年），以該校缺乏日本精神爲由接管之，在校長有坂一世的經營下，倡導文武教育，以發展德術兼備作爲教育方針，在學業及運動方面曾孕育出優秀的人才。台灣光復後，基督長老教會接管淡江中學，迄今校內體制亦隨時代潮流而有所變更，然在宗教理想的支持下，該校以發展全人教育爲目標，且恪遵「信、望、愛」的校訓。 註44、63

Established in 1914 by George W. Mackay, son of the renowned missionary Dr. George L. Mackay, under the directive of the Presbyterian Church of Canada, Tanchiang High School is a Christian school aimed at raising the quality of students for theological schools in Taiwan. In 1936, the Japanese rulers took over the school under the pretext of its lack of Japanese spirit. Under the administration of the principal, Arisaka Isse, the school advocated both academic and physical education under the guideline of balanced moral and academic education. The school cultivated a great amount of talent in the academic field and in the realm of sports as well. After World War II, the administration of the school was handed over to the Presbyterian Church, which modified the internal system of the school to meet the needs of modern society. With a religious underpinning, the school continues to this day, with continued efforts to provide holistic education under the school's principle of faith, hope and love.

RH-102

日治時期自遠處眺望淡江中學之景觀

A distant view of Tanchiang High School during the Japanese era.

淡江中學的創立者偕叡廉先生
Geroge W. Mackay,
founder of Tanchiang High School.

RH-104

馬偕博士與淡江中學

馬偕博士，加拿大籍長老教會傳教士，於清同治 11 年（西元 1872 年）來淡水傳教，憑藉著驚人的意志力、輔以行醫救人的傳道，深得當地人士的敬重，其足跡遍佈台灣北部各地，共歷時 29 年，設立教會達 60 餘所。馬偕博士對於台灣新式教育的貢獻至今仍爲人傳頌。光緒 8 年（西元 1882 年）在淡水興辦了理學堂大書院（牛津學堂），次年又創辦了台灣最早的新式女子學校——淡水女學堂。明治 34 年（1901 年）馬偕博士過世，牛津理學堂乃更名爲淡水神學院；大正 3 年（1914 年）神學院遷於台北，原址創設了淡水中學，之後曾一度由日本人經營，稱之爲私立淡水中學校。台灣光復後，淡水中學校乃由台灣長老教會接收，更名爲淡江中學。

Dr. MacKay and Tanshui Middle School

Dr. George L. MacKay was a Presbyterian missionary from Canada. He came to Tanshui in 1872. Relying on his astonishing will power, his preaching, and particularly his ability to save people through his medical skills, he won widespread respect from the local people. He traveled all over northern Taiwan. He stayed in Taiwan 29 years, setting up more than 60 churches. Dr. MacKay's contribution to Taiwan's modern educational system is still widely remembered and acclaimed. In 1882, he set up the Oxford Academy. In the following year, he founded Taiwan's first modern girls' school, the Tanshui Girls' School. Dr. MacKay passed away in 1901. The Oxford Academy was renamed the Tanshui Theological Academy. In 1914, the theological academy was moved to Taipei. At the original site, the Tanshui Middle School was established. Later on, the middle school was operated by the Japanese and called the Tanshui Private Middle School. After Taiwan returned to Chinese control, the middle school was taken over by the Presbyterian church of Taiwan and was once again named Tanshui Middle School.

中西合璧的淡江中學校舍

Buildings of Tanchiang High School — Amalgamation of East and West

淡江中學之校舍，完成於西元1925年，由該校數學幾何老師羅虔益(K.W. Dowie)所設計，至今仍保存相當完整。其採用了很多台灣地方性建材，如紅瓦、釉花磚等，加上受本地傳統建築的影響，格局接近三合院，在細部裝飾及雕刻上，則有濃厚的中國風味。然正面及兩翼前的八角形塔，卻爲西方拜占庭式建築。這種成功地融合中西建築的表現手法，在台灣建築史上頗具重要性。

註117、118

The buildings of the Tanchiang High School, which were designed by the geometry teacher K. W. Dowie, were completed in 1925 and have remained intact even to this day. In the construction process, local Taiwanese materials, such as red tiles and enamel bricks, were utilized. Under the influence of Taiwan's traditional architecture, the layout of the buildings conformed to ancient Chinese tradition. The Chinese characteristics found their way in the detailed decorations and carvings of the buildings. However, the octagon of the front section is a Byzantine-style structure. Indeed, the successful amalgamation of the Chinese and Western architectural styles as exemplified by the buildings is a significant milestone in the history of Taiwan's architecture.

RH-107

隨主事者更替的淡江高女

Tanchiang Girls' High School

淡江高女的歷史可追溯至馬偕博士於西元 1883 年所創立的「淡水女學堂」，當時以訓練女子傳道人員爲教學目標，然隨馬偕的逝世而停辦。1907 年，女學堂復校後改變教育方針，以提供現代化女子教育的課程爲宗旨。1916 年，新校舍峻工，更名爲「淡水高等女學校」。1936 年，該校在日人有坂一世的經營下，以涵養婦德爲目標，除教授普通課程外，特重裁縫課。台灣光復後，與淡江中學合併，之後曾一度獨立爲純德女中，1956 年再度合併，迄今。

註 44、63、138

Tanchiang Girls' High School can be traced back to the Tanshui Girls' School founded by Dr. Mackay in 1883, with the view to cultivate female preachers. The school was closed when Mackay passed away. In 1907 the school was reopened, with modified educational guidelines, under which the school was to provide modern education for women. In 1916, new buildings were added, and the school was renamed Tanshui Girls' High School. In 1936, Arisaka Isse took over the administration of the school, and the school began to focus on cultivating the virtue of women. In addition to regular courses, the school paid great attention to needlework. After World War II, the school was merged with Tanchiang High School. Later, the school was separated from Tanchiang High School and became Tsunte Girls' High School. In 1956, the two schools merged again.

圖爲日治時代所攝私立淡水高女及觀音山景色

A scene of the private Tanshui Girls' High School and Mt. Kuanyin during the Japanese era.

RH-106

RH-105

圖爲日治時代所攝淡水高女校舍

Buildings of Tanshui Girls' High School during the Japanese era.

新莊公學校

新莊公學校，即今日之新莊國民小學，創設於明治 31 年（西元 1898 年）。為台北國語傳習所新莊分教場，後來獨立成爲興直公學校，不久又易名爲第一公學校、新莊公學校等，是新莊第一所西式教育的學校。 註 22、85

RH-108-A

Hsinchuang Public School

The Hsinchuang Public School is today's Hsinchuang Elementary School, founded in 1898. It was originally the Hsinchuang branch of Taipei's National (Japanese) Language School. Later on, it was made an independent institution, renamed the Kojiki Public School. Within a short a period of time, it was renamed the First Hsinchuang Public School, and ultimately Hsinchuang Public School. It was the first Western-style school of Hsinchuang.

山脚公學校

山脚公學校，即今日之泰山國民小學，創設於明治 31 年（西元 1898 年）。原爲淡水國語傳習所山脚分教場，爾後更名爲新莊山脚公學校。之後又改稱山脚國民學校，並先後在菁埔、坑子外等地設立分校，光復後改爲今名。

註 22、85

RH-108-B

Shanchao Public School

Shanchao Public School is today's Taishan Elementary School. Founded 1897, it was originally a branch of the Tanshui National (Japanese) Language Dissemination and Learning Academy. It was later renamed the Shanchao Public School of Hsinchuang, and later still, Shanchao Citizen's School. Branches were set up first at Janpu and Kengtzuwai. After World War II, it was given its current name.

典型哥德式——濟南教會

濟南教會位於中山南路與濟南路口，建於西元 1916 年。以紅磚爲主體，窗框、門框以砂岩疊砌，形式上屬哥德式建築風格。大面玻璃窗、鐘樓、尖頂、十字架是典型教堂建築的特色。

濟南教會之創設，可追溯從日本基督教會於西元 1896 年派牧師河合龜輔來台宣教開始，直至台灣光復止，先後歷經大谷虞、光小太郎及上與二郎牧師的牧會達 51 年。而期間更興建了今日台灣最具歷史、藝術價值的教堂—濟南教會大禮拜堂，時稱幸町教會。西元 1947 年，日籍信徒先後返日，教會由台灣基督長老會接收，且依所在地之道路名稱改爲濟南教會。

RA-027

日治時期的濟南教會，當時稱辛町教會

Chinan Church during the Japanese era when it was called Xin District Church.

Representative Gothic Style-- The Chinan Church

The Chinan Church is situated at the intersection of Chungshan South Road and Chinan Road. It was built in 1916. The building was mainly composed of red bricks, and the window frames as well as door frames were layered with sandstone. The architectural style was Gothic. Large shields of glass windows, a bell tower, a tapered steeple and a cross are the representative characteristics of church architecture.

The establishment of the Chinan Church can be traced back to the Japanese Christian Church, when they sent over a missionary, Pastor Kawai Kamesuke to Taiwan to evangelize. From that time until the end of World War II Tani Osore, Hikari, Kotaro, and Kamiyo Jiro all served as the church's ministers. This succession of ministers extended 51 years. During that period of time, they set up the church which has the most historical and artistic value in today's Taiwan. Now formally called the Chinan Tabernacle, it was in years past called the Xin district Church. In 1947, the Japanese followers gradually returned to Japan, and the church was taken over by the Taiwan Presbyterian Church. It was renamed the Chinan Church, according to the thoroughfare on which it is located.

臺南公館 Tainan Public Building

臺南公館，又稱臺南公會堂（今社教館），是一棟位於今公園路遠東百貨附近的二層樓建築，建於明治44年（西元1911年）。其後方著名的吳家花園：紫春園，係臺南富紳吳尚新在清道光10年（西元1830年）所建；公館後庭主要爲一大水池，池邊有兩座水榭，對岸以硓砧石堆成假山曰「飛來峰」，樹石亭榭景致優美，居鬧市而有閑雅幽邃之境，後來漸因周邊建築物侵入不復舊觀。臺南公館的立面處理與稍後興建的臺南州廳有許多共通之處。 註65、117、118

The Tainan Public Building, also called Tainan Public Assembly Hall (now the Society and Education Building), is a two-story building located on what is now Kungyuan Road near the Far Eastern Department Store. It was built in 1911. Behind it is the Tsichun Park, the garden of the famous Wu family; the wealth gentry Wu Shanghsin of Tainan built it in 1830. The back courtyard of the Public Building is mainly a large pool, with two water-side pavilions at each side, and at the edge across the pool was an artificial mountain made of intriguing stones piled up, called the Feilai Peak. The trees, rocks, pavilions and gazebos were extremely lovely, forming a refined, relaxed, isolated oasis in the center of the noisy city. Later, the former scenes could not be retained, because gradually all around them other buildings intruded. The treatment of the facade of the Tainan Public Building bears a lot of similarity with that of the Tainan County Government Building which was built slightly later.

日治時代的台南公館爲今台南社教館

Tainan Public Building (currently Social Education Building) during the Japanese era.

RH-110

兩廣會館

服務兩廣鄉親的會館

我國自唐代以來即有同鄉會館之設置，其目的即在照顧旅居外地的鄉親，提供短期住宿、小額信用貸款、民事糾紛仲裁等服務，並迎奉原鄉守護神，爲異鄉遊子身心憑依之處。

曾經爲台灣最大的會館

台南兩廣會館位在今台南市南門路孔子廟附近（清水寺街台南市政府對面），由當時台灣總兵吳光亮與福建巡撫岑毓英，向旅居臺地的廣東、廣西籍人士勸募六萬元建築而成，原稱爲嶺南會館，清光緒元年（西元 1875 年）岑毓英奉旨改建稱爲兩廣會館。匠師與建材均來自廣東原鄉。其華麗之建築風格不同於閩南（如圖示屋脊未起翹且兩側砌成封火山牆），曾爲台灣最大之會館，日治時期日人將其作爲教育博物館。惜在西元 1945 年 3 月 14 日遭盟機轟炸而夷爲平地。　**註 118、147**

RH-109

清代建立的兩廣會館，今已不存

Public Building for Guangdong and Guangxi during the Japanese era. It is no longer in existence.

The Public Building for Guangdong and Guangxi

A public building serving people from Guangdong and Guangxi

From the Tang Dynasty onwards, China has had faculties for public assembly of emigrants from the same province. Their purpose is to take care of emigrants during their travels or residence in territories outside their home province, to provide such services as short-term housing, credit or loans for small amounts of money, and mediation in civil disputes, as well as to welcome visits from the home province tutelary deities. It was a place on which wandering sons could rely for safety and security.

Once the largest public building in Taiwan

The Public Building for Guangdong and Guangxi was located near the Confucian temple on what is now Nanmen Road of Tainan City, across from the Tainan Municipal Government. It was a public meeting hall to serve Chinese who had migrated to Taiwan from Guangdong and Guangxi. It was built with 60,000 yuan collected from people of Guangdong and Guangxi traveling or resident in Taiwan, a project undertaken by Wu Kuangliang, a high-ranking military officer in Taiwan, and Tsen Yuying, the Governor of Fujian. It was originally called the Lingnan Assembly Building. In 1875 Tsen Yuying ordered the structure rebuilt, and the name was changed to the Public Building for Guangdong and Guangxi. The carpenters and building materials all came from Guangdong's Yuan County. Its delicate, elaborate architectural style is different from that of the Southern Min. (As the illustration shows, the roof's ridge does not sweep upward; the ends have been cut to form high terminal walls and chimney cover.) It was once the largest assembly building in Taiwan. During the Japanese period it was used as an educational museum. Unfortunately, the building was destroyed by the bombing of Allied Aircraft on March 14, 1945.

台大醫院前身
——台灣病院

台灣病院即今台大醫院前身，明治 28 年（西元 1895 年）創建於大稻埕千秋街（今貴德街），1897 年遷至常德街現址。1911 年 8 月遇颱風毀損，乃於次年改建，歷經 12 年，於 1924 年落成，當時爲遠東地區最具規模的醫院，同時也爲日本研究熱帶病理學的權威機構。硬體設備暨醫療器材均超越日本本土爲亞洲之冠。昭和 13 年（西元 1938 年）4 月改隸爲台北帝國大學醫學部附設醫院，戰後成爲國立台灣大學醫學院附設醫院。

台灣病院爲醫院建築專家近滕十郎的經典之作，形制係仿文藝復興時期風格，牆身利用紅磚與洗石子，做出紅白相間的滾繞裝飾，此建築特色爲中間正立面四組成對門廊柱延伸出的立面與量體凹凸的變化，門廊與衛塔高出左右一層，在長條型建築中構成中央突出的主體。

註 72、78、117

RH-111

日治時代的台灣病院

Taiwan Infirmary during the Japanese era.

Taiwan Infirmary

—— The Forerunner of NTU Hospital

Taiwan Infirmary was the forerunner of our present National Taiwan University (NTU) hospital. In 1895 its construction began on Chianchiu Street (now Kuite Road) of Tataoying. In 1897 it moved to its present location on Changte Street. It was severely damaged in a typhoon in August of 1911, and was therefore rebuilt the following year. Construction was completed 12 years later, in 1924. At the time it was the largest hospital of any in the Far East; it was also the headquarters of Japan's Tropical Diseases Study Group, a research group which attained very authoritative status. Their facilities and treatment equipment were the best in Asia, better than those in Japan. In April, 1938, the hospital was renamed the Taipei Imperial University Medical School Affiliated Hospital. After the war it became the National Taiwan University School of Medicine Affiliated Hospital.

The Taiwan Infirmary was a classic work by a specialist in hospital architecture, Kinto Juro. Its structure imitates a Renaissance style. The walls use red brick and scrubbed stone, making a winding decorative display in alternating red and white. A characteristic of this architecture is the facade which extends from the set of four portico columns in pairs from the exact central facade. The interaction between the facades and the columns causes an emerging and receding effect, the portico and the surrounding towers being higher by one level. The long linear elements of the architectural design emerge as central thematic unit.

臺灣總督府阿緱醫院

即屏東病院舊稱，爲今屏東市自由路省立屏東醫院現址。明治43年（西元1910年）建，爲雨淋板外牆木構造建築，由前鳳山病院舍資材撤移所建，乃因應阿緱（屏東）地方的開發及醫療設施的缺乏，而將原鳳山病院的院舍、醫療設備拆遷至阿緱。建築面積811坪，其建築基地8668坪，係王進成等十五人捐贈而成。初僅有內、外兩科，逐漸擴增眼科、婦產科、X光科、小兒科而成爲屏東地區頗具規模的醫院。據《臺灣省通志》記載：「昭和11年（西元1936年）時，該院設有內、外、眼、小兒、婦產等五科；置有醫師七人、藥局長及藥劑師各一人，暨其他職員數十人；設有一、二、三等病床共92床，設備尚稱完整。」第二次世界大戰期間曾經受損，戰後改爲省立屏東醫院，並經漸次修復。照片中的建築物於民國44年11月因電線走火引發火災後已遭拆除。

註3、33、180

Ah-hou Hospital of the Taiwan Governor's Office

Originally named Pingtung Hospital, Ah-hou Hospital was located on Tse Yu Road at the address of today's Pingtung Provincial Hospital. In 1910, the hospital was established as a wooden structure with exterior weather boards, using construction materials from the buildings of the previous Fengshan Hospital. To facilitate the development of Ah-hou (Pingtung) and to cope with a shortage of medical facilities, the buildings and medical facilities were dismantled and relocated to Ah-hou. The hospital covering a construction area of 811 ping and a land area of 8, 668 ping was established, thanks to the contribution of Wang Chin-cheng and 14 other donors. Initially, the hospital had only the departments of medicine and surgery. With the gradual addition of the departments of ophthalmology, gynecology, radiology and pediatrics, the hospital became a large hospital in Pingtung. The History of Taiwan states,"In 1936, the hospital had five departments--internal medicine, surgery, ophthalmology, pediatrics and gynecology--with seven doctors, a chief pharmacist and an assistant pharmacist, and dozens of other employees. Along with over 92 first-class, second-class and third-class beds, the hospital could be regarded as a well-equipped hospital."The hospital was damaged during World War II and was reconstructed as the Provincial Pingtung Hospital after the war, followed by several stages of renovation. The building in this picture was demolished in November 1955, in the wake of a fire caused by a short circuit.

RH-113

日治時期醫護人員比例

	台籍	日籍	其他	共計
醫　　師	2168	1249	9	3426
牙科醫師	493	245	0	738
護　　士	508	312	0	820

（統計年代：1945 年）

The Number of Medical Personnel during the Japanese Era

	Tai-wanese	Japanese	Others	Total
Doctors	2168	1249	9	3426
Dentists	493	245	0	738
Nurses	508	312	0	820

(Statistics compiled in 1945.)

嘉義慈惠院

前身爲清代嘉義育嬰堂，明治 39 年（西元 1906 年）10 月改稱爲此名，院舍爲磚造平房，診療所爲木造雨淋板外牆二層建築。該院救護區域原爲二十廳時期的斗六、嘉義、鹽水港三廳轄內；明治 43 年（西元 1910 年）3 月修改地方官制，改爲調整行政區劃後歸嘉義廳管轄；除鹽水港一部改歸臺南廳，其他仍舊。診療所之對象分「恩賜診療」、「實費診療」兩種，前者對於貧困無力求醫者給與施療，由財團明治救濟會（△）提供經費支援；後者係爲一般社會服務。
註 29、51、122

△：該會是以日本明治天皇逝世時，日皇室對台灣地方事業助成捐款爲基礎而成立。昭和 2 年(1927)時，撥發林本源博愛醫院、澎湖普濟院、台南新樓病院、護國十善會、馬偕醫院、高雄天主公教會孤兒院、礦溪醫院等單位救濟金。昭和 5 年(1930)起，將八千元委交台灣社會事業協會推行該會事業，並對該事業協會每年補助經費五千元。

RH-112

圖爲日治時代的嘉義慈惠院，門楣上懸掛著「恩賜」與「實費」兩種就醫對象

Chiayi Tzihuei Hospital during the Japanese era. The sign on the lintel specified two categories of patients: those paying subsidized fees and full fees.

Chiayi Tsz-hui Hospital

Originally called the Chiayi Children's Education Hall during the Ching dynasty, the Chiayi Tsz-hui Hospital gained its present name in October of 1906. The ward was a one-story brick structure, and the clinic was a two-story wooden building with outer walls of weather-proof wood panels. At the time, Taiwan consisted of 12 prefects, and the area benefiting from this hospital's service was originally within the jurisdiction of the three Prefects of Touliu, Chiayi, Yanshuikang. In March of 1910, the local governmental structure was modified, and administrative districts were redefined; this institution was then placed under Chiayi's jurisdiction. Everything else remained the same except that Yanshuikang partially came under the jurisdiction of Tainan County. The clinic's target clients fell into two types: subsidized fees and full fees. The former was treatment supported by the Meiji (△) Corporate Charitable Foundation for patients who suffered from poverty, hardship or helplessness; the latter were regular services performed for the general community.

△: The Meiji Relief Foundation was established, after the demise of Emperor Meiji of Japan, by the contribution of Japan's royal family made to facilitate the development of local public-interest organizations in Taiwan. In 1927, the foundation provided relief for Lin Pen Yuan Hospital, Puchi Hospital of Penghu, Hsinlou Hospital of Tainan, the Charity Association, Mackay Hospital, orphanages of the Kaohsiung Anglican Church, and Kuahsi Hospital. In 1930, the foundation entrusted its operation with the Social Affairs Association, which received 8000 yen for the commission and an annual subsidy of 5000 yen from the foundation.

軍中廣播電台昔日爲澎湖衛戍病院

澎湖陸軍衛戍病院是日治時期日人駐防澎湖島的軍事醫療單位，此棟衛戍病院大樓建於大正7年（西元1918年），是今天軍中廣播電台的舊地。此棟建築牆面以紅磚爲主，並有白色仿石條之裝飾帶，圓拱造型自二樓連至一樓，搭配石砌台階及斜面屋頂，爲當時常見之建築形式。 註43、165

RH-114

圖爲日治時代澎湖衛戍病院

Weishu Hospital of Penghu during the Japanese era.

The Weihsu Hospital in Penghu-- The Present-day Military Broadcasting Station

During the Japanese era, the Weihsu Hospital served the Japanese soldiers stationed in Penghu. Erected in 1918, the hospital building was the former site of the present day Military Broadcasting Station. The building walls were constructed mostly of red bricks, decorated with white artificial stones. With its arched design extending from the second floor down to the first, together with stone stairways and sloped roof, the building was typical of the architectural style popular in Taiwan during the period of Japanese rule.

台灣首座西式旅館
——鐵道飯店

Taiwan's First Western - style Hotel —— The Railway Hotel

鐵道飯店是臺灣首座西式旅館，現址爲今臺北火車站前新光三越摩天大樓、大亞百貨。明治41年（西元1908年）10月，爲配合西部幹線鐵路通車所興建，同年11月1日落成，由鐵道部經營，爲磚石混合構造三層樓建築，德國馬薩式樣(Mansard style)。其平面呈口字形；三樓爲傾斜高峭加老虎窗的大屋頂；屋脊有華麗的裝飾鐵件；內部裝飾及餐器都非常講究，亦爲當年臺灣最豪華的飯店，環境巧緻雅逸，非一般旅館所能企及，戰爭末期被盟軍飛機炸毀。

鐵道飯店正面朝西，爲開封街東側端景，臨街大門開向今館前路，其紅磚主體襯以水泥砂漿條狀水平帶飾之形式，爲明治時期的建築所常見。

註2、65、67、68、117、118、125

The Railway Hotel was Taiwan's first Western-style hotel. It was located in front of the present Taipei Train Station, where the Hsinkuang Mitsukoshi super skyscraper and the Far Eastern Department Store now are. In coordination with the western train line's coming into operation, it was built in October, 1908, and on November 1 of the same year construction was complete. It was run by the Bureau of Railways. Comprised of a mixture of brick, it was a three-story building in the German Mansard style, designed by the only architect in the General Government who had studied abroad in Germany, Matsusaki Bancho. Its surface was marked by square patterns; the third floor was a large, high, sloping roof containing round, tiger windows, and all along the ridge beam were fancy ironwork decorations. The interior decor and the dining facilities were all done with fastidious care, so that this was the most luxurious hotel in Taiwan at the time. The setting was refined and elegant, something that the ordinary hotel could not hope to attain. It was destroyed in bombing raids by Allied airplanes in the last phase of the war.

The main facade of the Railway Hotel faced west; it was the prominent feature of the eastern terminus of Kaifeng Street. The front door near the street opened towards what is now Kuanchien Road. Its thematic design in red brick, with decorative surfaces featuring lines of cement and sand, was commonly seen in Meiji- style architecture.

RH-115

日本勸業銀行臺北支店

勸業銀行臺北支店最初係大正 12 年（西元 1923 年）設立於館前路開封街北側轉角，昭和 8 年（西元 1933 年）襄陽路新址落成改遷於此。此建築是由該行建築課設計，東京大林組施工，鋼筋混凝土構造，窗台及入口處的材料，則來自日本德山的花崗石及長州大理石，外牆貼人造石片，質感甚佳，爲混合埃及、馬雅及日本風格之折衷式樣建築，且造型渾厚，帶有埃及風格之柱列是最醒目的特徵。光復後改爲臺灣土地銀行，列爲第三級古蹟。右側高塔建築係位於襄陽路館前路口之三井物產會社。

註 66、72、117、118、121、126

圖爲日治時代 1933 年改遷之後的日本勸業銀行，現爲台灣土地銀行

RA-028

Japanese Kangyo Bank in 1933 after its relocation. It is currently the address of Taiwan Land Bank.

The Taipei Branch of the Japanese Kangyo Bank

Kangyo Bank's Taipei Branch was first established in 1923 on the north side on the corner of Kuanchien Road and Kaifeng Street. In 1933, they moved to the new site on Hsiangyang Road. This building was designed by the architectural division of the bank, and the construction was carried out by the Dairinso Group of Tokyo. Built of steel reinforced concrete, the materials for the window ledges and the doors were granite from Tokuyama and marble from Choshu, both in Japan. Artificial stone slabs were applied to the outer surfaces; the texture was very excellent. The architecture was a combination of Egyptian, Maya, and Japanese styles. Its most striking feature was the heavy feel conveyed by the row of thick columns in the Egyptian style. After Retrocession this building became the Taiwan Land Bank, and was listed as a cultural landmark of the third grade. The high towered building at the right is the Sanching Wuchan Company at the intersection of Hsiangyang Road and Kuanchien Road.

台北米糧之主要源頭——新莊

The Main Source of Taipei's Rice — Hsinchuang

日治時期，日本政府收購後村圳之灌溉渠重新經營（西元1909年），其間曾推廣綠肥及有機肥的使用；大正10年（西元1921年）更推廣蓬萊米，大舉提昇了米質及產量（約占當時台北地區稻米產量的二分之一），自此新莊米名聞遐邇。爲了儲存新莊地區生產的米糧，台北州農會於大正13年（西元1924年）在新莊街建立了一座可容米萬袋的「新莊農業倉庫」。

註85

During the era of Japanese rule, the Japanese government purchased the irrigation system of Houchunchen and recommenced operation in 1909. During that period of time, they promoted the use of green manure and organic fertilizer. In 1921, they started to promote the plantation of the Penglai variety of rice, greatly increasing the quality and quantity of rice production (roughly amounting to half of the rice production of the Taipei area of the time). From then on, Hsinchuang's rice became very famous. To store the rice which Hsinchuang produced, the Taipei Prefectural Agricultural Association built up the Hsinchuang Agricultural Granary 1924, which could accommodate 10,000 rice bags on Hsinchuang Street.

RH-081

圖爲日治時期儲存新莊米的新莊農業倉庫

Warehouse of Hsinchuang Farmers' Cooperative used for the storage of Hsinchuang rice during the Japanese era.

新莊圖書館

新莊圖書館成立於大正 12 年 9 月 21 日。館長由當時的街長兼任，創立之初藏書約 261 冊；大正 14 年，增至 917 冊，是日治時期新莊地區的文庫。民國 64 年，新莊老街為了改建成今日的市場，乃拆除了慈祐宮對面的圖書館、公會堂及其公園旁的大樹。

註 45

RH-006

日治時期新莊圖書館，今已被拆除

Hsinchuang Library during the Japanese era. It has been demolished.

Hsinchuang Library

The Hsinchuang Library was established on September 21, 1923. The neighborhood overseer also served as the curator of the library. At its inception, the library had a collection of 261 volumes. In 1925, its collection had increased to 917 books. At this time is served as the document depository for the Hsinchuang area. In 1975, in order to build the current market on old Hsinchuang street, the local government demolished the library across from the Chiyou Temple, as well as the public meeting hall and all the old trees next to the park.

嘉義廳前通與農會事務所

嘉義廳位於今嘉義市中山路市政府前，廳前通應爲市政府前之直行道路。位於該道路的農會事務所設於昭和19年（西元1944年）1月，辦理生產指導、提供運銷、農會金融等業務，今日農會的型態可追溯至此。 註192

RH-116

圖爲日治時代嘉義廳農會事務所及廳前大街

This picture depicts the office of Chiayi Farmers' Cooperative and the street in its front during the Japanese era.

Chiayi Prefecture Hall and the Farmers' Association

The chiayi prefecture hall was located at the present-day Chiayi city government office along the road in front of the prefecture hall, the office of the farmers' association was established in 1944 during the 19th yesr of the Showa era, managing affairs such as production counseling, distribution and sales, as well as financial assistance to the farmers' association. It is believed that the present-day farmers' associations were patterned after the farmers' office.

日治時期西門町市場——紅樓

The Hsimenting Market during Japanese Era —— The Red Building

西門町市場，在臺北西門圓環邊。該地屬清代新起街；日治後爲新起町，故稱新起街市場，俗稱西門町市場。明治29年(西元1896年)9月在鄰址建一簡單市場，爲臺北市新市場之濫觴。明治41年改建西門圓環邊，正面八角形磚造二層建築，俗稱八角樓，又有「紅樓」別稱，其左方連接丁字形斜屋頂平房一座(魚肉蔬菜市場攤棚)，由近藤十郎設計，同年11月落成。光復後，改爲紅樓劇場。

註2、66、72、117、125、126

The Hsimenting Market lies next to the Hsimenting Roundabout. During the Ching, the area belonged to Hsinchi Street. After Japan took over Taiwan, it was called Hsinchi Ting (Ting meaning street in Japanese), so the market was called Hsinchi Street Market, commonly known as the Hsimenting (or West Gate Street) Market. In early September of 1896, the Japanese built a simple market next to it, which was the predecessor of the Taipei New Market. In 1908, they built a new Market next to Hsimenting Roundabout.

The octagon-shaped building is two floors tall, built with red bricks. It is commonly called the Octagon Building, and nicknamed the Red Building. On its left was an adjacent T-shaped building with an A-frame roof. (In the attic there were sheds for fish meat and fresh vegetables.) The building was designed by Kondo Juro It was completely finished in November of 1908. After the Japanese left Taiwan, the market was changed to the Red Building Theater House.

RH-117

圖爲日治時代所攝的台北西門町市場，日治時期西門町市場——紅樓

Market at Hsimendin, Taipei during the Japanese era. Hsimendin Market during the Japanese era–Red Building.

日治時期的市場管理

台灣最早的市場是由民間自發聚集而成，官方僅設置公斗公量制，以維持市場交易，並沒有明文的規章。到了日治時期，日人爲了摒除以往市場雜亂之弊病，以及整頓交通起見，在台灣設置井然有序的市場。明治 37 年（西元 1904 年）更發佈「台灣總督府令第 65 號」，規定各地市場爲公共建造物，由該地之街庄長或廳長管理，清朝所遺之牛墟也交由街庄長管理，其賦稅則充作街庄之公共費用。

註 8、14、20

日治時代的新莊市場

Hsinchuang Market during the Japanese era.

Market Management During the Japanese Era

The earliest market of Taiwan was formed through voluntary gatherings of the people. The authorities only established the system of weights and measures to maintain the flow of exchange in the market. They didn't enumerate clear-cut regulations. During the Japanese era, in order to get rid of the problems of chaos in the market and to straighten up the traffic, the Japanese established orderly marketplaces in various locales. In 1904, they issued the No. 65 Taiwan Government Office Decree, stipulating that marketplaces everywhere are public structures and are governed by the local chief or prefecture magistrate, and the taxes collected serve as the public funds for the locale.

日本人經營的台中吉本商店

台中櫻橋通即今台中市中正路。照片中的吉本商店是當時首屈一指的百貨食品行；緊臨的台中座爲一戲院（即今日龍心百貨所在地）。 註29

RH-118

圖爲日治時代的台中櫻橋通，即今中正路

In this picture was Yingchiao Road during the Japanese era, which is Chung Cheng Road of Taichung today.

The Japanese-run Chipen Store in Taichung

The Japanese-run Chipen Store, as shown in the picture, was the most popular store in Taichung during the period. Located on Yingchiao Road (present-day Chungcheng Road), the store stood next to a movie theater (present-day address of the Lunghsin Department Store), and offered groceries and other food products.

汐止街泉源商行

「泉源商行」位於汐止鎮茄冬路上，其前門題有「周泉源」三字，應爲周家之商號，此棟華宅荒蕪許久，多年前已拍賣給招商局。

主屋有四層樓，四樓貼有面磚，爲昭和時期流行的建築；三樓以下則爲大正時期所建。屋前有一大庭院，花木扶疏，可以想見當年之繁盛。 註123

RH-119

圖爲日治時代所攝的汐止泉源商行

Chuanyuan Store in Hsichih during the Japanese era.

The Chuenyuen Shop of Hsichih

The Chuenyuen Shop is located on Chiehtung Road in Hsichih Township. On the main gate were enscribed the words Chou Chuen Yuen, probably the Chou family trademark. This extravagant building has long been abandoned. Years ago it was auctioned to the Commercial Exchange Bureau.

The main house has four floors. On the fourth floor, the house is decorated with tiles which were the fashion of the Showa era. The first three floors were built during the Taisho period. There is a huge yard in front of the house, with lush and exuberant flowers and trees, revealing the prosperity the house enjoyed in its prime.

設施
Construction

現代化都市的表徵──公園
Parks- Symbols of Urban Development

公園可作爲遊憩、休閒，亦有涵養水源、保存古蹟、自然景觀和生態環境等功能，更可融合人文及知性活動，呈現多元化的都市公園內涵。「公園」是西方城市現代化的產物，日治時期日人便以建設台灣都市公園，作爲展現其一部分治台成果。

Parks can be used for entertainment, recreation, conservation of water, preservation of historic sites, and appreciation of natural scenery and preservation of ecological systems. They can also incorporate humanistic and educational activities to reflect the essence of multifaceted urban parks. Parks are products created by the modernization of Western cities. During the Japanese era, parks in Taiwan were established as a showcase of Japan's successful administration of Taiwan.

驛站巡禮 History of Train Stations

本章將呈現日治時期所建之若干驛站圖片，並著墨於驛站的建築、風格及質材，旁及各驛站之發展沿革。本章另搜集由日治時期台灣總督府所發行的各驛站郵戳，每一枚刻章皆爲手工刻製，泥色歷久不衰，特將此羅列，以饗讀者。

This chapter presents pictures of some train stations set up by the Japanese, focusing on their architectural styles and materials, as well as their historical background. Also depicted in this chapter are stamps of the train stations. These enduring stamps, produced by hand, are presented for the enjoyment of the readers.

燈塔沿革 History of Lighthouses

燈塔除指引海上迷津之功能外，也爲軍事防禦要地，本章將引述台灣若干重要的燈塔，以一覽其電力設施更進及其背景故事之外，也想帶領讀者佇立島嶼邊陲，領略台灣燈塔之美。

In addition to giving directions for vessels in the sea, lighthouses also served as military strongholds. This chapter introduces the major lighthouses in Taiwan, as well as their power facilities and background stories, so that the readers can better appreciate the beauty of Taiwan's lighthouses.

橋的記憶 Memory of Bridges

橋讓路變長，延伸了視野，從此疆列彼界，扮演歷史的傳遞者，也是亙古的記憶！

Bridges are extensions of roads and our vision. They also serve as bridges with the past in our memory.

橋的記憶
Memory of Bridges

臺北橋

臺北橋，初建於光緒 15 年（西元 1889 年），原爲木構橋樑，因兩度遭颱洪沖毀，大正 10 年（西元 1921 年）9 月第二度重建，大正 14 年 6 月完成，傳爲英國工程師設計。橋長 434.55 公尺，寬 8.55 公尺，中爲快車道，兩旁有人行道，橋身護欄以臺北市徽爲圖案，採砌石混凝土橋墩，每孔 61.04 公尺之七節鋼桁架大橋，雄偉壯麗，爲當時北臺灣橋樑之首。圖係由三重方面所拍攝，背景爲大稻埕沿河房屋，河中每見舟帆往來。此橋橫跨淡水河，爲大稻埕通三重埔、新莊之縱貫公路孔道，民國 55 年（西元 1966 年）7 月動工改建，跨徑仍同，現已四度改建完成。　註 2、5、65、66、107、108、114、115、117、125

RH-120

圖爲日治時期的台北橋

Taipei Bridge during the Japanese era.

The Taipei Bridge

The Taipei Bridge was first built in 1889. It was originally a wooden bridge. Because it was twice destroyed in typhoon-related flooding, it was reconstructed, a process which began in September of 1921, and was completed in June of 1925. It is said that the project was undertaken by a British engineer. This bridge was 434.55 meters long and 8.55 meters wide; in the center were fast lanes, and there were pedestrian walkways on either side. Taipei Municipal Insignia were displayed on the protective wall on the side of the bridge. Cut stone in cement formed the bridge's buttresses; each of the seven arches of the steel supporting span was 6.04 meters. It was a magnificent sight, at the forefront of bridges in Taipei City at that time. This illustration was taken from a vantage point in Sanchung; the background shows the buildings in Tataoying along the river. Boats were often seen sailing up and down the river. This bridge crossed the Tanshui River, linking up Tataoying with Sanchung and Hsinchuang. In July, 1966, construction was begun to refurbish the bridge, and although a throughway has been left open the whole time, it is to this day still surrounded all round by construction sites.

明治橋

第一代明治橋（今中山橋前身），跨越基隆河，爲鋼桁架鐵橋，明治 34 年（西元 1901 年）10 月完工，是通往臺灣神社的橋樑，橋長 90 公尺，鋼筋混凝土橋面，中央是馬車道有分隔島，兩側爲人行道，兩旁欄杆設計桐葉紋飾，鋼桁架後方即臺灣神社的第一座鳥居（類似入口牌坊）。昭和 5 年（西元 1930 年）拆除改建第二代鋼筋混凝土固定拱構造橋，花崗石護欄，配置青銅路燈，造型典雅秀麗，戰後改名中山橋，民國 57 年（西元 1968 年）改建拓寬成今貌。

註 65、66、115、117、118、125、137

RH-132

The Meiji Bridge

The first generation of the Meiji Bridge (the forerunner of the present Chungshan Bridge) crossed the Keelung River. It was a steel girder bridge. Work was completed in October, 1901. This bridge went to the Taiwan Shinto Shrine. It was 90 meters long. The surfaces of the bridge were steel reinforced concrete. In the center, the horse lane had a dividing island, and on either side were pedestrian walkways. The balustrades at either side showed a maple leaf design. At the end of the steel frame there could be found the first of the Shinto Temple's offering stations (similar to an entrance pylon). In 1930, the bridge was demolished and rebuilt; the second-generation steel-reinforced concrete bridge was an elegant, refined creation, with a solid frame, protective walls of granite, and coordinated bronze street light accessories. After World War II, it was renamed Chungshan Bridge. In 1968 it was rebuilt, and widened to its present condition.

昭和橋

今光復橋前身，爲跨越新店溪之搖柱式鋼構橋塔吊橋，橋長 367.8 公尺，寬 4.5 公尺，載重 10 公噸，昭和 8 年（西元 1933 年）8 月底竣工。此橋通車後，促使臺北與板橋之交通大開，加速板橋地區的發展與繁榮，也成爲海山郡（板橋、三峽、鶯歌等五街庄）門戶的代表。其橋塔與橋墩台的鉸接是一個力學的接觸點，橋側以加勁桁構加強橋面剛度，展現工程的力學之美。光復後於民國 48 年（西元 1959 年）將混凝土橋面全面翻修後，因主索銹蝕，民國 57 年 11 月後禁止大型車輛通行，於民國 66 年底完工，爲三孔預力混凝土斜張吊橋。

註 65、107、108

RH-121

Showa Bridge

The forerunner of today's Kuangfu Bridge, this steel suspension bridge crossed Hsintien River. It was 367.8 meters long and 4.5 meters wide, with a loading capacity of 10 tons. Construction was completed at the end of August, 1933. When this bridge opened to vehicles, it greatly assisted transportation between Taipei and Panchiao, thus helping the city to develop and flourish more quickly. The bridge became a symbol for the representatives of Haishan Township (Panchiao, Sanhsia, Yingke and other villages). The pivots between the bridge's towers and its bases and platforms form mechanical points of contact; the sides of the bridge are reinforced with bars which in turn increase the rigidity of the bridge surface, showing the mechanical beauty in its engineering. In 1959, the bridge's cement surface was completely replaced, because it was found that the major elements were rusted. Subsequently, after November 1968, large vehicles were prohibited from crossing the bridge. The end of 1977 saw the completion of work on the bridge, which had become a three-arch inclined plane suspension bridge made of prestressed cement.

濁水溪鐵橋

濁水溪鐵橋，在彰化、斗六兩廳（今彰化、雲林、南投三縣）交界，跨濁水溪（別稱虎尾溪、西螺溪），長 875 公尺，介於二水、林內兩站之間，爲縱貫鐵路通車初期最長的橋樑，於明治 39 年（西元 1906 年）完工，次年 6 月通車，較同形式的下淡水溪（高屏溪）鐵橋要早 33 年，明治 44 年（西元 1911 年）8 月曾遭颱洪沖毀。

註 34、66、137

明治末期的濁水溪鐵橋

Railway Bridge over Chuoshuei River during the Japanese era

RF-126

The Railway Bridge over Chuoshui River

The Railway Bridge over Chuoshui River was at the borders between Changhua and Touliu Prefectures (now Changhua, Yunlin and Nantou Counties). It crossed the Chuoshui River (also called Tiger Tail River and Hsilo River). It was 875 meters long, and ran between the two stops of Ershui and Linnei. In the early period of the long-distance railroad it was the longest bridge on the line. Work on the bridge was finished in 1906, and it was opened for use in June of the next year. It was built 33 years earlier than the similarly structured Railway Bridge at Lower Tanshui River (Kaoping River). In August of 1911, it was destroyed in flooding brought about by a typhoon.

西螺大橋

橫跨於台灣中部的濁水溪是南北交通的一大障礙。其於二水以下因進入平原，河面更寬達2～3公里。日治時期所開築的縱貫鐵路，特別自彰化偏向東南，經二水跨越濁水溪；縱貫公路則於集集築橋聯接竹山。二水以下則全賴渡船往來。

由於渡船載運量低、速度慢，更受暴雨影響，因此自日治時代起，總督府即擬於西螺與溪州之間築公路大橋，直至日本發動戰爭停止時，共築成橋墩30座與兩側河岸之橋臺。台灣光復後，地方上不斷要求築橋，及爲因應軍事與經濟之需求，同時美國恢復經援，省府經諮商獲美方同意資助鋼材，築橋工程遂重新開始。

民國39年(西元1950年)，西螺大橋工程委員會與工程處成立，分別由侯家源（省交通處長）、洪紳擔任主委及處長，美商懷特公司協助設計。總工程於民國41年12月25日完工，42年1月28日正式通車。通車當日觀禮民衆達十萬人(西螺鎮人口三萬)，西螺鎮則舉行提燈、煙火、戲劇、音樂、體育等長達三天的慶祝活動。

西螺大橋全長1939.1公尺，爲當時遠東第一長橋，並號稱爲僅次於美國舊金山金門大橋的公路橋。橋體採穿式桁樑設計，每孔跨距超過60公尺，在預力鋼樑混凝土橋樑技術發展成熟前常用於長跨距之橋樑（如縱貫鐵路山線之大安溪、大甲溪橋，屏東線鐵路之下淡水溪橋、以及舊台北大橋)，全橋共用鋼料5,300餘噸，大橋完成時漆成灰綠色，現改爲紅色。橋面淨寬7.32公尺，爲鋼筋混凝土，共用混凝土2,400立方公尺。除公路外，並舖設台糖之762㎜鐵路，使西部糖業鐵路網可經由台中通至屏東完全聯接，並且可作戰時爲縱貫鐵路之輔助。西螺大橋完工後使彰化王田至雲林斗南之間公路里程自99公里減至58公里。

整座大橋的鋼材總值149萬美元，由美國安全總署直接在美撥款訂購。造橋工程及其他材料則花費新台幣1,410萬元，其中310萬由省府自籌，餘額由安全分署自美援相對基金撥用（因而兩側橋頭均鐫有「中美合作」字樣之銘牌，今日猶存)。全部參與工程人員500餘人，在施工期間無死亡及重傷，當時政府頗以爲傲。

至民國60年代之後，台灣經濟起飛交通流量大增，民國64年，每日通過此橋之車輛平均爲6,949輛，此後每年並以20%成長率增加中；而因大橋之限高(4.3公尺)與限重(15公噸)，使大型貨櫃拖車無法通行，因此，政府於68年拆除台糖鐵路鐵軌，將大橋改爲純公路橋。

The Great Hsilo Bridge

Crossing central Taiwan's Chuoshui River is a major obstacle in north-south travel. Because everything downstream from Ershui opens up into a plain, the river broadens as wide as 2 to 3 kilometers.

The long-distance railroad constructed in the Japanese period veered off from Changhua at a southeast angle in order to cross the Chuoshui River at Ershui; the long-distance highway constructed a bridge at Chichi and crossed to Chushan. Any transportation downstream from Ershui was totally dependent on boat crossing.

Due to the low carrying capacity and speed of boat ferrying, and because of the disruptive influence of torrential rains, the government of the Japanese period decided to build a highway and bridge between Hsilo and Hsichou. When work was stopped due to the Japanese war effort, the construction of 30 buttresses and the two on-shore platforms had been completed. After Retrocession, there were endless demands for local bridge construction. So, in order to meet defense and economic requirements, and at the same time because the United States resumed economic aid, the Taiwan Provincial Government conferred and obtained American agreement to provide economic assistance and steel supplies, and the bridge construction experienced a renewed beginning.

In 1950, the Great Hsilo Bridge Construction Committee Engineering Office was established, with Hou Chia-yuan (the Head of the Provincial Transportation Office) and Hong Shen as Committee Chairman and Office Head, respectively. The American White Company assisted in the design. The entire project was completed on December 25, 1952, and the bridge officially opened to traffic on January 28, 1953. There were as many as 100,000 people in attendance to witness the ceremonies at the opening. (The population of Hsilo was 30,000.) Throughout a three-day cele bration, Hsilo Township held events such as lantern festivities, bonfires, dramatic and musical performances, and athletic competitions.

The Great Hsilo Bridge is 1,988 meters long overall; at that time it was the longest bridge in the Far East. Moreover, it was second only to the Golden Gate Bridge in San Francisco in the United States as a highway bridge. The design adapted comprised transecting bridge beams. Each arch spanned a distance of more than 60 meters. The prestressed steel reinforced concrete bridge beam technology achieved a mature development of what previously was a commonly used kind of bridge beam for spanning long distances (such as the Ta-an River and Tachia River Bridges on the mountain route of the long-distance railway, or the Lower Tanshui River Bridge on the Pingtung Railway line, or the old Great Taipei Bridge). In all, more than 5300 tons of steel girder were used in the bridge. When the great bridge was completed, it was entirely painted a gray-green color, which has since been changed to red. The 7.32 meter wide bridge surface is of steel-reinforced cement, using a total of 2400 cubic meters of concrete. Besides the highway, a 762-mm. railway line belonging to the Taiwan Sugar Production Company crossed the bridge, so that the railway network for the sugar industry in the western parts could go through Taichung and thereby to Pingtung, allowing for total interconnectivity. This is furthermore beneficial in providing a supplemental rail route to the long-distance railway, if needed for military use. After the work on the Great Hsilo Bridge was completed, the distance between Changhua County's Wangtien and Yunlin County's Tounan, as traveled on the highway, was reduced from 99 kilometers to 58 kilometers.

The overall cost of the steel materials for the bridge was valued at US$ 1,490,000; it was directly allocated by a United States securities office, and went directly from the allocation to the purchase. The other expenses for materials and engineering cost NT$ 14,100,000. Of that, NT$ 3, 100,000 was funded directly from the Provincial Government; the rest was covered by a branch securities office, handled by the American Cooperative Assistance Foundation. (Because of this, both ends of the bridge carry a metal placard on which is written Chinese and American Cooperation, which still is there today.) More than 500 workers participated in the project, yet no deaths or serious injuries took place during the construction period. This was a major source of pride for the government.

The 1970s saw rapid economic development in Taiwan, creating a greater traffic flow. In 1975, there was an average of 6,949 vehicles passing this bridge each day. Since then, such number was on the rise by 20% each year. However, due to the limit of height (4.3 meters) and weight (15 tons) imposed for the bridge, the bridge became off limits for large container cars. Therefore, the government torn down the rail track of Taiwan Sugar Company and converted the bridge into a pure highway bridge.

高雄大橋現址

日治時期高雄之「大橋」即爲今日橫跨愛河，連接前金區及鹽埕區的中正橋。這座橋是爲配合大橋通（今中正四路）的三線道工程而興建，於昭和 13 年（西元 1938 年）完工。

註 55

RH-122

圖爲日治時代之高雄大橋（今中正橋）

Kaohsiung Bridge (currently Chung Cheng Bridge) during the Japanese era

Present-day Location of the Kaohsiung Bridge

The Japanese-era Kaohsiung bridge is presently called the Chungcheng Bridge, which spans the Ai ("Love") River, connecting the districts of Chien-chin and Yencheng. The bridge was completed in 1938 (the 13th year of the Showa era), in conjunction with the expansion of Tachiao Road (present-day Chungcheng Shih Road) to three lanes.

屏東人的歷史記憶——
下淡水溪鐵橋

前身為大正 2 年(西元 1913 年)臺灣製糖會社第三(阿緱)工廠所架設之輕便軌道鐵橋，以利甘蔗原料搬運及旅客交通，長度達 1525 公尺，其長度超過日本境內任何一座橋樑。此橋於昭和 14 年（西元 1939 年）建造，耗資 130 萬日圓，為一座造型優美的「花樑桁架橋」。橋長 1700.4 公尺，寬 7.5 公尺，由 24 節鋼桁架組成，鋼樑皆由日本製造運臺安裝，在西螺大橋完成前為本島第一長橋，仍係臺糖鐵路與公路的（省道臺一線高雄屏東間）共同橋樑。此橋完工後，台灣縱貫鐵路南端終點便自九曲堂延伸至屏東市；昭和 16 年(西元 1941 年)，延伸至枋寮。近來為適應交通需要，在下游 200 公尺處另建新的下淡水溪橋（高屏大橋），民國 67 年（西元 1978 年）10 月完工。民國 76 年 4 月新雙線高屏溪橋竣工，民國 78 年 6 月高屏間鐵路雙軌化通車，舊鐵橋雖停用，因富有歷史價值仍保留未拆。

註 65、66、70、106、107、108、115、137

RH-123

The Historical Memories of the Pingtung People ——

The Railway Bridge over the Lower Tanshui River

The forerunner of this bridge, was a light gauge rail line, built in 1913 for the Taiwan Sugar Processing Company's Factory# 3 (Ahou). The light rail was suited for the transport of sugar cane materials and visiting travelers. Its length was 1,525 meters, which surpassed the longest bridge within Japan proper. The bridge was built in 1939, at a cost of 1,300,000 yen, and was a lovely example of decorative girder bridge construction. This bridge was 1700.4 meters long and 7.5 meters wide, and composed of 24 steel girders. The beams were all manufactured in Japan and transported to Taiwan for installation. Before the completion of the Great Hsilo Bridge, this was the longest bridge on the island, and is still a bridge combining railroad and highway (Provincial Highway One between Kaohsiung and Pingtung). After the completion of the bridge, the last stop at the southern terminus of the long-distance railway was extended from Chiuchutang to Pingtung, and in 1941 was further extended to Fangliao.

In recent times, a new bridge (Kaoping Bridge) over Lower Tanshuei River was established some 200 meters away in the downstream area in October, 1978 to accommodate transportation needs. In April, 1987, construction of a new double-track railway bridge over Kaoping Creek was completed, and in June, 1989, the double-track rail line between Kaohsiung and Pingtung began operation. Although the old railway bridge stopped operation, it has not been demolished due to its historic signficance.

下淡水溪上的新橋
The New Bridge over the Lower Tanshui River

高屏鐵路雙軌工程爲台灣 14 項建設之一，而以「新雙線高屏溪橋」的工程最爲艱鉅。「新橋」連接高屏溪（昔稱下淡水溪）兩岸的九曲堂與六塊厝，全橋於 74 年 6 月 4 日完工，同年 6 月 17 日切換單線，22 日正式雙線通車，取代原舊橋之工作。

Construction of the double-gauge railroad between Kaohsiung and Pingtung was one of the 14 public works projects in Taiwan. Its most difficult component was the New Double Line Kaoping River Bridge. The new bridge linked Chiuchutang and Liukuaitsu on the two banks of the Kaoping River (formerly called the Lower Tanshui River). The entire bridge was complete on June 4, 1985, and opened one lane on June 17, officially opening both lanes on June 22 of the same year, thus replacing the work on the original old bridge.

鵝鑾鼻燈塔百年風霜

清末時期，鵝鑾鼻附近海域常有船隻觸礁沈没，因此各國籲請清廷設立燈塔。光緒元年（西元 1875 年），清海關開始在鵝鑾鼻籌建燈塔，至光緒 8 年（西元 1882 年）完成。此座燈塔由英國技師所設計，共耗銀 40 餘萬兩；塔身爲白色鐵造，裝置一等定光五蕊煤油燈，500 支燭光，向七星礁方向射紅色弧示警。另外爲防原住民侵擾，燈塔建築成砲壘形式，以塔基作爲砲台，圍牆上設有槍眼，牆外設有壕溝，並置槍械自衛，甚至派兵守衛多年。西元 1895 年甲午戰爭時，燈塔遭清殘兵縱火燒毀。

日人治台後，於明治 30 年（西元 1897 年）開始重修燈塔，翌年 5 月燈塔再度啓用。明治 43 年（西元 1910 年）改裝煤油白熱燈，光力增強至 2 萬 6 千支燭光，高五丈九尺，光達距離二十三里，當時爲東洋第一燈塔；至昭和 6 年（西元 1931 年）時改爲頓光燈。

日治時期，鵝鑾鼻燈塔被列爲台灣八景之一，第二次世界大戰末期，曾遭盟軍飛機所炸毀。

光復後，於民國 36 年（西元 1947 年）經海關改修，暫裝六等電石氣閃光燈，每 4 秒一閃，翌年改裝五等直流電閃光燈器，又次年改閃光時間爲每 10 秒一閃，仍爲白光，光力 3 千支燭光。民國 51 年燈塔改建，塔頂換裝新式大型四等旋轉透鏡電燈，每 10 秒一閃，光力高達 180 萬支燭光，是台灣目前光力最強的燈塔。

註 71、145、154、158、159、160

The 100-Year History of the Oluanpi Lighthouse

During the late Ching Dynasty, boats often ran aground on the Hengchun Peninsula and sank. Therefore, many countries repeatedly asked the Ching government to set up a lighthouse. In 1875, the Ching customs service began to make plans for the construction of the Oluanpi lighthouse. It was completed in 1882. This lighthouse was designed by English engineers, costing more than 400,000 taels.

The main structure of the lighthouse was built of iron and painted white. Inside the lighthouse was equipped with class-one, five- stemmed kerosene lamps, emitting 500 candlepower of light, signaling red warning lights out in the direction of the Chihsing Reef. Furthermore, in order to prevent the aborigines from invading, the lighthouse was built in the shape of a fortress, with the foundation built as a turret. Gun holes were built in the walls, and a trench was dug around the walls. For many years, the Ching Dynasty not only equipped the lighthouse with weaponry, but also deployed guards here. In 1895 during the Sino-Japanese War, the lighthouse was burnt down by the departing Ching soldiers.

After Japan took over Taiwan, the Japanese began to renovate the lighthouse starting in 1897. The lighthouse was again in use in May of the following year. In 1910, the lighthouse was re-equipped with white kerosene lamps, increased to a candlepower of 26,000. In 1931, it was upgraded with incandescent light.

During the era of Japanese rule, the Oluanpi Lighthouse was listed as one of the Eight Vistas of Taiwan. At the end of War World Two, the lighthouse was destroyed by allied fighter planes.

After World War Two, the customs service began to fix up the lighthouse in 1947, temporarily installing acetylene lamps, which flashed every four seconds. The following year, it was equipped with five direct-current electric flashing lamps. Then, in 1949, it was changed to flash once every ten seconds, with a luminosity of 3000 candlepower. In 1962, the whole lighthouse underwent renovation. The top of the lighthouse was replaced with a large four-tiered rotating mirrored lamp, flashing once every ten seconds. Its light power was 1.8 million candlepower, making it the most powerful lighthouse in Taiwan.

RH-124

日治時期所攝鵝鑾鼻燈塔

Oluanpi Lighthouse during the Japanese era.

富貴角燈塔
Fukui Point Lighthouse

這座燈塔是台灣最北端燈塔，原稱爲富基角燈塔，建材全由日本船運來台，明治30年(1897)完工，是一座八角形的鐵塔，裝有二等三重芯煤油燈。明治44年改裝煤油白熱燈，光力增強。昭和2年(1927)改稱富貴角燈塔。昭和5年換裝白色頓光電燈。二次大戰時受到轟炸受損，塔身也銹蝕腐壞。到了民國43年(1954)拆除，暫設方形鋼架塔代替。民國51年改建爲八角形混凝土塔，裝置小型三等旋轉透鏡電燈。

註71

Located at the northern tip of Taiwan, the lighthouse was originally called Fuchi Point Lighthouse, with the entire construction materials shipped from Japan. Construction of this lighthouse, featuring a steel-frame octagon with a class-two triple-wick kerosene lamp, was completed in 1897. In 1930, a white dioptric lamp was installed. The lighthouse was bombed and damaged during World War II, and the structure was seriously eroded. In 1954, the lighthouse was demolished and temporarily replaced by a square steel tower. In 1962, the tower was reconstructed as an octagonal concrete tower equipped with a small class-three revolving prism electrical lamp.

彭佳嶼燈塔
Pengchiayu Lighthouse

這座燈塔位於彭佳嶼島上，是目前台灣區海拔最高的燈塔。自明治39年(1906)開始建造，因爲製造廠交貨延遲，冬季時東北季風強盛而受到阻礙，延至明治42年才建造完成。在建造期間曾設有臨時燈桿，到建設好後才拆除。燈塔是圓形磚造，裝有白熱石油燈，並設有霧砲。 註71

Located on Pengchiayu Isle, the lighthouse has a higher elevation than other lighthouses in Taiwan. The construction of the lighthouse began in 1906 and was not completed until 1909, due to shipping delivery by the manufacturer and to the strong northeasterly seasonal winds in the winter. A makeshift lamppost was erected during the construction period and was removed following the completion of the lighthouse. With a circular masonry structure, the lighthouse was equipped with an incandescent oil lamp and fog beacons.

高雄燈塔的歷史背景

高雄燈塔位於旗津區旗後山頂。清咸豐8年（西元1858年）天津條約訂定後，開放打狗港，船舶商務的往來便日趨頻繁，爲了行船的安全起見，同治年間即有興建燈塔的提議，直至光緒9年（西元1883年）才由鳳山副將王福祿聘英籍技師著手興建此一燈塔，由海關籌設兼管。此燈塔原爲方形磚造，兼負有觀測氣象之任務，大正7年（西元1918年）日人將其改建爲白色上端圓柱，下端八角形之燈塔，高11公尺，光度爲94,000燭光，照射距離可達20.5浬，爲外海明顯的導航目標。今列爲三級古蹟。

註54

RH-125

至今有114年歷史的三級古蹟——高雄燈塔

Kaohsiung Lighthouse- a class-three historic site with a history of 114 years

The Historical Background of Kaohsiung Lighthouse

The Kaohsiung Lighthouse is located on the hilltop behind Chichin. After the Tienchin Treaty was signed in 1858, Kaohsiung harbor (then called Takou, or Beating the Dog) was opened up. The exchanges between commercial boats became ever more frequent. To ensure the safety of the boats, there were appeals for building up a lighthouse during the Tungchi reign of the Ching Dynasty. But not until 1883 was an English engineer employed by the deputy commander Wang Fu-lu to initiate the construction. The customs took charge of monitoring the assembly and management of the lighthouse. This square-shaped lighthouse was built with bricks, and it also shared the duty of meteorological observation. In 1918, the Japanese changed the upper part of the lighthouse into a white cylinder, and the lower part into an octagon. The whole construction was 11 meters high, its light power 94,000 watts. As an obvious directional target, its lighting spread an area of 20.5 nautical miles. Nowadays, it has been categorized as a Grade 3 historical landmark.

西嶼燈塔(漁翁島燈塔)
West Isle Lighthouse (Fisherman Isle Lighthouse)

西嶼燈塔位於澎湖漁翁島南端，光緒元年(1875)改建成全台第一座西式燈塔，使用煤油照明，有宿舍派人駐守，並改稱「漁翁島燈塔」。大正4年(1915)，改建成現存的規模，並改用電石氣閃光燈。昭和13年(1938)，改用煤油白熱燈。二次大戰間遭美軍攻擊，略有受損，戰後隨即修復完畢。民國55年(1966)，改裝四等旋轉透鏡交流電燈，光力增強。現在被列爲國家第二級古蹟。

註71、90、132、135

Located at Wanjentuipi in Keelung Harbor and established in 1900, the lighthouse is a masonry circular tower with a white and iridescent kerosene arc lamp. Later, the lighting device was replaced by an acetylene lamp in 1913. Subsequently, the lighting device was replaced in 1932 by an AC electrical lamp, in 1956 by a white-red flash lamp, and in 1969 by a class-four electrical bulb (containing enhanced illuminative power). In 1989, the red light of the lighthouse was changed into white light. The original red arc of Keelung Lighthouse which was used to mark the location of Hsinta Reef off the harbor was removed in 1989 after the reef was blasted and removed.

基隆燈塔
Keelung Lighthouse

此燈塔位在基隆港口萬人堆鼻，明治33年(1900)建成，是一座磚砌圓形燈塔。原裝白紅定光煤油燈，大正2年(1913)改用電石氣燈。昭和7年(1932)改裝交流電燈。民國45年(1956)換成白紅連閃光電燈。民國58年改用四等電燈，光力增強。民國78年將紅光改爲白光。基隆燈塔原置有紅色光弧，用來標示港外新瀨暗礁位置，民國78年炸去暗礁後撤除。

註71

West Isle Lighthouse was located in southern Fisherman Isle of Penghu. In 1875, the lighthouse, which was renamed Fisherman Isle Lighthouse, was reconstructed as the first Western-style lighthouse, employing kerosene illumination. Also, living quarters were built to accommodate lighthouse personnel. In 1915, the lighthouse was reconstructed at its current scale, and the lighting device became an incandescent flash lamp. In 1938, the lamp was replaced by a incandescent kerosene lamp. During World War II, the lighthouse was attacked and damaged by US forces. In 1966, the lighthouse was equipped with a class-four revolving prism AC lamp, which offered more illuminative power. The lighthouse is currently designated as a class-two historic site.

日治時期的都市公園

City Parks during the Japanese Era

日治時期，日人在台建設的公園可分為兩大類：一為都市公園；二為國家公園。都市公園為近一、二百年西方都市文明急速發展後的產物，後來逐漸納入現代化的都市計劃之中。日人自明治維新後，受西方文化影響漸深，一心追求現代化，於是都市公園設施的興建便與日人在台的現代都市計劃之間有著密切的關係，一方面提供市民休閒、娛樂的公共場所；一方面綠化城市，改善都市景觀；然而潛在的意涵則是標誌著都市的現代文明性，以顯示日人統治所帶來的進步。

日人在台的公園設施以明治 31 年（西元 1898 年）時所建的台北圓山公園為最早，至昭和 9 年（西元 1934 年）時，全台已有 23 座主要的公園。以台北市為例，日治時期原本預定的公園達 17 處，面積約占 388 公頃，加上原有的公園面積約 49 公頃，合計 437 公頃，約占市區計劃利用面積的 9%，再加上計劃建設的兒童遊樂園、廣場及小公園，則可達 10%。

註 124、157、162

During the period of Japanese occupation, there were two major types of parks established by Japanese in Taiwan: one kind was the urban park, and the other kind was the national park. Urban parks are the product of the rapid development over the past one or two hundred years in Western urban civilizations. Subsequently, they have gradually entered into city-planning schemes for modernization. From the time of the Meiji Restoration, which was deeply influenced by Western culture, and whole-heartedly pursued modernization, the establishment of urban parks had an ever more intimate relationship to modern city-planning by Japanese people on Taiwan: On the one hand, it provided city dwellers with a place for rest and recreation, and enjoyment of the city; on the other hand, it made cities green and improved their appearance. Nonetheless, mixed in with these concepts was the idea of furnishing an indicator of the city's modern civilization, in order to show the progress that Japanese rule had brought with it.

Japanese people on Taiwan first started providing parks in Taiwan in 1898, with the Taipei Yuanshan Park. By 1934, there were already 23 major parks. Taking Taipei as an example, during the Japanese period, there were originally 17 parks planned, with a total area of about 388 hectares. With the already existing park area of 49 hectares, the total increased to 437 hectares, almost 9% of the area of the entire city as planned. With the Children's Park, public square, and small parks as planned, the percentage increased to 10%.

造園計劃 北、中、南
Park Projects in Northern, Central and Southern Taiwan

台北新公園：新公園係明治32年(西元1899年)台北市區改易時所開闢，總面積23,664坪，原名台北公園，因晚於圓山公園，故稱新公園以區別。其地點適中，林蔭濃密，是市中心納涼散心的好場所。近來因國內政治環境的變化，為撫平二二八事件受難家屬心靈創痛，消弭族群對立情結，選定公園內興建紀念碑，於去年（西元1995年）事件居滿四十八年之際落成，今年，台北市政府甫將之易名為二二八和平公園。

註2、65、66、68、72、115、126

Taipei New Park: With a total area of 23,664 *ping*, New Park was originally named Taipei Park and was established in 1899 during the repartitioning of the city areas of Taipei. The park got its name because its establishment was predated by Yuanshan Park. It is a nice place where people can enjoy the shade and take a walk, thanks to its bushy trees and appropriate geographical location. Due to changes to the political climate in Taiwan in recent times, a monument was erected to rectify the pain suffered by families of victims killed during the February 28 Incident and to ease ethnic confrontation. The monument was erected in 1995, 48 years after the incident. In 1996, the Taipei City Government renamed the park the February 28 Peace Park.

RH-127

圖下方為公園西側的水池、小橋景致；右上總督府前為公園旁（現懷寧街）之二層建築物；左上為已移置園內之急公好義石坊。

In the lower section of the picture is the scene of a pool and a small bridge in the western section of the park. In the upper right is a two-story structure beside the park (Huaining Street today) and in front of the Taiwan Governor's Office. In the upper left is the Stele of Generous Deeds, which was moved inside the park.

RH-128

圖左為博物館後方軸線上樹立之後藤新平立像（二二八和平紀念碑現址），此像正南、東北尚有第四任總督兒玉源太郎戎裝騎馬石像、臺灣銀行首任頭取（董事長）柳生之半身銅像，戰後已悉被拆除。後藤新平立像基座後來改為鐘塔，直至 1995 年，為改建二二八和平紀念碑而拆除。

Behind the museum in the left of the picture is the statute of Goto Shinbei (currently in its place is the February 28 Incident Monument). In the south and northeast were stone statues of Kodama Gentaro, the fourth governor of Taiwan during the Japanese era, in military uniform on horseback, and a half-length bronze statue of Yanaiki, the first Chairman of Taiwan Bank. These statues were demolished after World War II. The foundation of the statue of Goto Shinbei was reconstructed as a clock tower, which was demolished in 1995 for the construction of the February 28 Incident Monument.

由博物館後側左望西南方，由近而遠依次（由左自右）爲圓形水池、露天的音樂台、總督府。

This picture presents a scene viewed from the left from behind the museum in the northwest. In this picture, there is a round pool in the foreground, an outdoor stage for musical performances in the middle, and the Taiwan Governor's Office in the distance.

RH-129

RH-130

昭和 10 年(西元 1935 年)所攝圓形音樂台及露天座位，時音樂台爲木造八角尖頂。遠處爲臺大醫院。左上係該院位於中山南路旁之焚化爐煙囪。

Taken in 1935, this picture shows a circular musical stage with a wooden octagonal roof and outdoor seats. In the distance is the National Taiwan University Hospital, and in the upper left is the chimney of the hospital incinerator located on Chungshan South Road.

台中公園：日治時期台中闢有公園二處，即今日的中山公園及體育場（即一號公園），日人對台中公園（昔稱）的規劃是和台中市的發展密不可分的，當時日人引進歐美都市計劃概念，企圖將台中市築成台灣第一個棋盤型街道城市，以台中公園作爲台中市之中心，當時台中市區內每條道路的開闢都是以台中公園内小丘上的石墩爲起點，進行測量。公園始建於1903年，初建於舊市區東方，並由台中地方士紳籌募經費擇定建地，並將北門城樓「明遠樓」移建於大敦之上（今易名爲望月亭），至同年10月28日建成，佔地28883坪。5年後日人又委託「櫻井」建築商設計一座亭閣，即今中正亭（原名湖心亭），爲園景之中樞，同時也成爲台中市象徵性的地景。明治41年縱貫鐵路通車慶祝典禮，特擇於台中公園舉行。

公園設立初年之主要設施包括：昭忠牌、兒玉將軍像、池亭、後藤新平像、猿檻及動物小屋並廣植樹木等。整座公園之規劃甚具現代性，不但具有休閒、娛樂、賞景的價值，更具有涵養水源及保存古蹟之功能。

台中公園即今日之台中市中山公園。原爲橋仔頭望族林家的花園，於明治36年（西元1903年）闢建成公園，佔地14餘公頃。公園大門左方有一砲台山，山上有望月亭，左側爲舊時北門樓的遺址。園內另有一日月湖，湖上建有長橋與湖心之小島相通，島上尚有一座湖心亭（今名中正亭），供人休憩賞景。

註29、113、122、127、156

圖爲日治時代的台中公園　RH-136

Taichung Park during the Japanese era.

Taichung Park: During the Japanese era, there were two parks in Taichung, one in today's Chungshan Park, the other in the Stadium (or No. 1 Park). Japan's planning for Taichung Park (previous name) was closely integrated with the development of Taichung City. During that time, the Japanese intended to develop Taichung city as the first city with road grids by introducing Western concepts of urban planning. Taichung Park was treated as the center of Taichung City. The development of each road within the city began with measurement from a stone podium on the small hill of Taichung Park. Established in 1903, Taichung Park was located in the east side of the old city area. The local gentry raised a fund for the acquisition of the land, and the Mingyuan Lou, the gate tower of North Gate, was moved to Tatun (which is called Moon Gazing Pavilion today). Construction of the park, covering an area of 28,883 "pings" (95,478 square meters), was completed on October 28 of the same year. Five years later, the Japanese retained Sakurai Construction Co. to design a pavilion, which is Chung Cheng Pavilion today (previously called Huhsin Pavilion). The centerpiece of the landscape of Taichung Park, the pavilion also became a landmark for Taichung City. The initiation ceremony for north-south railway in the 48th year of the Meiji period was held in Taichung Park.

Major facilities of the park in the beginning included Japanese a statue of General Gentaro, pavilions, a statue of Goto Shinbei, monkey cages and animal houses, along with extensive plantation of trees. Created on the basis of modern planning, the park was good for recreation, entertainment and appreciation, as well as for conservation of water and preservation of historic relics.

The Taichung Garden of the Japanese era is the present-day Chungshan Park in Taichung City. Originally the private garden of the prestigious Lin family in Chiaotzaitou, the garden occupied more than 14 hectares of land and was converted into a public park in 1903. To the left of the garden's main gate was a hill, on which stood the remnants of the former Peimen Pavilion. Another attraction within the garden was a pavilion (present-day Chungcheng Pavilion) built on an islet in the middle of Sun Moon Lagoon.

台南公園：即今日的台南中山公園，爲大正 6 年（西元 1917 年），台南都市改正計劃下的產物，規模比台北公園、台中公園略小，只有 14.63 公頃，爲台南市最大的森林公園，是台南市最重要的開放空間之一。園區內尚有一燕潭在東，南爲叢林，碧綠蒼翠。大正初年園區增廣後，將原有的台南府城大北門遺址及附近城垣遺址納入。乙未割台前公園僅有東區（即燕潭），而潭北高台爲刑場，日人擴大園區範圍加建亭榭園景並廣植樹林，奇花異卉至今仍保有大部分全貌，爲台灣各大都市中容貌最完整者。

台南公園闢建四年完工，位於當時的北門町，園內除池塘古蹟外，尚有噴水池、運動場、招魂碑及小動物園等設施，西元 1930 年時總面積尚有 45000 坪，其林泉園池加上常綠闊葉林頗具南台灣風情，台南公園的設計結構乃配合台南市的都市計劃，爲日人巧心佈置的城市「綠帶」。

註 31、113、127、131、156

RH-137

Tainan Park: Established in 1917, Tainan Park, which is Chung Shan Park today, was a product of Tainan's urban development plans. With an area of 14.63 hectares, the park was smaller than Taipei Park and Taichung Park. Yet, it was the largest forest park and the most important open space in Tainan City. In the east part of the park was Yen Pool, and in the south were dense woods with beautiful green trees. In the early years of the Taisho period, the park was expanded to include the relics of Large North Gate and of other fort walls in the vicinity. Before Taiwan was ceded to Japan, the scope of the park was limited to the eastern section. The stage in the northern section was an execution site. The Japanese expanded the park with additional pavilions, landscapes, and trees and flowers, most of which survive today. Compared with other parks in Taiwan, Tainan Park preserves the most complete appearance of Japanese creation.

Located in Located in the peiman District of the era, Tainan Park, whose expansion took four years, featured pools, water fountains, playing fields, a spirit-conjuring tablet, and a small zoo. In 1930, the total area of the park was 45,000 *pings* (148,756 square meters). The trees, gardens and pools in the park, along with the broad-leaved forest, reflected the culture of southern Taiwan. The design of the park was conducted to accommodate the urban planning of Tainan, and the park was an elegant "green belt" of the city created by the Japanese.

圖爲日治時代的台南公園 RH-131

Tainan Park during the Japanese era.

南國情調——台北植物園

植物園位於日治時期南門町（今南海路），面積 52000 坪，其前身爲臺北苗圃，明治 29 年（西元 1896 年）1 月開始經營，最初設於小南門外，其間曾遷大龍峒、圓山兩地，明治 33 年購得植物園現址土地，實驗栽培本島森林固有之林木及國外樹種，明治 44 年改稱林業試驗所，附屬於總督府民政部殖產局，專事本島林業調查及研究工作。園內遍植喬木、灌木一千餘種，池沼水閣穿插其間，頗有林泉之勝，園內當時尚建有商品陳列館（戰後改設歷史博物館，並經改建）、建功神社、武德殿等建築，園宏境靜，遊人如織。圖爲高大的椰子樹林及各種熱帶苗木所呈現的南國情調。今以科學館、藝術館、教育資料館等文教機構林立，有南海學園之稱。

註 2、65、114、125、137

日治時代的台北植物園

RH-133

Taipei Botanical Garden during the Japanese era.

The Tropical Atmosphere--Taipei Botanical Gardens

The Botanical Gardens on South Gate Street (currently Nanhai Road), with an area of 312,000 square feet, formerly was Taipei Nursery.

In January 1896, it began operation. At the beginning it was designed to be at the outside of the small southern gate, but it also moved to Talungtung and Yuanshan. In 1900 the land at the present Botanical Gardens was purchased, as an area for experimental cultivation of forestry species native and non-native to the island. In 1910, the name was changed to Forestry Experimentation Institute, and was affiliated to the General Government Bureau of Civil Government, Office of Cultivation and Production; it specialized in survey and research work for the forestry industry on the island. The park was filled with more than a thousand types of trees and shrubs, and there was a pond in the midst of them. It was a splendid setting of vegetation and water.

At the time, an exhibition hall for merchandise was in the park (after the war, with some rebuilding, this became the Museum of History), as well as a Shinto shrine, a military shrine, and other buildings. The park was large and its surroundings were quiet; it attracted many visitors. The tropical atmosphere was brought about by the very large palm tree grove and all kinds of tropical plants.

Nowadays, with cultural resource agencies such as the Science Hall, Hall of Arts, and Educational Materials Hall, it is called the Nanhai Park of Learning.

史前貝塚滄海桑田
——圓山公園的變遷

Prehistoric Shell Mound at Yuanshan Park —— Dramatic Changes over the Ages

圓山爲一獨立小丘，舊名龍峒山，位在基隆河左岸（南岸），與劍潭山隔河相對，有史前文化貝塚遺址，清咸豐舉人陳維英別墅「太古巢」所在。圓山公園（今中山北路三段）闢於明治 29 年（西元 1896 年），較新公園（今二二八和平公園）早三年，爲臺北市最早開闢的公園，其地偎山面水，境頗幽雅。昭和初年在園内增設玩樂機具，面積 4.88 公頃，成爲兒童之休閒娛樂中心天地。昭和 7 年（西元 1932 年）3 月公告大臺北市區計畫，此範圍成爲一號公園預定地，面積約占 19.9 公頃，包括動物園、兒童樂園、圓山運動場在内。戰後改稱中山公園，近年動物園遷移後整建爲臺北市立兒童育樂中心。圖左爲明治橋（今中山橋），其右側基隆河對岸即圓山公園。

註 2、12、15、53、65、68、121、126、137

Yuanshan is a little hill standing off alone by itself. Its former name is Lungtung Mountain. It is located on the left (south) shore of the Keelung River, and stands across from Chiantan Mountain on the other side of the river. Prehistoric shell mound remains are located here. This is the location of the great Ching *chujen* scholar Chen Hsiung-ying's villa, Taikuchao. The Yuanshan Park (presently at the third section of Chungshan North Road) opened in 1896, three years earlier than the New Park (presently the February 28 Peace Park); it was the first park in Taipei to be opened. This site abuts the mountains and looks out on water, so it is a rather elegant vista. In the 1920's some entertaining attractions were added in the park, which had an area of 4.88 hectares, and became the Children's Recreational Paradise. In March, 1932, the greater Taipei city-planning project was announced, and this area was designated as the number one park area, with an area of around 19.9 hectares. It included a zoo, a children's recreational park and the Yuanshan sports arena. After the war, it was renamed Chungshan Park. In recent years after the zoo moved, this area has been redesigned as the Taipei City Children's Recreational Center. The illustration shows the Meiji Bridge (now the Chungshan Bridge) at the left, and on the right is the Yuanshan Park on the other side of the Keelung River.

RH-134

日治時代遠眺台北圓山公園

Yuanshan Park in the distance during the Japanese era.

由私營改爲官營
—圓山動物園
Yuanshan Zoo
—— From Private to Public

臺灣第一座動物園創於大正3年（西元1914年）4月，爲日本人大江氏所興設之民營小型動物園，次年5月，臺北廳爲紀念大正天皇即位，收購大江的動物園加以充實，改爲官營圓山動物園，並配合總督府慶祝治臺始政20年舉辦的臺灣勸業共進會活動，於大正5年4月20日正式開幕，大正9年實施市制，翌年定名爲臺北市動物園。該園面積13745坪，除豢養臺灣本地所產動物，並網羅各國珍禽異獸之外，因氣候關係，園內多飼養熱帶動物。

註2、15、53、66、67、125、126

The first zoo in Taiwan was created in April 1914. A small, privately run zoo, it was conceived and executed by a Japanese man, Mr. Oe. In May of the next year, in order to commemorate the Taisho Emperor's accession to the throne, the Taipei City Government purchased Mr. Oe's zoo and expanded it, changing it to an officially run zoo, and in cooperation with activities celebrating the 20th anniversary of rule over Taiwan organized by the General Government's, in conjunction with the Taiwan Kangyo bank, on April 20, 1916, official opening ceremonies were held. Municipal government management began in 1920, and the next year the name changed to Taipei City Zoo. This zoo's area covered 82,470 square feet. Besides keeping animals native to Taiwan, it also collected rare animals from other countries. Because of the weather, mostly tropical animals were collected.

RH-135

鵜鶘，也叫「淘河」，是一種捕食魚類的水鳥，羽毛呈灰白色、嘴長，牠的脖子下面有一個大喉囊。

With ash-gray feathers, a long bill and a large pouch under the jowl, pelicans are waterfowl that feed on fish.

中正橋畔的風光霽月

Chungcheng Bridge with a Clear Landscape

川端橋即今台北中正橋，沿岸爲川端公園，接連臺北競馬場及臺北農場（川端苗圃、第一苗圃），昔時周遭極爲幽靜，山明水秀。明治 43 年（西元 1910 年）即在河域設天然游泳場，並可划船，圖右即租船帳篷，戰後盛況仍不遜於基隆或淡水之海水浴場。昭和年間臺北市役所（市政府）所主辦的花火（煙火）大會，即在川端町紀州庵前施放。圖爲川端橋東端朝上游方向南望所見景色。

註 2、12、13、15、47、65、108、125

Chuantuan Bridge is presently known as Chungcheng Bridge. Along the shores of the river was the Chuantuan Park, which was adjacent to the Taipei Horse Racing Track and the Taipei Farm (Chuantuan Nursery, First Nursery). In the past this was an area of exceeding loveliness wherever one looked, with clear mountains and clean water. In 1910 a swimming area was provided in the river area, and also a place for boating. At the right in the illustration one can see the tent where boat rentals were offered. After the war, this was still a nicer spot than the seaside swimming areas at Tanshui and Keelung. From the 1920's on, the Taipei Municipal Government sponsored Fire Festivals, which were held in the streets around Chuantuan. The illustration shows the scenery looking south and upstream from the eastern end of the Chuantuan Bridge.

圖爲日治時代的川端公園

RH-138

Chuantuan park during the Japanese era.

北投公園

即今新北投公園，明治44年（西元1911年）開闢，位在原鐵路淡水支線新北投火車站的正前方。北投公園依山勢建構而成，內有噴泉，園北端有北投溫瀑，頗富自然野趣，圖爲園內圓形噴泉水池附近景觀。

註51、65、66、125

RH-139

日治時代的北投公園

Peitou Park during the Japanese era.

Peitou Park

This is presently New Peitou Park. Located right in front of the New Peitou Train Station on the original railroad's Tanshui branch line, it was opened in 1911. The Peitou Park was constructed to fit the contours of the mountain. There was a fountain in the park, and in its northern reaches there were the Peitou hot springs. It is an interesting, natural park. The illustration shows the scenery in the park near the round fountain and pool.

彰化公園

彰化公園位在彰化市楠町（今卦山里縣立文化中心、縣議會一帶），面積約40025坪，大正初年由彰化舊城所改，包括東門外八卦山麓，光復後改稱中山公園。圖爲公園內彰化神社鳥居前園林蒼翠、蓮塘曲折的景致，環境靜幽、綠樹成蔭。

註2、65、66

日治時代的彰化公園

RH-140

Changhua Park during the Japanese era.

Changhua Park

Changhua Park was located at Nanmachi (presently in the vicinity of the Kuashanli County Cultural Center and the County Assembly) in Changhua City and had an area of around 240,150 square feet. It was built in 1911 by old Changhua City, and comprised the foothills of Pakua Mountain outside the East Gate. After Retrocession, the name was changed to Chungshan Park. The illustration shows the green area near the torii (gateways) of Changhua Shinto Shrine in front of the park, with a lotus pool winding through the elegant setting. The scene is serene, with many green, shady trees.

日治時期 鼓山公園規劃

Kushan Park during the Japanese Era

鼓山公園（今日的中山公園），位在高雄縣旗山鎮，和其他的公園最大的不同在於它並未位居市中心或火車站，主要是因高雄港的修築而改變了市中心區位。

鼓山公園的地形特殊、風景幽美，位在楠梓仙溪右岸，旗山街市之西，與旗尾山隔溪遙相對峙，而因山形似大鼓故名「鼓山」。此公園符合日治時期建築公園中大公園的特色，不但符合普通公園——即市民遊樂休閒場所的特色，亦兼有古蹟保存的功能（園內有清代「同志赴義」古碑，爲閩粵之間從械鬥到合作留下見證），更具有大公園中特殊公園的部分性質，如擁有美麗的自然景觀和生態環境。鼓山公園依山勢而規劃爲五層，從第四平台的涼亭旁可至最高點的「鼓山頂」，俯瞰旗山市街與對岸旗尾連峰。

日人規劃此公園乃爲配合對高雄港及高雄市的都市設計，遂以完整而氣勢開闊的手法建立此大型公園，爲空前之大手筆，日治之前原址儘爲「鼓山塚」即蕃薯寮居民墓地，足見統治者的氣勢，顯然壓過根深的民風。

Unlike other parks, the Kushan Park (present-day Chungshan Park), located in Chishan Town, Kaohsiung County, was not built in the city center nor near a train station. This was mainly due to the construction of the Kaohsiung Harbor, which altered the location of the city's central district.

The scenic Kushan Park is located left of the Tzehsinghsien River and to the west of Chishan Street. Across the river is the Chiwei Mountain, which, when seen from afar, looks like a drum, and hence the name Kushan (literally, "Drum Mountain"). Kushan Park was built in accordance with the architectural styles of the Japanese era; not only did it provide a recreation spot for local residents, it also served to preserve historical relics. A stone tablet from the Ching Dynasty may be found inside the park, which was erected as a testimony to the peaceful co-existence between the peoples on Taiwan from Fujian and Guandong provinces on the island. In addition to its recreational and historical benefits, the park also featured beautiful scenery and fascinating wildlife. The park is divided into five stories laid out along the Kushan mountain slopes. The entire Chishan city and the peak of Chiwei Mountain across the river may be seem from the peak of Kushan, which is accessible from the park's forth terrace.

During the Japanese era, the construction of the park was planned in conjunction with the urban planning requirements of Kaohsiung City and the development of the Kaohsiung Harbor. The scale of the construction was unprecedented. Prior to the construction, the mountain served as burial grounds for the residents of Fanshuliao.

澎湖公園及松島事件

日本人對松島艦有特殊的歷史情感，緣於明治 28 年（西元 1895 年）日本在中日馬關條約尚未議定之際，即先行派遣以松島艦爲主力艦之艦隊，自澎湖良文港（今湖西鄉龍門港）登陸，爲日本佔領澎湖之開路先鋒。其後在明治 41 年（西元 1908 年）4 月 30 日，松島艦載有日本海軍官校實習官兵學生來澎，突發火藥庫爆炸而沉沒，連同艦長矢田由松在內共計 222 人喪生，死傷慘重，爲當年國際矚目之意外事件，次年爲紀念此事件，闢建澎湖公園。

炸沉後之松島艦經打撈，將其主砲管豎立爲紀念碑（一說此砲爲事件後才製造），立於當時馬公公園內，共高約 30 公尺，口徑約 17 吋，望之如一柱擎天，其後在昭和 8 年(西元 1933 年）時，因日本國內缺乏五金而被拆下作爲軍需物質。公園田地亦在光復後，闢建爲市場、餐廳、加油站，滄海桑田變幻無常。

註 191、194

圖爲日治時代的澎湖公園松島紀念砲塔 RH-141

Matsushima Monument in Penghu Park during the Japanese era.

Penghu Park and the Matsushima Incident

The naval vessel Matsushima carried special historic meaning for the Japanese. Prior to the signing of the Treaty of Shimonoseki between China and Japan in 1895, Japan had sent a fleet in which Matsushima was the main battleship to seize Penghu by landing on Wenkang (Lungmenkang, Huhsi Township), Penghu as a precursor to Japan's rule over Taiwan. Later, on April 30, 1908, Matsushima visited Penghu with naval officers and cadets on board. A sudden explosion of the powder magazine sank the ship and claimed 222 lives, including the captain's. The heavy casualties received worldwide attention at the time. Penghu Park was established in memory of this accident.

The main cannon of the vessel was erected as a monument following the retrieval of the vessel from the bottom of the ocean. (Another theory holds that the cannon was cast after the accident occurred.) With a height of some 30 meters and a diameter of 17 inches, the cannon looked like a huge stick reaching all the way up to the sky. The monument was demolished in 1933 and used as materiel, due to a shortage of metal in Japan. After the KMT takeover of Taiwan, the park area was developed into a marketplace, restaurants, gas stations, etc., attesting to the vicissitudes of life.

驛站巡禮
History of Train Stations

臺北火車站三代沿革

清代臺北最早的火車站係設於大稻埕河溝頭，稱爲「大稻埕火車票房」(今鄭州路中興醫院址)。日治以後，因修改鐵路線，火車站改設於今忠孝西路，初名臺北停車場。明治 38 年 (西元 1905 年) 改爲磚石建築，建材多取自臺北府城拆卸的城壁，中央部分二層樓高，正脊的兩端裝置避雷針，屋頂有鐵柵飾件。自運輸量擴增後，原有規模漸難應付，乃於昭和 13 年 (西元 1938 年) 予以改建。第二代的臺北火車站於昭和 15 年 5 月落成，營運至民國 75 年 (西元 1986 年) 3 月 1 日，爲配合鐵路地下化工程再度拆建。現今的第三代臺北車站在民國 78 年落成啓用，較原車站東移 170 公尺。

位居海陸要衝

左側爲大阪商船辦事處的二層建築，與火車站分庭抗禮，在此出售船票服務旅客，屋頂可見該社標誌及旗幟；廣場西南角隅另有近海郵船的辦事處。由於鐵公路與航運機構匯集，所以這裡是來往臺灣、日本各地的交通要津。站前廣場上曾有坐姿雕像圓環，後來又被拆除。

大阪商船株式會社，爲日治時期本島海運航業主力之一，自明治 29 年 (西元 1896 年) 起開闢定期航線，航行臺灣基隆與日本神户間，中途停靠門司港 (北九州)；該公司從大正 3 年 (西元 1914 年) 9 月起，有六艘船行駛，每月往返十二次。

註 2、66、68、70、72、114、117、118、125

RH-142

臺北火車站前廣場約 8000 坪，廣場上三輪車群集，有不少搭載著剛出站的旅客正要離開。車站後面 (北方) 的山勢依稀可見。

The square in front of the Taipei Train Station was an area of around 48,000 square feet. Pedicabs crowd together in the square. In the background of the station (to the north), the mountains are readily apparent.

Three Generations of Change at the Taipei Train Station

In the Ching Dynasty, Taipei's largest train station was established at the riverfront in Tataoying, and called the Tataoying Train Ticket Office (where the Chunghsing Hospital presently stands on Chengchou Road). Following Japanese occupation, due to repairs on the rail line, the train station was rebuilt at its present site on Chunghsiao West Road, and at first it was called Taipei Train Terminal. In 1905 a new building was constructed, made of bricks which were mainly taken from the torn- down city walls. Its central portion was two stories high, with lightning rods on either end of the main roof ridge, which was covered with decorative metal work. Yet the scale of the train station was insufficient to keep pace with increased transportation volume. Therefore, in 1938, reconstruction commenced. The second generation Taipei Railway Station was completed in May, 1940, and continued in operation until March 1, 1986, when it was torn down once again, in coordination with the project to put the rail line underground. The present, third generation of Taipei Railway Station went into operation on completion in 1989; it is 170 meters east of the original station.

The Vital Point between Sea and Land

The illustration on the left shows the Osaka Merchant Lines Office Building, a two story building which rivaled the Railway Station, selling boat tickets and serving travelers. At the roof level can be seen this company's sign and flag. At the southwest corner of the square, there is another office for sea postal delivery. With rail and boat transportation services clustered together here, this was the central artery for intercourse between all places in Taiwan and Japan. In front of the square, there was a sculpture carved in the form of a ring, which since has been torn down.

The Osaka Merchant Lines Corporation was one of the most powerful sea transportation companies during the times of Japanese rule in Taiwan; from 1896 it operated regular sea lines between Keelung, Taiwan and Kobe, Japan, with stops in Moshi, in Northern Honshu. From September, 1914, this company had six ships in the fleet making this round trip 12 times a month.

臺北火車站初期只設三個月台。圖由第二月台西望站內設施，蒸汽機車頭正緩緩入站，另一處月台是在後站。

There were just three platforms in the Taipei Train Station at this time.
The illustration, looking west from the second platform, shows a steam engine entering the station in a cloud of steam; another platform is in the background.

RH-143

新北投驛（新北投火車站）

由於發展北投地區的溫泉觀光事業。淡水線鐵路於大正 5 年(西元 1916 年)自北投站興築一段長 1.2 公里的支線鐵路通往溫泉區，此支線的起點，稱爲新北投站。圖中的站房係於昭和 12 年（西元 1937 年）重建而成，民國 77 年淡水線鐵路停駛後本站拆除，站房結構爲商人購去，重建於彰化花壇(今台灣民俗村)。新北投站原址現爲捷運新北投站。

註 75

RH-144

The New Peitou Railway Station

Due to the development of the Peitou area hot springs and tourist industry, in 1916 the Tanshui branch rail line extended a 1.2 kilometer line of the railroad from the Peitou Station to go to the hot springs area, and this new terminus was called the New Peitou Station. The station in the illustration was reconstructed in 1937.

In 1988, when service from the Tanshui branch rail line was stopped, this station was demolished. The station's structure was purchased by an entrepreneur, and was rebuilt at Huatan in Changhua. The original location of the New Peitou Station is now the site of the Mass Rapid Transit system's Peitou Station.

蘇澳火車站

宜蘭線於大正 6 年（西元 1917 年）興建，大正 13 年（西元 1924 年）通車，由八堵至蘇澳，全長 95 公里，爲單線鐵路。民國 69 年北迴鐵路開通後，宜蘭線和北迴線交接於距離原宜蘭線蘇澳站 3.2 公里的蘇澳新站。

宜蘭——蘇澳間鐵路在大正 8 年（西元 1919 年）3 月完成，是宜蘭線中最早通車的一段。蘇澳車站是宜蘭線終點，位於市街南側，此圖取景採東望蘇澳灣方向鳥瞰市街、火車站，背景是七星山、北方澳，圖右小丘後的北方澳現爲蘇澳軍港，編屬海軍中正基地。

註 106

RH-145

圖爲遠望日治時代的蘇澳驛附近的港灣

In the distance was the bay area in the vicinity of Su'ao Train Station during the Japanese era.

Su'ao Train Station

With a total length of 95 km, the one-track Ilan rail line linking Patu and Su'ao was begun to be built in 1917 and was opened in 1924. Since 1980 when the North Link Railway opened, the Ilan line has connected with the North Link Railway at the New Su'ao Station, some 3.2 km from the Su'ao Station of the old Ilan line.

The train line between Ilan and Su'ao was completed in March of 1919. It was the first segment to carry rail traffic on the Ilan line. The Su'ao Train Station was the terminus of the Ilan line. It was located on the south side of City Street. This photo was taken looking east towards Su'ao Bay, and shows a bird's eye view of City Street and the Train Station, with Chihsing Mountain and the Northern Bay in the background. In the right of the illustration, the Northern Bay behind the small hill is now the Su'ao Military Harbor, belonging to the Chungcheng Navel Base.

第一代宜蘭火車站（宜蘭驛）

宜蘭線鐵路於大正 6 年（西元 1917 年）12 月開工，其中宜蘭——蘇澳段於大正 8 年 3 月完成，是最早通車的一段；八堵至蘇澳爲單線鐵路，全線於大正 13 年通車、全長 95 公里。宜蘭站爲和洋混合風格，採日本式唐破風入口木構造建築，站舍與艋舺（建於 1918 年）、彰化車站極爲相似，幾爲翻版。

註 5、66、117

RH-146

The First Ilan Railway Station

Work to put the Ilan line into use began in December, 1917. The segment from Ilan to Su'ao was finished in March, 1919. It was the first section to open to rail passage. Ilan Station was a mixture of Japanese and Western styles; it used a Japanese-style wooden structure with ornamented ventilation openings. The station was almost an exact replica of the one in Mengka (built in 1918) and the one in Changhua.

第二代花蓮火車站（舊東線鐵路花蓮港驛）

東線鐵路在日治時期稱爲臺東線鐵道，早於明治 43 年（西元 1910 年）6 月即築成花蓮港（花蓮舊稱）至鯉魚尾（今壽豐）一段，大正 5 年（西元 1916 年），完成至璞石閣（今玉里）之第一期工程。花蓮港驛址在今中山路，其改建工程於昭和 6 年（西元 1931 年）12 月竣工，始於爲鐵公路轉運要站，其建築亦爲全台火車站風格中甚爲突出者，此站於昭和 19 年（西元 1944 年）10 月遭空襲盟機炸毀，戰後曾再重建。民國 40 年改稱花蓮站，民國 69 年（西元 1980 年）2 月北迴鐵路通車，花蓮火車站新站啓用後，旋遭廢置。

註 34、35、39、65、66

RH-147

The Second Hualien Railway Station (the Old East Line Railway Hualien Harbor Station)

The East Line Railway in the period of Japanese occupation was the Taitung Line Railroad. As early as June of 1910 the segment from Hualien Harbor (the old name for Hualien) to Liyuwei (now called Shoufeng) was built; in 1916 the first period of construction was completed as far as Pushike (now Yuli). The Hualien Harbor Station was located at the present Chungshan Road. Its refurbishment was completed in December, 1931. It was a vital point on the railway line. The architectural style of this train station was also quite outstanding. In October, 1944, it was destroyed in an Allied bomb attack, but was rebuilt after the war, and in 1951 was renamed the Hualien Station. In February, 1980, rail passage was opened on the northern return line, and Hualien Train Station's New Station came into use, so the old one was no longer needed.

第一代 基隆火車站（基隆驛）

清代基隆火車票房，在今四號碼頭南端西側，是當時基隆、新竹間鐵路端點終站房，號稱全臺鐵路起首第一場面，最初僅爲土角造，面積73坪，設備簡陋。日治後，迨基隆築港第二期工程進行，火車站位置亦亟待更張，俾配合港灣設備，乃遷建曾仔寮街（明治町，火車站現址），明治41年（西元1908年）10月落成，初名基隆停車場，建築形態與臺北停車場相仿，爲鋼筋磚砌文藝復興式樣二層建築，所用木材以省產檜木爲主。

基隆火車站一樓中央大廳，設有售票房、店舖、旅客嚮導所等，兩翼爲候車室，二樓分爲三室，中間是貴賓候車室，左、右二室充作客廳，屋頂鋪金屬瓦、開軒窗（又稱老虎窗），中央有尖頂鐘塔，屋脊裝置鐵飾。該站曾經多次修繕，日治後期屋脊鐵飾即被取下，戰後的記錄照片則已不見軒窗。

註23、24、50、51、66、115、118

RH-148

The First Keelung Train Station

The Keelung Ticket Office of the Ching Dynasty was on the western side of the south end of the present# 4 wharf. At the time it was the terminal for the line between Keelung and Hsinchu, known as the number one spot of the entire Taiwan Railroad line. At first it was just a simple structure made of mud brick, with an area of 438 square feet. During Japanese rule, the train station was slated for relocation and renewal, pending the beginning of the Keelung Harbor construction project's second phase of work; in coordination with the establishment of the harbor plan, it was moved to Tsengaliao Street (Meiji Street, where the Train Station is presently located). Construction was completed in October, 1908. Originally it was called Keelung Train Terminal. The design imitated that of the Taipei Train Station, a two-story building of steel-reinforced cut brick in a Renaissance style. The wood materials used mostly came from juniper trees native to the island.

The one-story central hall of the Keelung Train Station had a ticket office, shops, travelers information, etc. The two wings were waiting rooms for the trains. The second floor was divided into three rooms; the middle one was a waiting room for the first-class travelers, whereas the left and right rooms were for parlors.

The roof was covered with metal tiles, and had tiger windows; in the center was a pointed bell tower, and the roof ridge was decorated with ironwork. This station was repaired and improved many times. After the Japanese period, the ironwork on the roof was removed, so in documentary photos after the war, the tiger windows cannot be seen.

交通重站——第一代嘉義火車站

初名嘉義停車場，爲日本瓦斜屋頂雨淋板外牆之木構造單層建築。明治 29 年（西元 1896 年），嘉義——臺南段竣工後，本站正式啓用，其路段是繼臺南到打狗之後，初期南部軍用輕便軌道向北延伸的第二個通車路段。明治 37 年（西元 1904 年）2 月，臺南至斗六段縱貫鐵路完成通車，本站便爲縱貫鐵路沿線的大站，也是糖廠北港線（有客運業務）、阿里山森林鐵路的起點，運務繁忙。昭和 8 年（西元 1933 年）拆除改建新站舍。

註 50、51、64、66、67

RH-149

At the Crossroads of Transportation--The First Chiayi Train Station

At first called the Chiayi Train Terminal, this was a one story wooden structure with rainproof wood panels as outer walls, and with a Japanese-style slanting tile roof. In 1896 the segment from Chiayi to Tainan was completed, and this station opened officially.

The route continued from Tainan to Takou (Kaohsiung). It followed in a second track along the light gauge railway which in the early years had been extended from the north for military use. In February, 1904, the section of the long-distance railroad from Tainan to Touliu was completed and opened to train passage, and this station was a major stop along the long-distance rail line. It was also the terminus of the Taiwan Sugar Company's Peikang line (which carried passengers as well) and of the Ali Mountain Forest Railroad. A large number of people passed through this station. In 1933 it was demolished in order to build the present station.

第一代高雄火車站

今高雄港貨運火車站初名打狗（高雄舊稱）停車場，位於鼓山區哈馬星，明治 33 年（西元 1900 年）建，爲日本瓦斜屋頂雨淋板外牆之木構造單層建築。臺灣南部最早的鐵路軌道，開始於明治 28 年 12 月，舖設於臺南、打狗間，是日本軍方所經營之軍用輕便軌道，當時並設置台灣陸軍補給廠打狗出張所（辦事處），明治 32 年 6 月置臨時臺灣鐵道敷設部打狗出張所。在屏東線未完成以前，打狗停車場曾爲縱貫鐵路本線最南端的車站，昭和 16 年（西元 1941 年）4 月，大港埔的高雄新驛（今高雄火車站現址）啓用，此站遂改爲高雄港驛。

註 50、66、106、174

RH-150

First-generation Kaohsiung Train Station

Originally called Takou (the old name of Kaohsiung, meaning"beating the dog") Train Station and located in Hamahsing, Kushan District of Kaohsiung, the current freight station of Kaohsiung Harbor was a one-story structure with sloping Japanese roofs and exterior weather boards. The earliest rail track in southern Taiwan was constructed in December 1895 as a light railway operated by the military to connect Takou and Tainan. During that time, the Takou office of the Taiwan Army Vehicle Service was established. In June 1898, the Takou office of the Tai-wan Temporary Railway Construction Department was established. Before the completion of the Pingtung rail line, Takou Train Station used to be the southernmost train station of the North-South Railway. The train station later became Kaohsiung Harbor Station in April, 1941 when the new station of Takangpu (currently the location of Kaohsiung Train Station) began operation.

旗山火車站——蕃薯寮停車場

蕃薯寮停車場，爲前「台灣製糖株式會社」所屬的旗山火車站，約建於西元 1910 年，址在今高雄縣旗山鎮中山路 1 號，今已拆除。

圖中的鐵路軌道軌距僅 762 公厘，屬「輕便鐵道」，原設爲貨運鐵路，載運「台灣製糖株式會社」(明治 35 年，西元 1902 年設立於橋仔頭) 的甘蔗原料。大正 11 年 (西元 1922 年) 3 月，爲了便利民衆交通出入，依據新頒的「台灣私設鐵道補助法」，開始兼營客運。

圖右火車頭與車廂均較小，即俗稱之「五分仔車」。

圖爲日治時代的旗山火車站，今已拆除 RH-151

Chishan Train Station during the Japanese era has been demolished.

The Chishan Railway Station--The Fanshuliao Terminal

The Fanshuliao Terminal was Chishan Railway Station when it belonged to the former Taiwan Sugar Company. It was built around 1910, at #1 Chungshan Road in Chishan Village, Kaohsiung County. It has already been torn down.

The illustration shows that the track gauge was about 762 mm, thus making it a light gauge railroad. It was originally used to transport goods and raw materials in the sugar industry for the Taiwan Sugar Company (which was established in 1902 at Chiaotou). In March of 1922, in order to facilitate people's access according to the newly passed Supplementary Law for Taiwan Privately Operated Railroads, it began to double as a passenger line.

In the right of the illustration, the engine and cars are exceedingly small; these are what were commonly called handspan cars.

參考書目 Reference Books

註 1　請參考　《臺灣省通志》卷一土地志疆域篇，臺灣省文獻委員會，1970•6
註 2　請參考　《臺灣省通志》卷三政事志建置篇，臺灣省文獻委員會，1972•12
註 3　請參考　《臺灣省通志》卷三政事志衛生篇，臺灣省文獻委員會，1972•6
註 4　請參考　《臺灣省通志》卷三政事志外事篇，臺灣省文獻委員會，1971•6
註 5　請參考　《臺灣省通志》卷四經濟志交通篇，臺灣省文獻委員會，1969•6
註 6　請參考　《臺灣省通志》卷四經濟志金融篇，臺灣省文獻委員會，1970•6
註 7　請參考　《臺灣省通志稿》卷四經濟志商業篇，臺灣省文獻委員會，1958•6
註 8　請參考　《臺灣省通志》卷四經濟志工業篇，臺灣省文獻委員會，1971•6
註 9　請參考　《重修臺灣省通志》卷四經濟志交通篇，臺灣省文獻委員會，1993•1
註 10　請參考　《重修臺灣省通志》卷五武備志防戍篇，臺灣省文獻委員會，1990•12
註 11　請參考　《重修臺灣省通志》卷七政治志建置沿革篇，臺灣省文獻委員會，1991•6
註 12　請參考　《臺北市志》卷三政制志建設篇，臺北市文獻委員會，1966•8
註 13　請參考　《臺北市志》卷三政制志公共建設篇，臺北市文獻委員會，1988•10
註 14　請參考　《臺北市志》卷六經濟志商業篇，臺北市文獻委員會，1965•1
註 15　請參考　《臺北市志》卷八文化志名勝古蹟篇，臺北市文獻委員會，1970•10
註 16　請參考　《臺北縣志》卷二疆域志，臺北縣文獻委員會，1960
註 17　請參考　《臺北縣志》卷三地理志上，臺北縣文獻委員會，1960
註 18　請參考　黃平立編撰，《馬公市志》，馬公市公所印
註 19　請參考　《臺北縣志》卷二〇水產志，臺北縣文獻委員會，1960
註 20　請參考　《臺北縣志》卷二三商業志，臺北縣文獻委員會，1960
註 21　請參考　《臺北縣志》卷二四交通志，臺北縣文獻委員會，1960
註 22　請參考　《臺北縣志》卷二五教育志，臺北縣文獻委員會，1960
註 23　請參考　《基隆市志》港務篇，基隆市文獻委員會，1957•8
註 24　請參考　《基隆市志》公用事業篇，基隆市文獻委員會，1956•6
註 25　請參考　《基隆市志》沿革篇，基隆市文獻委員會，1956•4
註 26　請參考　《基隆市志》地政篇，基隆市文獻委員會，1957•8
註 27　請參考　《新竹縣志》卷五政事志，新竹縣文獻委員會，1957
註 28　請參考　《苗栗縣志》卷一地理志，苗栗縣文獻委員會，1968•11
註 29　請參考　《台中市志》，台中市政府，1978•6
註 30　請參考　《台南市志》卷一土地志勝蹟篇，台南市政府編印，1985
註 31　請參考　《台南市志》卷三政事志建設篇，台南市政府編印，1979•6
註 32　請參考　《高雄市志》卷八、卷九交通志，高雄市文獻委員會編印，1986
註 33　請參考　《屏東縣志》卷三政事志衛生篇，屏東縣文獻委員會，1971•5
註 34　請參考　《宜蘭縣志》卷首中大事記，宜蘭縣文獻委員會，1960•3
註 35　請參考　《花蓮縣志》卷一五交通，花蓮縣文獻委員會，1974•6
註 35　請參考　《花蓮縣志》卷一大事記，花蓮縣文獻委員會，1974•10
註 36　請參考　《花蓮縣志》卷四地形，花蓮縣文獻委員會，1970•6
註 38　請參考　《花蓮縣志稿》卷七下工商水利（商業），花蓮縣文獻委員會
註 39　請參考　《花蓮文獻》(2)，花蓮縣文獻委員會，1953•10
註 40　請參考　《澎湖縣志》卷二開拓志，澎湖縣文獻委員會，1972•7
註 41　請參考　《澎湖縣志》卷十一教育志，澎湖縣文獻委員會，1972•7
註 42　請參考　《澎湖縣志》卷十一人文志，澎湖縣文獻委員會，1972•7
註 43　請參考　《澎湖縣志》卷十三人文志，澎湖縣文獻委員會，1978•7
註 44　請參考　《淡水鎮志》，淡水鎮公所編印，1989
註 45　請參考　《臺北州管概況及事務概要》，臺北州役所編，1923
註 46　請參考　《臺北市役所》，臺北成文重印，1985•3 台一版
註 47　請參考　《臺北市政 20 年史》，臺北市役所編，1930
註 48　請參考　《高雄州要覽》（成文復刻版），高雄州役所，1985 年台一版
註 49　請參考　《臺灣總督府公文類纂》第 19 號 14 門，雜類，1897
註 50　請參考　《臺灣鐵道史》上卷，臺灣總督府鐵道部，1910•9

參考書目 Reference Books

註 51　請參考　《日據下之臺政》，臺灣省文獻委員會，1977•4
註 52　請參考　《日據前期臺灣北部施政紀實》，臺灣省文獻委員會，1986•10
註 53　請參考　《臺北市發展史㈣》，臺北市文獻委員會，1983•6
註 54　請參考　《高雄市文化資產採訪專輯》，高雄市文獻委員會，1982•6
註 55　請參考　《高雄市舊地名探索》，高雄市文獻委員會，1983•6
註 56　請參考　《高雄市發展史》，高雄市文獻委員會，1988
註 57　請參考　《耆老口述歷史（上）—台中市鄉土史料》，臺灣省文獻會，1994•11
註 58　請參考　《耆老口述歷史㈤—台南市鄉土史料》，臺灣省文獻會，1994•8
註 59　請參考　《第一居臺灣本土文化學術研討會論文集（下）》，國立臺灣師範大學文學院人文教育研究中心，1995•4
註 60　請參考　《臺灣之工業論集》卷二，台銀經濟研究室，1958
註 61　請參考　《基隆港》，基隆港務局編，1948•10
註 62　請參考　《基隆港建港百年紀念文集》，基隆港務局，1985•11•9
註 63　請參考　《淡水教會 120 週年紀念冊(1872－1992)》，淡水基督教長老會出版，1992•10
註 64　請參考　《台糖五十年》，臺灣糖業股份有限公司，1996•5
註 65　請參考　《臺灣懷舊》，創意力文化事業有限公司，1990•11
註 66　請參考　《臺灣回想》，創意力文化事業有限公司，1993•1
註 67　請參考　《臺灣全記錄》，錦繡出版社，1990•5
註 68　請參考　《臺北古今圖説集》，臺北市文獻委員會，1992•6
註 69　請參考　《臺灣省立博物館之研究與修護計劃》，漢光建築師事務所，1991•6
註 70　請參考　《臺灣鐵路百週年紀念》，臺灣鐵路管理局，1987•6
註 71　請參考　《臺灣之燈塔》，海關總稅務司署，1989•12
註 72　請參考　《臺北古城之旅》(臺灣深度旅遊手冊 5)，遠流，1992•3
註 73　請參考　《宜蘭》(臺灣深度旅遊手冊 8)，遠流，1991•10
註 74　請參考　《臺灣最佳去處全集》，户外生活圖書，1983•1
註 75　請參考　《陽明山地區鄉土教材專輯》，士林國中，1984
註 76　請參考　《臺閩地區古蹟簡介》，内政部印行
註 77　請參考　《澎湖縣順承門修復調查研究》，漢寶德建築事務所
註 78　請參考　《臺北建築》，臺北市建築師公會
註 79　請參考　《臺中市管内概況》，成文，1924
註 80　請參考　《臺中州管内概況及事務概要》，成文，1940
註 81　請參考　《臺灣事情㈠》，日本臺灣總督府編印，1916
註 82　請參考　臺灣教育會編，《臺灣教育沿革志》祥生出版社，1973•3•29 複刻版發行
註 83　請參考　國立臺灣大學歷史學系編輯，《日據時期台灣史國際研討會論文集》，國立臺灣大學歷史學系，1993•6
註 84　請參考　郭延以，《近代中國史綱》，香港中文大學，1979
註 85　請參考　尹章義，《新莊發展史》，新莊市公所，1980
註 86　請參考　尹章義、陳宗仁，《新莊政治發展史》，新莊市公所，1989•3
註 87　請參考　黄純青、林熊祥主修，《臺灣省通志稿》成文，1982•3
註 88　請參考　畢慶昌等，《新竹新志》中華叢書委員會，1958•6
註 89　請參考　張炎憲、戴寶村、李筱峰主編，《臺灣史論文精選（下)》，玉山社，1996•9
註 90　請參考　周宗賢主編，《臺灣史國際學術研討會－社會、經濟與墾拓論文集》，國史館，1995•8
註 91　請參考　汪洋，《臺灣視查報告書》，成文，1982•3 台一版
註 92　請參考　陳正祥編，《臺灣地名手冊》，臺灣省文獻會，1959•6
註 93　請參考　陳正祥，《臺灣地名辭典》數明產業地理研究所研究報告第 105 號，1960
註 94　請參考　洪敏麟，《臺灣地名沿革》，臺灣省政府新聞處編印，1985
註 95　請參考　洪伯溫，《臺北地誌新探》龍文，1993•12•30
註 96　請參考　賴順盛等編，《台中市發展史》，台中市政府，1989•6
註 97　請參考　許文洲，《台中港都市計劃評估研究》，東海大學社會研究所碩士論文，1981
註 98　請參考　洪慶峰總編、戴寶村主編，《台中港開發史》，台中縣立文化中心，1987•5•1
註 99　請參考　楊壬生主編，《高雄市今昔圖説》，高雄市文獻委員會，1990•3•31

註 100 請參考 呂伯璘編，《高雄市民政史料初編》高雄市文獻委員會，1993•6•30
註 101 請參考 曾玉昆，《高雄市各區發展淵源（上)》，高雄市文獻委員會，1992•6
註 102 請參考 曾玉昆，《高雄市地名探源》，高雄市文獻委員會，1987
註 103 請參考 王金塗、蘇月琴編輯，《高雄縣地名初探》，高雄縣文化中心，1995•4
註 104 請參考 呂順安主編，《高雄縣鄉土史料》，臺灣省文獻委員會，1994•11
註 105 請參考 李淑芬，《日本帝國南進政策中的高雄建設》，國立成功大學歷史語言研究所碩士論文，1995•6
註 106 請參考 洪致文，《臺灣鐵道傳奇》，時報，1992•12
註 107 請參考 胡美璜等，《中華公路史下部》台灣商務印書館 1984•7
註 108 請參考 陳俊，《臺灣道路發展史》，交通部運輸研究所，1987•10
註 109 請參考 張勝彥、吳文星、溫振華、戴寶村，《臺灣開發史》，國立空中大學，1996•1
註 110 請參考 程大學編著，《臺灣開發史》，衆文，1991
註 111 請參考 潘英，《臺灣拓殖史及其族姓分布研究》，自立，1992
註 112 請參考 黄昭堂著，廖智譯，《臺灣民主國之研究》，現代學術基金會
註 113 請參考 莊永明，《臺灣紀事（下)》，時報，1989•10•10
註 114 請參考 何皓，《殖墾時代臺灣攝影紀事(1895－1945)》，武陵出版社，1988•4
註 115 請參考 向陽、劉還月，《快門下的老臺灣》，林白出版社，1989•5
註 116 請參考 劉還月，《回首看臺灣》，漢光文化事業，1988•6
註 117 請參考 李乾朗，《臺灣近代建築》，雄師圖書，1980•12
註 118 請參考 李乾朗，《臺灣建築史》，北屋出版事業，1980•7
註 119 請參考 李乾朗，《臺灣近代建築之風格》，室內雜誌社，1992•9
註 120 請參考 李乾朗，《臺北古城門》，臺北市文獻委員會，1993•3
註 121 請參考 李乾朗，《臺北市古蹟簡介》，臺北市政府民政局，1993•6
註 122 請參考 關山情主編，《臺灣古蹟全集》，戶外生活雜誌社，1980•5
註 123 請參考 王志鴻、周守眞，《臺北縣的舊街》，臺北縣立文化中心，1994•3
註 124 請參考 朱萬里編著，《臺北市都市建築史稿》，臺北市工務局，1954
註 125 請參考 莊永明，《臺北老街》，時報文化，1991•7
註 126 請參考 趙莒玲，《臺北市古街之旅》，臺北市政府新聞處，1992•6
註 127 請參考 林衡道主編，《臺灣古蹟第一輯》，臺灣省文獻委員會，1977•4
註 128 請參考 黃鼎松編著，《苗栗史蹟巡禮》，苗栗縣立文化中心，1990•5•20
註 129 請參考 張景森，《臺灣的都市計劃(1895－1988)》，業強，1993•7
註 130 請參考 郭瓊瑩研究主持，《臺北市都市開放空間系統之建立暨規劃原則之研究》臺北市政府研究發展考核委員會，1984
註 131 請參考 徐明福計劃主持，《台南市古蹟使用調查與評估》，文建會，1996•5
註 132 請參考 米復國計劃主持，《臺灣南部地區（嘉義縣、嘉義市、台南縣、高雄縣、高雄市、屏東縣、澎湖縣）古蹟使用調査與評估》，行政院文化建設委員會，1996•4
註 133 請參考 洪敏麟，《台南市市區史蹟調查報告書》，臺灣省文獻委員會
註 134 請參考 張家菁，《花蓮市街的空間演變：臺灣東部一個都市聚落的形成與發展》，國立臺灣師範大學地理研究所碩士論文，1993•6
註 135 請參考 陳耀明，《澎湖鄉土史話》，澎湖縣文獻委員會，1981
註 136 請參考 王國瑞編著，《臺灣林業史》，金氏圖書公司，1980
註 137 請參考 應大偉譯，《一百年前的臺灣寫眞》，圓神出版社，1995•5
註 138 請參考 游鑑明，《日據時期臺灣女子教育》，師大歷史碩士論文，1987
註 139 請參考 王國璠編著，《臺北市史畫集》，臺北市文獻委員會，1980•6
註 140 請參考 劉寧顏主編，《日據初期司法制度檔案》，臺灣省文獻委員會，1982•6
註 141 請參考 陳水逢，《日本近代史》，商務，1988•1
註 142 請參考 鄭學稼，《日本史》，黎明，1985•10
註 143 請參考 江樹生，《鄭成功和荷蘭人在臺灣的最後一戰及換文締和》，漢聲出版社
註 144 請參考 楊仁江，《台閩地區第一級古蹟檔案圖說》，內政部印行
註 145 請參考 鍾桂蘭、古福祥纂修，《屏東縣誌》，成文，1983•3
註 146 請參考 王啓宗，《臺灣的書院》，文建會

參考書目Reference Books

註147　請參考　周宗賢，《血濃於水的會館》，文建會
註148　請參考　蔡相煇，《臺灣的王爺與媽祖》，台原，1922•8
註149　請參考　矢内原忠雄著，周憲文譯，《帝國主義下之臺灣》，帕米爾書店，1987•5
註150　請參考　井出季和太著，郭輝譯，《日據時代下之台政》，臺灣省文獻委員會，1977•4•10
註151　請參考　信夫清二郎著，周啓乾譯，《日本近代政治史》卷四，桂冠，1990•12
註152　請參考　原口清著，李永熾譯，《日本近代國家之形成》，水牛，1986•2•15
註153　請參考　黃世孟譯，越澤明原著，《滿洲都市計畫史之研究》，國立臺灣大學土木工程學研究所都市計畫研究室，1986•9
註154　請參考　武内貞義，《臺灣（改訂版）》，新高堂書店，1927
註155　請參考　武内貞義，《臺灣（增補版）》，臺灣刊行會，1929
註156　請參考　武内貞義《臺灣㈠》，中國方志叢書，臺灣地區第133號，成文，1985・3台一版
註157　請參考　井出季和太，《臺灣治績志》，臺灣日日新報社，1937
註158　請參考　吉田東伍，《增補大日本地名辭書》，富士房，1990
註159　請參考　島定知編，《臺灣勝地誌》，成文，1985•3
註160　請參考　杉山靖憲編，《臺灣名勝舊蹟誌》，臺灣總督府發行，1916
註161　請參考　安倍明義，《臺灣地名研究》，蕃語研究會，1938
註162　請參考　田中一二編，《臺北市史》臺灣通信社，1931
註163　請參考　石阪莊作，《基隆港》，成文，1917
註164　請參考　菅野秀雄，《新竹州沿革史》，成文，1938
註165　請參考　井田麟鹿，《澎湖風土記》，日本臺灣總督府，1910
註166　請參考　本田喜八等編，《高雄州地誌》，1930
註167　請參考　藤森照信，《日本的近代建築（上)》，東京：岩波書店，1993•11一刷
註168　請參考　藤森照信，《日本的近代建築（下)》，東京：岩波書店，1994•5第三刷
註169　請參考　武井豐治，《古建築辭典》，東京：理工學社，1994•5
註170　請參考　村松貞次郎，《日本近代建築的歷史》，日本放送出版協會，1997•10
註171　請參考　石板莊作，《おらが基隆港》，1932
註172　請參考　島海靖，《日本近代史——國際社會の中の近代日本》，放送大學，教育振興會，1992•3•20
註173　請參考　河野收編，《近代日本戰爭史》，日：東京堂，平成7年4月20日
註174　請參考　《昭和史全記錄》，東京：每日新聞社，1989•3
註175　請參考　京都市文化觀光資源保護財團編集，《近代京都的名建築》，京都：同朋舍，1994•5
註176　請參考　《臺灣統治綜覽》，臺灣總督府，1908
註177　請參考　《臺灣總督府警察沿革誌》，臺灣總督府警務局編，1933
註178　請參考　《臺灣の警察》，臺灣總督府警務局，1931
註179　請參考　《近代都市計劃の百年とその未來》，日本都市計劃學會編，1988
註180　請參考　《臺灣の衛生》，臺灣總督府警務局編，1939
註181　請參考　早川透，〈都市經營論一新高都市建設事業と開發会社〉，《臺灣時報》第26年第1號
註182　請參考　松本虎太，〈臺灣中部築港計劃の將とその役割〉，《臺灣時報》1939•6
註183　請參考　黃俊銘，〈日據時期臺灣近代建築的路上觀察學〉，《桃園縣立文化中心年刊(83)》，1995•6
註184　請參考　林鶴亭，〈安平史蹟〉，《台南文化新刊》，台南市文獻委員會，1976•12
註185　請參考　莊金德，〈日據初期臺北之警治〉，《台北文物》第6卷第2期，1957•6
註186　請參考　陳純雪，〈日據時期臺灣的警察制度〉，《警察學報》抽印本
註187　請參考　黃世孟，〈日據時期臺灣都市計劃政經脈絡及歷程分期之探討〉，《國立成功大學規劃學報》第十四期，1987
註188　請參考　溫振華，〈日據時期台中市之都市化〉，《思與言》，1988
註189　請參考　黃海泉，〈梧棲沿革誌〉，《中縣文獻》第一期，1955
註190　請參考　黃世孟，〈新高港都計劃與台中港特定區計劃範型之比較分析〉，《日據時期臺灣史國際學術研討會論文集》，國立台灣大學歷史系，1993•6
註191　請參考　《耆老口述歷史——澎湖縣鄉土資料》，台灣省文獻委員會
註192　請參考　《嘉義縣志》，嘉義縣文獻委員會
註193　請參考　《花蓮縣志》卷二一名勝古蹟，花蓮縣文獻委員會，1975•6
註194　請參考　《澎湖縣志》，澎湖縣政府出版
註195　請參考　李俊華，〈臺灣日據時期建築家鈴置良一之研究〉，中原大學建築研究所碩士論文，未刊稿，2000•7

臺灣影像歷史系列

開台尋跡

A Collection of the Visual History of Taiwan

Strolling the Old Trails

編輯顧問：吳文星、李欽賢、林衡道、施添福、夏目志郎、高橋正己、陳秋坤、陳國棟、陳淑華、童春發、黃秀政、劉大元（依姓氏筆劃順序排列）
政策執行委員會：總會長王桂榮－台美基金會、江以誠、李金庫、林美欄、林威亮、紀文豪、許震超、陳大昇、陳立宗、陳根清、游聰發、簡德順、簡德旺、蘇仁慈
總 編 輯：施淑宜
特約撰文：劉謦豪、程嘉文、潘玉芳、王志鴻、黎晉禎、姚其中、莊姵柔、陳景宏
初版執行編輯：夏靜凝
再版文字編輯：徐佳蓉
美術編輯：蔡瑷竹
法律顧問：王存淦、John Kenehan, Esq.
攝　　影：彭延平、張修政、陳耀欽
印　　務：陳榮財、張惠卿
英文翻譯：曾文中、王志遠、劉瑞芬、Brent Heinrich、Scott Davis
英文校訂：Brent Heinrich（韓伯龍）
日文名詞校訂：李欽賢
封面設計及題字：施淑宜
封面影像合成：陳治綱、蕭翔鴻
照相打字：美吉電腦照相排版有限公司
打字排版：正豐電腦排版有限公司
製版印刷：紅藍彩藝印刷股份有限公司
裝　　訂：堅成裝訂股份有限公司
出 版 者：台灣傳承文化事業股份有限公司
初版日期：民國85年11月
再版日期：民國93年11月
地　　址：臺北市信義路四段450巷9號8樓
電　　話：886-2-27200629,27200637
傳　　真：886-2-27200643
網　　址：www.taiwanheritage.com
郵政劃撥：帳戶：台灣傳承文化事業股份有限公司
帳號：19877111

Editing Consultants : Wen-Hsing Wu, Chin-Hsien Lee, Tien-Fu Shih,Willing S.Natsume,Takahashi Masami,Chiu-Kun Chen,Guo-Dong Chen,Shu-Hua Chen, Masegeseg Jingror, Hsiu-Cheng Hunag, Da-Yuan Liu
Executive Committee : Kenjohn Wang(Chaiman of Taiwanese American Foundation), I-Cheng Chang, Chin-Ku Lee, Linda Lin, William Wei-Lyan Lin, Wen-Hao Chi, Cheng-Chao Hsu, Steven Chen, Lee Chen, Ken-Ching Chen, Chong-Fa Yu, Te-Sun Chien,Te-Wang Chien, Ren-Tzu Sue
Editor-in-Chief : Connie Shu-Yi Shih
Special Contributor : Ching-Hao Liu, Chia-Wen Cheng,Joyce Pan, Chih-Hung Wang, Chin-Chen Li, Chin-Chung Yao, Pei-Rou Chuang, Jing-Hong Chen
1st Edition Executive Editor : Ching-Ning Hsia
Letter Editor : Opal Hsu
Arts Editors : Trista Tsai
Law Consultant : Tsun-Kan Wang,John Kenehan, Esq.
Photographers : Yen-Ping Pang, Hsiu-Cheng Chang, Yao-Chin Chang
Printing Coordinator : Tony Chen,Irene Chang
English Translators : Joseph Tseng, Chih-Yuan Wang,Laureen Liu Brent Heinrich, Scott Davis
Binding : Jian-Chen Printing Bookbinding Co., Ltd.
English Proofreader : Brent Heinrich
Japanese Terminology Proofreader : Chin-Hsien, Lee
Cover Designer & Calligraphy : Connie Shu-Yi Shih
Cover Image Composer : Chi-Guan Chen, Sean H. Shiao
Photo Typing : Mikey Computer Photo Type-Setting Co., Ltd.
Typing / Type-Setting : Cheng Feng Computer Type-Setting Co., Ltd.
Engraving / Printing : Red & Blue Color Printing Co., Ltd.
Publishing Company : Taiwan Heritage Co., Ltd.
Date or Publication : November 1996 1st Edition / November 2004 2nd Edition
Office Address : 8F., No.9, Lane 450, Sec. 4, Hsin-Yi Rd., Hsin-Yi District, Taipei 110, Taiwan
Tel No. : 886-2-27200629/27200637 **Fax No.** : 886-2-27200643
Website Address : www.taiwanheritage.com
Postal A / C Name : Taiwan Heritage Co., Ltd.
Postal A / C No. : 19877111

■定價：新台幣3600元
■本書紙張採用特製150磅象牙雪銅
■如有缺頁、破損，請寄回本公司更換

*Price : US$110.00
*The paper used for printing is specially mat-finish coated
*In case of skip leaf and damages, please send the book back by mail to the publishing company for replacement.

ISBN:986-7302-06-0

台灣影像歷史系列
A Collection of the Visual History of Taiwan

■見證——台灣總督府(1895～1945)
Witness–The Colonial Taiwan (1895～1945)

■台灣總督府官葉
Postcards Issued by Taiwan Governor's Office

■典藏手繪封
Postcard Drawings–The Rare Collection

■斯土繪影(1895～1945)
The Drawings of That Land–The Interpretation of Taiwan(1895～1945)

■高砂春秋——台灣原住民之文化藝術
The Exquisite Heritage–The Culture and Arts of Taiwan Aborigines

■蓬萊舊庄——台灣城鄉聚落(1895～1945)
The Abodes in the Bygone Era–Taiwan's Town and Country Settlements(1895～1945)

■海國圖索——台灣自然地理開發(1895～1945)
The Landscape of the Island Country–The Development of the Natural Geography of Taiwan(1895～1945)

■開台尋跡
Strolling the old Trails

■台灣古書契(1717～1906)
Archaic Land Documents of Taiwan(1717～1906)

■殖產方略——台灣產業開發(1895～1945)
The Schemes of Production–Taiwan's Industrial Development(1895～1945)